"Call a Spade a Spade"

Alan Dundes
General Editor

Vol. 2

PETER LANG
New York • Washington, D.C./Baltimore • Bern
Frankfurt am Main • Berlin • Brussels • Vienna • Oxford

Wolfgang Mieder

"Call a Spade a Spade"

From Classical Phrase to Racial Slur
A CASE STUDY

PETER LANG
New York • Washington, D.C./Baltimore • Bern
Frankfurt am Main • Berlin • Brussels • Vienna • Oxford

Library of Congress Cataloging-in-Publication Data

Mieder, Wolfgang.
"Call a spade a spade": from classical phrase
to racial slur: a case study / Wolfgang Mieder.
p. cm. – (International folkloristics; v. 2)
Includes bibliographical references (p.) and index.
1. Spade (The English word). 2. English language–Idioms. 3. Racism in language.
4. Proverbs, English. 5. Figures of speech. I. Title. II. Series.
PE1599.S67 M54   422–dc21   2002004102
ISBN 0-8204-6176-8
ISSN 1528-6533

Die Deutsche Bibliothek-CIP-Einheitsaufnahme

Mieder, Wolfgang:
"Call a spade a spade": from classical phrase
to racial slur: a case study / Wolfgang Mieder.
–New York; Washington, D.C./Baltimore; Bern;
Frankfurt am Main; Berlin; Brussels; Vienna; Oxford: Lang.
(International folkloristics; vol. 2)
ISBN 0-8204-6176-8

Cover design by Lisa Dillon
Cover illustration, "IPSO VTILES VSV," (Useful only by use), is an emblem from
Sebastián de Covarrubias Orozco's (1539–1613) *Emblemas morales*
(Madrid: Luis Sanchez, 1610), II, 71.

The paper in this book meets the guidelines for permanence and durability
of the Committee on Production Guidelines for Book Longevity
of the Council of Library Resources.

© 2002 Peter Lang Publishing, Inc., New York

All rights reserved.
Reprint or reproduction, even partially, in all forms such as microfilm,
xerography, microfiche, microcard, and offset strictly prohibited.

Printed in the United States of America

Contents

	Editor's Preface	vii
	Introduction	1
I.	Early Scholarship on the Phrase (1851–1978)	7
II.	From Aristophanes to Erasmus of Rotterdam	33
III.	The Expression in Dictionaries of Quotations	47
IV.	The Phrase in Proverb and Idiom Collections	61
V.	Spade = Shovel, Eunuch, Card, and "Black"	87
VI.	Literary Texts from the 16th to the 20th Century	113
VII.	Scholarly Use of the Proverbial Expression	143
VIII.	Use of the Phrase in the Mass Media	153
IX.	Innocuous Proverbial Phrase or Racial Slur?	179
X.	The Phrase in Advertisements and Cartoons	199
XI.	Four Demographic Studies of the Expression	213
	Bibliography	235
	Name Index	243

Editor's Preface

Folkloristics includes the study of various genres of folklore and each of these genres has inspired its own separate scholarship. The sum total of all the scholarship devoted to the dozens of folklore genres is accordingly too enormous to be encompassed by any one folklorist. This is one reason why most folklorists choose to concentrate on one particular genre, such as myth or epic or superstition. As a result, there are subfields of specialization within folkloristics. Folklorists who are mythologists, for example, study myth and certainly the books, monographs, and essays treating myth number in the thousands.

One of the most fascinating genres of folklore is the proverb, the study of which is called paremiology. The true proverb is usually in sentential form consisting of a minimum of a topic and a comment. Hence there can be two-word proverbs (such as "Time flies," "Money talks," and "Speed kills"). There cannot be, by definition, a one-word proverb. Most proverbs are metaphorical, but a few are purely literal and these are sometimes called aphorisms ("Honesty is the best policy"). Proverbs do not seem to be found equally distributed among all peoples. Especially popular and widespread in Africa and Asia, proverbs seem to be largely absent among the native peoples of North and South America. In this regard, proverbs differ from myths inasmuch as all peoples have examples of this genre though, to be sure, no one individual myth is universal in the sense of being found among all peoples of the earth, past and present.

Paremiologists sometimes study other folkloristic forms which have been traditionally associated with proverbs and aphorisms. Such forms, typically found in standard collections of proverbs, include what are termed "proverbial phrases" and "proverbial comparisons." These labels are, unfortunately, misleading. The adjective "proverbial" has little to do with the proverb genre per se. Rather the adjective is in effect a synonym for "traditional" or "folk." Accordingly, the terms "folk metaphor" and "folk simile" are, in my opinion, more accurate labels for these forms. A true proverb normally sums up a situation, passes judgment, or recommends a course of action. Proverbial comparisons or folk similes, in contrast, merely describe. Moreover, such comparisons cannot be easily transformed into proverbs. For example, "as blind as a bat" which has the form "as_____as_____" is a typical folk simile. But it is quite different from the proverb "Love is blind." Now while one could certainly say "A bat is blind," it would not be regarded as an authentic traditional proverb. By the same token, one could say "as blind as love," but that would not be regarded as an authentic traditional folk simile.

Folk metaphors are a bit closer to the proverb genre, but they too differ significantly from the true proverb. With the true proverb, a fixed phrase (as opposed to free phrase) genre, the wording cannot change. In other words, it is fixed. With a folk metaphor, however, the subject or agent can change and so can the tense of the verb. For this reason, folk metaphors are usually reported in a more or less neutral infinitive form, for example, "to call a spade a spade." The range of possibilities is extensive. I can call a spade a spade, you can call a spade a spade, he or she can call a spade a spade, etc. Yesterday, I called a spade a spade; tomorrow I will call a spade a spade, today I could have called a spade a spade, etc. That said, I shall now attempt to call a spade a spade!

Among all the paremiologists of the world, there is one and only one who is generally acknowledged to be *primus inter pares* and that one paremiologist is Professor Wolfgang Mieder of the University of Vermont. Author, co-author, editor of more than one hundred books and hundreds of articles, Wolfgang Mieder is unquestionably the most prolific folklorist of his generation and perhaps of any generation. His mastery of the international scholarship on proverbs (and folk metaphors and folk similes) is unequalled by any folklorist, living or dead, and is not likely ever to be equalled. Anyone with the slightest doubt about this claim has only to consult the more than seven thousand entries in Mieder's extraordinary bibliographies of proverb scholarship: *International Proverb Scholarship: An Annotated Bibliography* (1982), 613 pp.; *International Proverb Scholarship, Supplement I* (1990), 436 pp.; *Supplement II* (1993), 927 pp.; and *Supplement III* (2001), 457 pp. These entries cover not collections of proverbs, but scholarly considerations of proverbs, considerations, I might add, written in a dazzling array of diverse languages. Professor Mieder has single-handedly made the vast range of proverb scholarship accessible to anyone interested in the genre. This plus his superb editorship of the yearbook *Proverbium* dedicated to encouraging proverb research, not to mention his countless investigations of individual proverbs or studies of all aspects of paremiology has established Professor Mieder as one of the great folklorists of the twentieth and twenty-first centuries. Anywhere in the world where there is a serious interest in the proverb, the name of Wolfgang Mieder is revered!

The story of how Professor Mieder came to be the world's leading authority on proverbs is one that deserves to be told. Born in 1944 at

Leipzig, he moved with his family to Lübeck in the late 1940s. After attending gymnasium, he took the unusual step at the age of sixteen of going to the United States to attend high school. This was at Wayne Memorial High School in Wayne, Michigan. Mieder then stayed on in the United States to attend college. He earned a B.A. in French and German from Olivet College (in Olivet, Michigan) in 1966. He then went to the University of Michigan for his M.A. in German. It was then that he made a strange decision, one that drastically changed his career trajectory but happily pointed him in the correct direction towards his eventual life's work. He decided to transfer from the University of Michigan to Michigan State University for his doctorate in German. Now there is nothing wrong with Michigan State. It is a great university, but it is generally not considered to be a better university than the University of Michigan, one of America's premier public universities. Most native-born Americans would probably not have moved to Michigan State from Michigan. Quite the contrary. They would have been more likely to move the other way round, from Michigan State to Michigan. Kansans, for example, would not rate Kansas State University over the University of Kansas; Floridians would not rank Florida State University over the University of Florida; and Californians would not rate any of the California State universities over any of the University of California campuses. But Wolfgang Mieder, thinking in terms of the German university system, assumed that Michigan State was more prestigious than the University of Michigan. As it all turned out, it was the right move for him.

At Michigan State University, one of the members of the Department of German was Stuart A. Gallacher (1906-1977) who had been a student of Archer Taylor (1890-1973), the greatest American paremiologist of the early twentieth century. As it happened, Professor Gallacher offered a seminar on the proverb and Mieder enrolled in that seminar. And the rest, as the folk say, is history! No doubt if Wolfgang Mieder had remained at the University of Michigan, he might have become a perfectly respectable expert in German language and literature, but paremiology certainly would not be the world-class discipline it has become, thanks largely to Professor Mieder's efforts.

After receiving his Ph.D. in 1970, Mieder taught for one year at Murray State University in Kentucky before moving to the University of Vermont where he has been a fixture ever since. With his remarkable productivity in both German literature and the proverb, he was rapidly promoted, becoming full professor in 1978, only eight years after earning his doctorate. And lest anyone think Professor Mieder didn't assume his share of administrative duties, it should be noted that he has served as chairperson of the Department of German and Russian since 1977. This administrative burden obviously did not in any way impede the steady flow of major publications over the past quarter century. During that time, Professor Mieder became more and more involved in American folklore, proverbs in particular. Although he continued to publish books and articles on German subject matter, usually in German, he has gradually become increasingly intrigued by American data. This is also reflected in the fact that he (finally) became an American citizen in the year 2001.

The present investigation *"Call a Spade a Spade"* is a unique study of a single folk metaphor. Tracing its path through the centuries from classical antiquity to modern times involved a tremendous amount of sleuthing. One of the keys to understanding any item of folklore is context. Unfortunately, the majority of early collections of proverbs and folk metaphors simply listed them in some kind of arbitrary order, usually alphabetical. Glosses were sparse and rarely was a given item quoted in any kind of natural speech act.

In this splendid extensive inquiry, we find dozens of contexts, carefully and accurately taken from a myriad of sources. It is by no means an easy task to locate the full range of citations of a particular proverb or folk metaphor. Standard dictionaries usually cite just one or two instances, if indeed that many. The amount of research required to produce this extraordinary documentation of the actual usage of "to call a spade a spade" is prodigious and truly staggers the mind. The naive reader may wrongly underestimate just how difficult and time-consuming it was to amass all the many citations that Professor Mieder has managed to assemble under one cover. In that sense, this study is a model of what is possible in the conduct of paremiological research, a level of perfection which I suspect few scholars would be able to attain.

Finally, the significance of this study does not rest solely in its exhaustive set of contextual citations. As Professor Mieder demonstrates, a relatively innocuous, if somewhat blunt, metaphor which apparently originated in classical antiquity has come to have possible racial nuances in the late twentieth century. This "case study" of one folk metaphor thereby illustrates how language is related to one of the central problematic issues of American culture, namely, racism. Once again, we can see the remarkable staying power of folklore as a given item apparently remains relatively intact over many centuries. At the same time, we are reminded of the ever-changing chameleon-like quality of folklore as new contextually-determined meanings of that item continually attest. This book constitutes yet another jewel in the crown of the modern *magister proverbium* Wolfgang Mieder!

Alan Dundes, *Editor*
Peter Lang International Folkloristics Series

Introduction

The study of the origin, history, dissemination, and meaning of a particular proverb or proverbial expression is no easy task. Scholars have dedicated entire monographs and substantial articles to the investigation of but one item of such traditional folk speech. There are, of course, numerous proverb and quotation dictionaries that list at least some historical references for individual phrases, and some even add a paragraph or a page of explanatory notes to them. And yet, once one probes more seriously into the source, transmission, and meaning of a proverb with its variants including those in different languages, it becomes obvious very quickly that a major research project will result that will draw on such fields as anthropology, communication, ethnology, folklore, history, literature, philology, religion, sociology, and others. The serious and comprehensive study of a singular proverb certainly entails a comparative and interdisciplinary approach based on diachronic and synchronic research methods.

The explanation of the well-known proverbial expression "to call a spade a spade" is no exception in this regard. As I started to work on its fascinating history and multiple meanings, I realized that my work would quickly grow into a project of considerable length. But I also recognized that this investigation could serve as a case study to illustrate the complexity of tracing one traditional phrase from classical antiquity to the modern age. The hundreds of references (cited with their various orthographical inconsistencies) of the "spade"-phrase assembled in this monograph are thus meant to show how involved such explanatory work on proverbial language can be. It might even serve as a model for many more projects along these lines. Such work is not only a valuable scholarly exercise but also a necessary undertaking if we wish to come to valid conclusions about the use, function, and meaning of proverbial folk speech.

Regarding the phrase under investigation here, it should be noted that "to call a spade a spade" is not a proverb but rather a proverbial expression. Proverbs are complete thoughts expressing an apparent truth, and they can stand by themselves as independent pieces of wisdom based on common experiences and observations. Proverbial expressions on the other hand are metaphorical phrases that have no claim to making a sapiential statement. They are simply used as expressive and figurative formulas that are integrated into the flow of oral or written language. As such they add stylistic and emotive color to speech patterns without imparting any wisdom or insight into life's challenges and tribulations. It is unfortunate that too many scholars do not differentiate between these two paremiological genres, and it will be seen that this confusion also exists in the many references cited throughout this study. In any case, the "spade"-phrase is a proverbial expression and not a proverb.

The present study has been divided into eleven chapters, and they represent in general what it takes to reach comprehensive conclusions about a particular phrase. Obviously not every analysis needs to be this involved, but in an ideal situation scholars need to cast their nets as wide as possible in order to amass enough textual references that will permit a clear picture of the history and meaning of the proverb or proverbial expression under investigation. And it is wise to begin by checking what has been learned about the proverbial utterance thus far. The first chapter of this monograph is therefore a review of the impressive research that has been done on the "spade"-phrase, albeit just in short and disparate notes. It began in the middle of the nineteenth century with scholars wanting to establish its classical origin. To be sure, they also tried to show how the old Greek phrase entered the English language and how it has survived in literary references to the present day.

The second chapter shows in much detail with citations from original Greek and Latin sources how the "spade"-expression originated with Aristophanes and was transmitted for several centuries until Erasmus of Rotterdam includes it in his famous *Adagia* collection of 1515. It is in this chapter where it becomes clear that it was a (conscious?) mistranslation of the Greek phrase by Erasmus that changed it from "to call a trough a trough" to "to call a spade a spade." In other words, while the root of the "spade"-phrase reaches back to Greek antiquity (perhaps Aristophanes is already citing a traditional phrase), the phrase as we know it clearly originates only with Erasmus. The many editions and translations of the *Adagia* then helped to establish the "new" proverbial expression in the English language with the traditional meaning of "to call things by their proper (right) names," "to speak one's mind," "to put things bluntly," "to say (tell) it as (like) it is," or "not to beat about (around) the bush."

The third and fourth chapters trace the "spade"-phrase through dozens of dictionaries of quotations as well as proverb and idiom collections. Such historical work is absolutely necessary to find as many references of the proverbial expression as possible. Many lexicographers and paremiographers copy from each other, but there are also those serious dictionaries and collections that will include additional literary references. Standard volumes definitely need to be checked, but one never knows what one might find in popular compilations and in the new compendia that constantly come on the market. In any case, the wealth of materials found in such volumes is of great value, even though they often lack precise bibliographical information. I have spent many hours and days hunting down such references, and they are listed in this book with complete and exact bibliographical citations.

The fifth chapter is of central importance in that it deals with the four semantic levels of the word "spade." There is the basic meaning of a spade being a type of a shovel. However, a spade can also refer to a eunuch, the suit of a card game (i.e., clubs, diamonds, hearts, and spades), and in American slang to African Americans or Blacks in general. These four meanings of the "spade"-word also carry over into the perceived interpretation of the proverbial expression "to call a spade a spade." It is for this reason that we need textual references of the phrase in context! This is the only way to find out the precise meaning of the expression in a particular situation. The spade meaning a garden implement is, of course, the most common semantic level. The "eunuch"-connotation on the other hand is quite rare, while there are many literary authors and speakers today who think that the "spade"-phrase refers to the card game. Finally, there is the problem that the word "spade" took on the slang meaning of "Blacks" in the 1920s. This has led to the new interpretation of the phrase as a racial slur, putting into question its appropriateness in modern communication.

Before dealing with this vexing problem in more detail, the sixth chapter presents many literary texts from the 16th to the 20th century, including such well-known authors as Ben Jonson, Robert Burton, John Taylor, Jonathan Swift, Washington Irving, James Fenimore Cooper, Charles Dickens, Anthony Trollope, Robert Browning, Oscar Wilde, Winston S. Churchill, John Galsworthy, Harry S. Truman, Aldous Huxley, and Kurt Vonnegut. The seventh chapter follows suit with numerous citations of the "spade"-phrase from scholarly publications in the form of books, scientific articles, book reviews, etc. The large eighth chapter presents a wealth of texts in contexts from the mass media in which the proverbial expression is used with considerable frequency. Finding all of these revealing references was not easy and took much time. However, the use of modern electronic databases makes this "hunt" an incredibly rewarding exercise. As we get ever more textual databases, proverb scholars will continue to reap great benefits from them. Many of the references cited in these chapters I would never have found without the help of the internet. Be that as it may, I present the contents of these three chapters with considerable pride, since they include a rather comprehensive picture of the use, function, and meaning of the "spade"-phrase in the printed media during the past five centuries.

The ninth chapter with its questioning title of "Innocuous Proverbial Phrase or Racial Slur?" is of utmost importance. It is here where I present references that show that the "spade"-phrase today has its very unique problems. While it continues to be used by people of diverse ethnic backgrounds (including African Americans) in its basic meaning of making a factual and blunt statement, it is also interpreted as a definite racial slur and used as such as well. This becomes clear also from the short chapter on the phrase in advertisements and cartoons. While it appears in its traditional sense in the advertisements, there are two cartoons that indicate an obvious racial interpretation. These texts and illustrations clearly show that the "spade"-phrase can be understood as a racial slur and that it is unfortunately used as such by bigots. It is not surprising then that the political correctness movement has labeled the proverbial expression "to call a spade a spade" a racial slur, arguing explicitly against its continued use.

The eleventh and final chapter continues this discussion by means of four demographic studies carried out at the Institute of Irish Studies at Queen's University in Belfast and among university students at Morehouse College in Atlanta, Georgia, the University of California at Berkeley, and the University of Vermont. The completed questionnaires showed that close to two-thirds of the students do *not* know the "spade"-phrase at all. And of the remaining third only about 30% or a third consider it a racial slur. That is a relatively small number indeed, and let's be thankful for that.

Nevertheless, while the "spade"-phrase clearly did not start as a racial slur, it can be interpreted as such. Perhaps there is no need to take an extreme "political correctness" position in the case of this classical phrase. In other words, there is no need to purge the language of the phrase in its traditional connotation. For the most part, people know and use it as a harmless expression for speaking plainly and bluntly without any thought or awareness of the fact that it can be used as a racial slur. This is, of course, especially true for English speakers from around the world for whom "spade" has no racial connotation. It would be wrong to accuse such speakers of having used a racial slur, especially if the context in which they employed the "spade"-phrase makes it perfectly clear that a racist interpretation is impossible. So let's be understanding of people who continue to make use of the proverbial expression in an absolutely innocuous fashion. Besides, our demographic studies show that the familiarity with the "spade"-phrase seems to be on a definite decline. Young people don't know it very well, and if they are aware of it, they hardly ever use it according to their answers on the questionnaires. It appears as if the phrase is fading in oral use, but then it appears with considerable frequency in written sources, both in literary works and the mass media. In other word, the "spade"-phrase is not dead yet!

So what should be done? It would be my subjective feeling after having completed this comprehensive study that the proverbial expression "to call a spade a spade" is in and of itself no racial slur. It can be used as a perfectly harmless expression for frank and blunt communication. However, since it can take on the meaning of a harmful racial slur, it should be used with care or better yet not at all. There are plenty of good and figurative substitutes available, to wit "to call things by their proper names" or "not to beat around the bush." We do not need the "spade"-phrase (certainly not as a slur!), and rather than perpetuating a problematic traditional phrase, we could drop it altogether at least in North America and Great Britain. While I understand it when people cite the "spade"-phrase in its traditional sense, I have consciously stopped using it. This seems to me the moral and humane thing to do after having written this intriguing story of the proverbial expression "to call a spade a spade."

No scholarly investigation is ever performed in isolation, and this study as well benefitted greatly from the help and expertise of many colleagues, students, and friends. I wish to thank above all my friend Fionnuala Williams from the Institute of Irish Studies at Queen's University in Belfast for circulating a valuable questionnaire and for sending me numerous references of the "spade"-phrase from literary sources and the mass media. I also owe much gratitude to my colleagues and friends Alan Dundes, Irmgard Immel, and Richard Sweterlitsch who distributed questionnaires to their students at the University of California at Berkeley, Morehouse College, and the University of Vermont. Special appreciation goes to my former student Olga Trokhimenko at Duke University who was of great help in finding references from various databases. Another former student, Jake Barickman, who now works at the library of the University of Vermont, also provided me with invaluable internet assistance. Many books were obtained through the interlibrary loan office at the University of Vermont, and I thank Barbara Lambert, Barbara Lamonda, Daryl Purvee, and Nancy Rosedale for their much-appreciated efforts. I also want to express my appreciation to my colleague Mark Usher for transliterating the Greek texts. Finally, let me thank my colleague and friend Dennis Mahoney and my assistant Janet Sobieski for their continued interest in my work. It is always a great pleasure to talk with them about my projects and to consider their valued opinions.

This book is dedicated to Sw. Anand Prahlad in memory of the time when he was a graduate student in a seminar on proverbs that I taught as guest professor at the University of California at Berkeley in 1981. Since then he has become a recognized proverb scholar in his own right, notably for his two books on *African-American Proverbs in Context* (1996) and *Reggae Wisdom: Proverbs in Jamaican Music* (2001). Due to his scholarly work we are much better informed about the importance of proverbs in various speech acts of African-American citizens. It is with pride and joy that I as his former teacher receive his steady flow of publications on the rich tradition of African-American proverb lore which includes the ultimate and liberating American proverb "Different strokes for different folks."

January 2002   Wolfgang Mieder
                                                                                                          University of Vermont

I.

Early Scholarship on the Phrase (1851-1978)

The scholarly occupation with the proverbial expression "to call a spade a spade" is nothing new. In fact, at the beginning of the twentieth century F. Edward Hulme had rendered somewhat of a summary of some of the findings regarding the origin and dissemination of the "spade"-phrase from classical antiquity to Erasmus and on to early English occurrences in his still quite informative study on *Proverb Lore* (1902):

> Those who pride themselves on a certain blunt directness of speech, and who declare that they always speak their mind, further define the position they take up by declaring that they call a spade a spade. There certainly are occasions when such a course is the only honest one, when a man has to make his protest and refuse to connive at any circumlocution or whittling away of principle. There are other occasions when a regard for the feelings of others makes such a proceeding sheer brutality, and it is, we believe, a well-established fact that the audience of those who pride themselves on speaking their mind ordinarily find that they are the victims of a somewhat unpleasant experience. Baxter declares, "I have strong natural inclination to speak of every subject just as it is, and to call a spade a spade, so that the thing spoken of may be fullest known by the words. But I unfeignedly confess that it is faulty because imprudent." "I am plaine," we read in Marprelate's "Epitome," "I must needs call a spade a spade," and Ben Jonson advises "boldly nominate a spade a spade."
>
> In the year 1548 Archbishop Cranmer was busily engaged on a design for the better unity of all the Protestant churches by having one common confession and one body of doctrine drawn out of Holy Writ, to which all could give their assent. Melancthon amongst others, was consulted by the archbishop, and was very favourable to the idea, but he strongly advised him, if the matter were to be carried to a successful issue, "to avoid all ambiguities of expression, call a spade a spade, and not cast words of dubious meaning before posterity as an apple of discord." Wise and weighty words that never fructified.
>
> John Knox, who was not by any means the man to go out of his way to prophesy smooth things or palliate wrong-doing by any euphuism or a prudent turning away of the head, declares, "I have learned to call

wickedness by its own terms, and to call a fig a fig and a spade a spade"; while Shakespeare, in his "Coriolanus," goes equally straight to the mark: "We call a nettle but a nettle, and the faults of fools but folly." Erasmus writes: "Ficus ficus, ligonem ligonem vocat" of a certain man.

Boileau in like manner writes, "J'appelle un chat un chat"; and Rabelais, "Nous sommes simples gents, puisqu'il plaist à Dieu: et appellons les figues figues, les prunes prunes, et les poires poires."

In the pages of Plutarch we read that Philip of Macedon, in answer to an irate ambassador, who complained to him that the citizens to the palace had called him a traitor, replied: "My subjects are a blunt people, and call things always by their right names. To them figs are figs, and they call spades spades." The adage is one of unknown antiquity, and may be found in the writings of Aristophanes, Demosthenes, Lucian, and other classic authors. Erasmus, in his "Apophthegmes," published in 1542 [i.e., Nicholas Udall's English translation], tells the story of the discomfiture of the embassy of the Macedonian court very quaintly: "When those persons that were at Lasthenes found themselfes greued and toke fumishly that certain of the traine of Phillipus called theim traitours, Phillipus answered that the Macedonians were feloes of no fine witte in their termes, but altogether grosse, clubbish, and rusticall, as the whiche had not the witte to cal a spade by any other name than a spade, alluding to that the common vsed prouerbe of the Grekes calling figgues figgues, and a bote a bote. As for his mening was that they were traitours in very deede. And the fair flatte truthe that the vplandishe or homely and play-clubbes of the countree dooen use, nameth eche things of the right names."

In Taverner's "Garden of Wysdome," published in 1539, the Macedonians are described as "very homely men and rudely brought vppe, which call a mattok nothing els but a mattok, and a spade a spade" — a very right and proper thing for Macedonians or anyone else to do on most occasions, but sometime a little too much like the unconscious brusqueness of children, who have in such matters no discretion, and who forget, or have never been taught, the more cautious precept that "all truths are not to be told on all occasions."

F. Edward Hulme, *Proverb Lore. Being a Historical Study of the Similarities, Contrasts, Topics, Meanings, and Other Facets of Proverbs, Truisms, and Pithy Sayings, as Expressed by the Peoples of Many Lands and Times* (London: Elliott Stock, 1902; rpt. Detroit, Michigan: Gale Research Company, 1968), pp. 78-80.

Hulme provides his eager readers with considerable historical and factual information, and he feels called upon to do a bit of moralizing while he goes along. His references will be taken up with more precise bibliographical information in later chapters, but as a whole his small treatise is quite satisfactory as a cursory survey of what was known about the "spade"-phrase around the turn of the previous century.

There had in fact taken place a rather impressive scholarly discussion of the proverbial expression in the second half of the nineteenth century. As early as the year 1851, W. Fraser submitted the following query to the renowned British journal *Notes and Queries*, and this question subsequently led to a string of seventeen answers by later readers until submissions regarding the origin and transmission of the phrase stopped in 1905:

1. *Call a Spade, a Spade.* — What is the origin of the common saying *to call a spade, a spade*? Is it an old proverb or quotation? In a letter of Melancthon's to Archbishop Cranmer respecting the formularies of the Anglican Church, dated May 1st, 1548, the following sentence occurs, which seems to be another form of it.

"In Ecclesiâ rectius, *scapham, scapham dicere*; nec objicere posteris ambigua dicta."

Is *scapham, scapham dicere*, I would also ask, a classical quotation, or a modern Latin version of the other expression?

W. Fraser

[Mr. Halliwell, in his *Dictionary*, says, "The phrase *To call a spade a spade* is applied to giving a person his real character of qualities. Still in use." "I am plaine, I must needs call *a spade a spade*, a pope a pope." — *Mar-Prelate's Epitome*, p. 2.]

Notes and Queries, 1st series, 4 (1851), 274.

As will be shown later, the Latin variant "scapham, scapham dicere" is indeed related to the "spade"-expression, and it was used as a direct equivalent by Erasmus of Rotterdam. His importance for the dissemination of the classical phrase in European languages will be shown in the second chapter. The same is true for various references from classical and English sources starting in the 16th century. They will all be cited in their literary contexts in subsequent chapters. The purpose of this chapter is simply to trace the scholarly investigations of the phrase "to call a spade a spade."

10 *"Call a Spade a Spade"*

In the same year of 1851, C. Forbes was able to add a significant amount of information regarding the origin and history of the phrase in the pages of *Notes and Queries*:

2. *Call a Spade, a Spade.* (Vol. iv., p. 274.) — I have found two early, but unauthenticated, instances of the use of the saying, in a note by J. Scaliger on the *Priapeia, sive Diversorum Poetarum in Priapum Lusus*:
"Simplicius multo est, ———— latinè
Dicere, quid faciam? crassa Minervæ mea est."
Carmen, ii. 9, 10.
"Agroikos eimi: ten skaphen skaphen lego" [all Greek texts have been transliterated and are cited in quotation marks]: Aristophanes. — Unde jocus maximi Principis, Philippi Macedonis. Quum ii, qui prodiderant Olynthum Philippo, conquestum et expostulatum ad ipsum venissent, quod injuriosè nimis vocarentur proditores ab aliis Macedonibus: "hoi Makedones, inquit, amatheis kai agroikoi eisi: ten skaphen skaphen legousi." — J. Scaliger. For which note see the "Priapeia," etc., at the end of an edition of Petronius Arbiter, entitled, *Titi Petronii Arbitri Equitis Romani Satyricon. Concinnante Michaele Hadrainide. Amstelodami. Typis Ioannis Blaeu.* M.DC.LXIX.
As I cannot at this moment refer to any good verbal index of Aristophanes, I cannot ascertain in what part of his works Scaliger's quotation is to be found. Burton, in his preface to the *Anatomy of Melancholy* ("Democritus Junior to the Reader"), repeats the saying twice, i.e. in Latin and English, and presents it, moreover, in an entirely new form:
"I am *aquae potor*, drink no wine at all, which so much improves our modern wits; a loose, plain, rude writer, *ficum voco ficum, et ligonem ligonem*, and as free as loose; *idem calamo quod in mente*: I call a spade a spade; *animis haec scribo, non auribus,* I respect matter, not words," etc. — Democritus Jr. to the Reader, Burton's *Anatomy of Melancholy*, Blake, MDCCCXXXVI. one vol. 8vo. p. 11.

C. Forbes

Notes and Queries, 1st series, 4 (1851), 456.

The note by Forbes is of much importance, since it refers to Aristophanes as one of the earliest sources of the expression. This literary text will, of course, be cited in the second chapter.

But for now, let us proceed with the references from *Notes and Queries* and observe how slowly but surely more references from English writings are added to the picture. Some of these will, of course, later be picked up by authors or better editors of various collections of quotations and proverbs (see chapters 3 and 4). We will cite them in more complete contexts in the sixth chapter on literary references from prose writings, drama, and poetry.

Five years later, in 1856, J.H.M. added a number of important citations from English sources to the string of references that show the early appearance of the phrase in that vernacular language:

3. "*To call a spade a spade.*" — Some of your correspondents are doubtless able to trace this expression, if not to its origin, to a much earlier period than I am in the following writers. Baxter, in his *Narrative of the most Memorable Passages of his Life and Times*, 1696, thus introduces it:

"I have a strong natural inclination to speak of every subject just as it is, and *to call a spade a spade*, and *verba rebus optare*, so as that the thing spoken of may be fulliest known by the words, which methinks is part of our speaking truly. But I unfeignedly confess that it is faulty, because imprudent."

This is the passage referred to by Mr. Blunt in his posthumous work, *Duties of the Parish Priest*.

A later writer of a very different school to Baxter — Dr. Arbuthnot — in his *Dissertations upon the Art of Selling Bargains*, says:

"In the native region of our itinerant salesman, there is an immemorial prescription *for calling a spade a spade*; they are not over curious in using circumlocutions or other *figurative* modes of speech, but choose rather to express themselves in the most *plain* and *proper* words of their Mother-Tongue."

Swift is quoted as using this expression, but I have no reference to the particular passage in his writings where it may be found.

Ray has given this amongst his *Proverbial Phrases*, but without a comment.

J.H.M.

Notes and Queries, 2nd series, 2 (1856), 26.

The references which this phrase sleuth cites, albeit as so often on the pages of *Notes and Queries* without proper bibliographical information (especially page numbers), are of particular importance since they clearly explain the meaning of the proverbial expression, i.e., to talk plainly and directly without any indirection whatsoever.

In the same year of 1856, a classical scholar who signs his name simply with "L." returns to more classical quotations of the phrase, especially Lucian. He also refers to Aristophanes and Erasmus of Rotterdam as the humanist scholar to whom the modern world is greatly indebted for having distributed proverbial language of antiquity through his *Adagia* (1500ff.):

4. *"To call a spade a spade"* (2nd S. ii. 26.) — In 1stS. iv. 456, a note of Scaliger is cited, in which this saying is traced to Aristophanes. The verse in question appears from the quotation of Lucian, *Quom. Hist. sit conscrib.*, to have been —
"Ta suka suka, ten skaphen skaphen legon."
See also Lucian, *Jov. Trag*, 32. Other references to his verse, which is nowhere ascribed by name to Aristophanes, are given in the note of C.F. Hermann, in his edition of the former treatise, p. 248. The proverb is inserted in the Adagia of Erasmus, under the head of "Libertas, Veritas."

L.

Notes and Queries, 2nd series, 2 (1856), 120.

Another year later, in 1857, Limus Lutum adds a citation from Plutarch to the discussion, and he also once again mentions Aristophanes:

5. *To call a Spade a Spade.* — Mr. Forbes (1st S. iv. 456.) cites the story about Philip of Macedon using this phrase from a Latin annotation of J. Scaliger. Scaliger got it from Plutarch's *Apophthegms*. Plutarch reports the saying thus:
"Skaious, ephe, phusei kai agroikous einai Makedonas, kai toi skaphoi skaphoi legontas."
Scaliger had some authority for assigning the expression to Aristophanes, although L. (2nd S. ii. 120.) implies that he had not. For Thirlwall, in a foot-note to his account of Philip's manner of treating the Olynthian traitors, quotes thus from Tzetses, *Chiliad*. viii. 208.:
"Ek komodias dexios eipon Aristophanous: Hoi Makedones, amatheis, skaphen phasi ten skaphen."

Limus Lutum

Notes and Queries, 2nd series, 3 (1857), 474.

Early Scholarship on the Phrase (1851–1978)

In 1858, a scholar using the initials A.B. was of much help in giving detailed information on Erasmus of Rotterdam's use of the phrase. It is important to note here that Erasmus is citing the variants "to call a fig a fig" and "to call a little boat a little boat." The translation of Erasmus' passages will eventually start the tradition of the phrase in English in particular:

6. *"Call a spade a spade"* (1ˢᵗ S. iv. 274. 456.) — Similar sayings are to be found in that storehouse of idioms, the Colloquies of Erasmus. At the end of the colloquy, "Philetymus et Pseudocheus," Phil. says: "At istam artem, nos crassiores, solemus vocare furtum, qui *ficum vocamus ficum, et scapham scapham.*" And in the dialogue "Dilucalum Philypnus": "Dicam igitur explanatè, nec aliud dicam ficum, quàm ficum."

A.B.

Notes and Queries, 2nd series, 5 (1858), 246.

Two years pass until William Bates continues the discussion, and he cites the passage in Erasmus' *Adagia* that was to have the largest influence on spreading the expression in the English language through translation:

7. TO CALL A SPADE A SPADE (1ˢᵗ S. iv. 274. 456.; 2ⁿᵈ S. ii. 26. 120.; iii. 474.) — To the illustrations of this phrase which have already been collected, the following may be added. Erasmus, in his *Adagia* (ed. Elzevir, p. 369.), citing the Latin saying,
    "Ficus ficus, ligonem ligonem vocat"
and its Greek equivalent
    "Ta suka suka, Ten skaphen skaphen legon"
refers to Aristophanes for the original idea, and adds
    "Nam ego, quemadmodum ait Comicus, rusticanus sum, et ligonem ligonem appello."
    These passages were doubtless in the mind of Rabelais when he wrote
    "Nous sommes simples gents, puisqu'il plaist à Dieu; et appellons les figues figues, les prunes prunes, et les poires poires." — *Pantagruel* liv. iv. chap. liv.,
and suggested to Boileau the *formula* by means of which, employed in a distich, the simplicity and terseness of which has rendered it proverbial, he has conferred on the name of Charles Rolet, — the *âme damnée* of the palace, the *Vollichon* of the *Roman Bourgeois* of Furetière, — an unenviable immortality: —

> "Je ne puis rien nommer, si ce n'est par son nom;
> J'appelle un chat un chat, et Rolet un fripon." *Sat.* i.
>
> William Bates
>
> *Notes and Queries*, 2nd series, 10 (1860), 58.

It should be noted here that the classical phrases of "calling a spade a spade" did in fact become proverbial in French as "appeler un chat un chat," and it is very much still in use today in this wording.

The next entry about the "spade"-expression does not come until 1880, when Wm. Freelove once again refers to Melanchthon and Archbishop Cranmer. What is clear from his comments is, however, that neither he nor the editors of *Notes and Queries* are aware of the citations that were published in the journal between 1852 and 1860. That is one of the problems that can be found again and again in the historical study of proverbial phrases. So that scholars have quick access to which expressions have been dealt with in the many volumes of *Notes and Queries*, I did put together the 420-page bibliography entitled *Investigations of Proverbs, Proverbial Expressions, Quotations and Clichés. A Bibliography of Explanatory Essays which Appeared in "Notes and Queries" (1849-1983)* (Bern: Peter Lang, 1984). The fifteen notes concerning "to call a spade a spade" that have appeared in *Notes and Queries* and which are reproduced here in their entirety are, of course, listed in this bibliography. But here are Freelove's comments:

> 8. TO "CALL A SPADE A SPADE." — In the year 1548 "Archbishop Cranmer was driving on a design for the better uniting the Protestant churches, viz. by having one common confession and harmony of faith and doctrine, drawn up out of the pure Word of God, which they might all own and agree in." Melanchthon, among others, was consulted by Cranmer on this occasion, and encouraged the archbishop to go on with his design, advising him, however, "to avoid all ambiguities of expression, saying, that in the church it was best to call a spade a spade, and not to cast ambiguous words before posterity as an apple of contention." Is there an instance of an earlier use of the phrase?
>
> Wm. Freelove
>
> *Notes and Queries*, 6th series, 2 (1880), 310.

Four phrase-hunters responded to the call for earlier citations the next year, and at least one of them was aware of the first query about the "spade"-phrase from 1851. While these scholars present some old information, albeit now in more detail and with English translation, there is also significant new material:

9. To "CALL A SPADE A SPADE" (6th S. ii. 310) is a phrase of ancient date and Grecian by birth, viz., "ta suka suka ten skaphen de skaphen onomazon" (Aristophanes, as quoted by Lucian in his dialogue, *Quomodo Historia sit Conscribenda*, par. 41). It is among the regal apothegms collected by Plutarch (*Reg. et Imper. Apophthegmata*, Philip, XV.), as having been made use of by Philip of Macedon in answer to an ambassador, who complained that the citizens, on his way to the palace, called him a traitor. "Aye," quoth the king, "my subjects are a blunt people, and always call things by their proper names. Figs they call figs, and a spade a spade" ("ta suka suka, ten skaphen de skaphen onomazousi"). Cf. Kennedy's *Demosth.*, vol. i. p. 249.

William Platt

Notes and Queries, 6th series, 3 (1881), 16.

10. When this saying first appeared in "N. & Q." it was in the Latin of Melancthon to Archbishop Cranmer (1st S. iv. 274), "In ecclesia rectius scapham, scapham dicere" (*Ep. as Cranm.*, Mai 1, 1548), the communication being made by Mr. Fraser. It has often been discussed since. The source of it is the answer of Philip to the Olynthian Lasthenes, when the former excused the Macedonians from the charge that they had called the Olynthians traitors by saying, "skaious phusei kai agroikous einai Makedonas, kai ten skaphen skaphen legontas" (Plutarch, *Apophthegm.*, p. 178 B, Par., 1624). The proverb also occurs in Lucian (*De Hist. Scribend.*, 41). Tzetses (*Chiliad.*, viii. 564-5) refers it to Aristophanes, "ek komodias dexios eipon (ho Philippos) Aristophanous hoi Makedones, amatheis, skaphen phasi ten skaphen." But I am not aware that any verse in the existing plays contains it. There is (*Clouds*, 1252-3), "ouk an apodoien oud' obolon an oudeni, hostis kaleseie kardopon ten kardopen," as Erasmus has it in his *Apophthegms*. Mr. Bates (2nd S. x. 58) refers to a rather earlier use of it than Cranmer in modern times, as it occurs in Rabelais (*Pantagr.*, l. iv. c. liv.). A somewhat later use is in the preface to the *Anatomy of Melancholy*, where Burton says, "I call a spade a spade" (C. Forbes, 1st S. iv. 456).

Ed. Marshall

Notes and Queries, 6th series, 3 (1881), 16-17.

11. Here is an instance of the use of the phrase earlier than the one quoted by Mr. Freelove: —

"When those persones that wer at Lasthenes found theimselfes greued, and toke highly or fumishly, that certain of the traine of Philippus called theim traitours, Philippus aunswered, that the Macedonians wer feloes of no fine wytte in their termes but altogether grosse, clubbishe, and rusticall, as the whiche had not the witte to cal a spade by any other name then a spade": —

"ta suka suka ten skaphen skaphen legon."

"Alluding to that the common vsed prouerbe of the Grekes, calling figgues, figgues: and a bote a bote. As for his mening was, that they wer traitours in [e]very deede. And the fair flatte truthe, that the vplandishe, or homely and playn clubbes of the countree dooen vse, nameth eche thing by the right names." — [Nicholas Udall, translator], *Apophthegmes of Erasmus*, 1542, reprint 1877, p. 189.

R.R,

Notes and Queries, 6th series, 3 (1881), 17.

12. This passage will be found in Plutarch's "Apophthegmata basileon kai strategon, Philippou tou Al. pat.: — skaious ephe fusei kai agroikous einei Makedonas, kai ten skaphen, skaphen legontas" ("Inepti, inquit, natura et agrestes sunt Macedones, utpote qui scapham scapham vocant."[)]

R.C.

Notes and Queries, 6th series, 3 (1881), 17.

It is of interest to note here that the English translator of Erasmus cites as a variant to the "spade"-phrase the expression "to call a thing by its right (proper) name," a proverbial expression very much still in use today as well.

Still in the same year of 1881, the scholar using the initials R.R. is able to cite an English reference from 1539, i.e., three years earlier than the Erasmus translation from 1542 to which he had referred earlier. Such are the joys of historical phraseology:

13. TO "CALL A SPADE A SPADE" (6th S. ii. 310; iii. 16 [he means 17]). — I now send an earlier version of my former quotation. It is doubtful whether any earlier instance of it [in English] can be found. "The Macedonians be very homely men and rudely brought vppe whiche can call a mattok nothyng els but a mattok, and *a spade a spade*." — Taverner's *Garden of Wysdome*, 1539, part i. chap. vi.

R.R.

Notes and Queries, 6th series, 3 (1881), 476.

And R.R. was right, for Taverner's 1539 use of the phrase is in fact the earliest English use that we know of today. Of course, that does not necessarily mean that a citation preceding it might not be found one day. Any English translation or adaptation of Erasmus' *Adagia* after 1515 would qualify.

Five years later in 1886, a phrase sleuth with the initials B.R. is pointing out that the translation of the Greek original referring to Philip and the Macedonians is actually incorrect. Contending that Plutarch mistranslated it, he goes so far as to claim that the Greek word should be rendered as "jakes" (privy, outhouse):

14. "TO CALL A SPADE A SPADE." — This seems a very pointless saying; for why should one *not* call a spade a spade? Attempts to explain or account for it have been made — some, if I recollect right, in 'N. & Q.'; but it does not appear to have occurred to any one to go to the fountain head, and challenge the correctness of the established translation of the story in Plutarch's 'Apophthegms,' from which it is derived.

The story is, that one Lasthenes having complained that Philip's followers had called him a traitor (which he was), Philip said, he must not mind it, the Macedonians were rough fellows, who called "ten skaphen skaphen": which all the translators (so far as I am aware) by a strange coincidence, or (which is more likely) because they have copied from one another, conspire to reader [i.e., render] "a spade"; although there is no authority (unless this be one) for using the word is [i.e., in] that sense; and I conceive (subject to correction by better scholars) that a noun of the instrument from an active verb like "skapto" would not be in this form; and the article "ten" seems inappropriate.

The primary meaning of "skaphe" is a ditch, hole, anything hollowed out; and we know that the word had a homely association, trough, bowl, tub; "skaphion" in Aristophanes, and *scaphium* in Juvenal means a nightpan, or slop-pail; it seems, therefore, to me almost certain that the proper version of Philip's saying is "to call the jakes the jakes," which does not want force, whatever else it may want.

B.R.

Notes and Queries, 7th series, 1 (1886), 366.

Two readers of *Notes and Queries* quickly responded to this new translation attempt. There was first of all Ed. Marshall, who had commented on the "spade"-phrase before. He is quite correct in concluding that the phrase in its accustomed translation would best remain as it is:

15. "TO CALL A SPADE A SPADE" (7th S. i. 366). — This possibly did not originate with the story in Plutarch, but formed part of an earlier line, known as the fragment of a comic poet, which has even been attributed to Aristophanes, who died two years before Philip was born. However, the best answer appears to be that which is suggested by the lines in the 'Æneid': —
    Fatis nunquam concessa moveri
    Adparet Camerina procul.
To the same effect is the Greek epigram ('Anth. Gr.,' lib. iv. p. 303, Francof., 1600): —
    "Me kinei Kamarinan, akinetos gar ameinon,
    Mepote kinesas ten meiona meizona theies."
    The Camarina in Sicily is not the only one which had best remain as it is.

Ed. Marshall

Notes and Queries, 7th series, 1 (1886), 496.

The point is well taken, for the expression "to call a spade a spade" had long become proverbial in English, and for its common use in that language it is irrelevant whether it is based on a mistranslation or not.

And yet, another scholar now suggested to that the correct translation might be "tub", a suggestion that was also made by R.B. in the same year of 1886:

16. Though "skaphe" does not mean a spade, it seems from Lidell and Scott that "skaphion" does, and the translator of Plutarch must have blundered between the two. But Lidell and Scott do not give "skaphe" any such meaning as B.R. suggests [i.e., jakes], and it surely ought to be found before the theory, probable as it may seem, can be entertained. Nor is B.R. quite correct in his rendering of "skaphion", or *scaphium*; strictly speaking, it is a *female urinal*. Why not be content with translating "skaphe" simply into *tub*?

C.F.S. Warren

Notes and Queries, 7th series, 1 (1886), 496–497.

Another ten years later, and perhaps with cultural literacy in Greek and Latin increasing in its decline, Frank Rede Fowke, with no knowledge of the previous scholarly exchanges in *Notes and Queries*, associates the word "spade" with playing cards:

17. "CALL A SPADE A SPADE." — In spite of the episcopal dictum that its synonym is "a sanguinary shovel," I incline to think that the spade of the proverb was that of playing cards. I should be glad of evidence for or aginst my opinion.

Frank Rede Fowke

Notes and Queries, 10th series, 3 (1905), 169.

As expected, this conjecture met with an immediate and sharp response by the well-known philologist and lexicographer Walter W. Skeat. He sets the record straight, as it were. And yet, there have been others who have associated the term "spade" of the proverbial phrase with the card game in more recent times. In due time, the black color of "spades" in the card game was influential in the creation of the slang term and slur of the modern "spade" referring to Blacks. This eventually would lead to the questionable persecution of the phrase "to call a spade a spade" in the name of political correctness. All of this will be explained in much detail in chapters five and nine, of course. Here for now are Skeat's comments:

18. "CALL A SPADE A SPADE" (10TH S. iii. 169). — When a querist admits that he does not know the origin of a phrase, it would be playing the game to refrain from guessing at it. Of course there is not the faintest reason for supposing that there is any allusion to a game of cards. Reference to King's 'Classical and Foreign Quotations,' advertised on the back of the final leaf in the very same number of 'N. & Q.,' will show that the saying occurs in Plutarch, who gave it in Greek. I cannot believe that playing-cards were common in Plutarch's time in Greece.

Walter W. Skeat

Notes and Queries, 10th series, 3 91905), 217.

With his scathing rebuttal, the eighteen scholarly interchanges in *Notes and Queries* between the years 1851 and 1905 come to an end. They contain much enlightening material as well as conjectures, much of which was also being picked up by compilers of quotation and proverb dictionaries, as pointed out by Walter Skeat in the last *Notes and Queries* entry in 1905.

20 *"Call a Spade a Spade"*

Some thirty years later, three classical scholars picked the whole discussion of the origin and dissemination of the phrase "to call a spade a spade" up one more time. At a meeting of the Cambridge Philological Society held in the Combination Room of Jesus College on 8 March 1934, J.M. Edmonds read a paper "On Calling a Spade a Spade," of which the following summary subsequently appeared in print:

Most editors have rightly connected Lucian's phrase in *Conscr. Hist.* 41 "ta suka suka, ten skaphen de skaphen onomason" with the fuller context paraphrased in his *Pseudolog.* 4, where he ascribes the whole citation to Menander, and with the line

"agroikos eimi ten skaphen skaphen legon"

from his *Jup. Trag.* 32, which occurs, in substance, in Synesius *Ep.* 159 and in Julian *Or.* 8. 208 a. As the saying in the latter form — with "agroikos" and without figs — is clearly anterior to Philip of Macedon, who according to Plutarch *Reg. Ap.* 178 used it of the traitor Lasthenes in 348, it cannot be Menander's. The following considerations, taken together, suggest that it came from the first edition of the *Clouds*, which, unlike the extant second edition, was acted, and is therefore the more likely of the two to have given a proverb to the language before Alexandrian times: (1) Apostolius (died 1480) gives the saying in two forms,

"ta suka suka ten skaphen skaphen legei"

and "kai ta suka suka lego kai ten kardopon kardopon," of which the latter clearly is related to the "kardopos-kardope" passage in *Nub.* 669 ff.; (2) Plutarch's pluralised paraphrase of the fig*less* version "skaious ephe (ho Philippos) kai agroikous einai Makedonas kai ten skaphen skaphen legontas" contains "skaios" as well as "agroikos", and in the *Clouds* Strepsiades not only calls himself twice, and is called by Socrates twice, "agroikos", but is three times called by Socrates "skaios", and this for not being able to learn his lessons; in one place, 628, he calls him both together, and in another, 655, calls him, not indeed "agroikos", but "agreios, kai skaios"; moreover three of these five occurrences of "skaios" or "agroikos" in the mouth of Socrates (or four of these six if we count "agreios" as equivalent to "agroikos") come near the passage where Socrates tells Strepsiades that he should say for kneading-trough (*see* Scholion) not "he kardopos" but "he kardope"; (3) the fig*less* version may well have been originally

"skaios de tis
kagroikos eimi ten skaphen skaphen legon,"

said by a Strepsiades bewildered by being told to say "he kardope" — as it were, 'I don't call it either, then; I'm a "skaios" and "agroikos" fellow and I call it a "skaphe", which it is'; (4) "skaphe" could mean kneading-trough in Comedy (*see* Poll. 10. 102); (5) It is only the connexion with the "kardope"-passage of Aristophanes which gives a reason for the choice of "skaphe"; (6) Tzetses (12th cent.) *Chil.* 8. 567 cites the fig*less* version and ascribes it to Aristophanes.

The conclusion is that Menander took the fig*less* version from the first edition of the *Clouds* — perhaps after the saying had won greater notoriety through its use by Philip — cut out the words "skaios" and "agroikos", and added the figs. The question, why figs? is answered by the consideration that once the saying was started in life with the "skaphai", for the choice of which there was good reason in its original place in Aristophanes, anything called sometimes by a more technical, fanciful, pedantic, or polite name would do, and while there are many kinds of figs they are all figs except to the gardener or the gourmet. This stage is seen not only in Menander, but in Rabelais, who, speaking of pears in bk. iv, chap. 54, cuts out the "skaphai" and adds two other fruits: 'Appelons les figues figues, les prunes prunes, et les poires poires.' These words were first printed in 1532, a year after the publication of Erasmus' *Apophthegms* — a collection based largely on Plutarch's *Regum Apophthegmata*, not to be confused with his *Adagia* of 1500 [should be the edition of 1515] —, where the fig*less* version is given in the Latin text in its Philippean context with "skaphen" mistranslated by *ligonem*, and the fig*ful* version added (doubtless from Lucian) in the note in the original Greek. Nicholas Udall translated Erasmus' *Apophthegms* into English in 1542, and though he renders the "skaphe" of Erasmus' note by 'bote' (which is one of its meanings) eternised Erasmus' mistake by translating the *ligonem* of the text by 'spade.' French was less fortunate than English, for it was not till a century later that Boileau published his famous version (*Sat.* i) — probably from Plutarch —, and then it was 'J'appelle un chat un chat et Rolet un fripon'.[1] This marks the further stage when anything *Whatever* will do. The attempt of some commentators to give "suka" and "skaphe" obscene meanings is defeated by the obvious meaning of the saying. In it figs must be figs and "skaphai skaphai", and while there is evidence that "skaphe" could mean kneading-trough, there is none that it could mean "skaphion".

The passage of Menander may be restored thus from Lucian and Plutarch (after Meineke 351 and Kock 545):

"Ego eim' Elegchos, andres hoi theomenoi,[2]
ton deur' anabanton ouk asemotatos theos,[3]
ho philos Aletheiai te kai Parrhesiai
monoisi t' echthros ton broton tois ten emen
glottan dediosi, panta d'eidos kai saphos
diexion hoposa sunoid' humin kaka,
ta suka suka ten skaphen skaphen legon."

[1] Information kindly supplied by Dr. Stewart.
[2] Cf. Soph. *Ph.* 585, Ar. *Vesp.* 1224, *Ach.* 497.
[3] Cf. Xen. *Hell.* 6. 4. 18 ("ouk elachiston dunamenos en tei polei").

J.M. Edmonds, "On Calling a Spade a Spade," *Proceedings of the Cambridge Philological Society*, 157-159 (1936), 5-7.

One would think that Edmonds might have known a few of the short comments in *Notes and Queries*, but he does not refer to them. His essay is, however, most useful in putting considerable order into the chronology and development of the phrase in classical times, establishing that Aristophanes is to be considered the first written source. More about all of this in the second chapter.

Two years after the publication of Edmond's paper in England, Bruce M. Metzger from Princeton had another go at it in 1938 in *The Classical Journal*, albeit without any references to the scholarship in *Notes and Queries* or to the Edmonds article. Consequently he decides that Menander and not Aristophanes might have fathered the phrase and repeats much of the information already included in former scholarship:

The idea involved in the English expression, "to call a spade a spade," is not original with us moderns. Both Greek and Latin writers have parallel phrases that pithily refer to the same notion of telling plain facts in plain language.

Plutarch believed that Philip of Macedon was the originator of a phrase that became quite popular. In his "Apothegms of Kings and Great Commanders" Plutarch[1] records Philip's reply to those who were complaining that some of the Macedonian's associates had called them traitors. Philip excused the speech of his companions by characterizing them as follows: "phusei kai agroikous einai Makedonas kai ten skaphen skaphen legontas." The point of the second clause is to be found in the fact that "skaphe" signifies "anything dug or scooped out," and thus might be used of a "trough," "basin," or "bowl" as well as of a "skiff" or "boat." "To call a spade a spade," then, using this word "skaphe", was similar to our reproach in referring to a nondescript boat as a "tub"; i.e., "to call a tub a tub."

Although Plutarch thought that Philip had coined this expression, the honor of being its father probably ought to be given to Menander. There is a fragment of his which combines two figures of speech expressing this idea (Frag. 545K):

"Elegchos eimi' ego
. . . . .panta t' eidos kai saphos
diexion hoposa sunoid' humin [kaka],
ta suka suka, ten skaphen skaphen legon."

Here not only is there a play on the word "skaphe" but on "sukon" as well. The play on the latter word arises from a specialized meaning of "fig." Greek physicians described the malady hemorrhoids as "suka", and hence to call "suka suka" is to be outspoken, not choosing dainty words to express coarse ideas. It is "calling a spade a spade."

Although we do not know who it was that first hit off this *jeu de mots*, certainly by the time of Philip it was in the air. Aristophanes seized upon "skaphe" for a pun.[2] Later it crops up in Lucian's *Jupiter Tragoedus* 32: "Oukoun akouson, o Zeu, meta parrhesias: ego gar, hos ho komoidos ephe, agroikos eimi ten skaphen skaphen legon." In fact, Lucian liked it so well that he gave it in its double form when listing the characteristics of a good historian:[3] "Toioutos oun moi ho suggrapheus esto, aphobos, adekastos, eleutheros, parrhesias kai aletheias philos, hos ho komikos phesi, ta suka suka, ten skaphen de skaphen onomason." We could wish that he had been more specific in his reference to the nameless "komoidos" or "komikos".

What the Greeks invented the Romans were not long in borrowing. Martial was intrigued by the terse phrase about "figs" and composed the following lines around it:[4]

> Cum dixi *ficus*, rides quasi barbara verba
>   et dici *ficos*, Caeciliane, jubes.
> Dicemus *ficus*, quos scimus in arbore nasci,
>   dicemus *ficos*, Caeciliane, tuos.⁵

Several centuries later Emperor Julian found this *lusus verborum* apropos to point his rebuke directed against Heraclius, a Cynic. It is slavelike, says the emperor, to disguise truth with words calculated to flatter those who listen. He continues: "All' ameinon an tis didachtheie me ta pragmata akouon auta mede ta ep' autois onomata kata ton komikon ten skaphen skaphen legonta...."⁶

Erasmus was a link in the chain that carried the idea in these expressions down to more modern times. Steeped in classical learning, he imitated the Graeco-Roman authors in his *Colloquium* between Pseudocheus and Philetymus. The latter says: *At istam artem nos crassiores solemus vocare furtum, qui ficum vocamus ficum, et scapham scapham.* Erasmus, as well as Lucian and Martial, evidently thought that if this sally was worth telling once it was worth repeating. He puts into the mouth of one of two characters in his humorous skit, "A Dialogue on Early Rising," one half of the phrase, viz. *Nec dicam ficum aliud quam ficum.*

Two centuries after Erasmus, Albert Bengel, a German scholar who wrote in Latin a commentary on the New Testament, makes use of the play on the word for "tub." He suggests in commenting on *Romans* I,26: *In peccatis arguendis saepe scapha debet scapha dici.*⁷

¹Cf. *Moralia* II, 178(b).
²Cf. *Equit.* 1315.
³Cf. *De Conscribenda Hist.* 41 (54).
⁴I,65. This pun evidently caught Martial's fancy, for he uses it in two other epigrams: IV,52 and VII,71.
⁵Some manuscripts read *tuas* here. Ancient grammarians disputed a great deal over the gender of *ficus*. The Teubner *Thesaurus Linguae Latinae* says (*s.v.*) that when *ficus* means *ulcus* it is *plerumque gen. masc.*
⁶*Orationes* VII, 208(a).
⁷Cf. *Gnomen Novi Testamenti, in loc.*
Bruce M. Metzger, "'To Call a Spade a Spade' in Greek and Latin," *The Classical Journal*, 33 (1938), 229–231.

Two months later Metzger's article drew a response in the same journal by John Paul Heironimus from the University of Wisconsin. Once again not being aware of previous scholarship, Heironimus goes into considerable detail regarding the mistranslation by Erasmus which subsequently is carried on by Richard Taverner's (1539) and Nicholas Udall's (1542) translation of Erasmus into English, thereby establishing the phrase as "to call a spade a spade" in the English language:

> The elegant circumlocutions by which our Victorian ancestors avoided naming a spade outright are happily no longer fashionable; they are to be found chiefly in areas of cultural lag such as pedagogical treatises, "journalese," and business English. I read recently of an amazing institution[1] which teaches Chicago clerks and stenographers to say "The typewriter is an indispensable office appliance" instead of "We couldn't get along without the typewriter." Such "improved" phrasing usually involved substitution of Latin derivatives for Anglo-Saxon, but the spirit which prompts it is not Latin; the Roman authors in general are not given to beating about the bush. Of course there are exceptions; Tacitus in particular objects to commonplace words. Thus *caligae* becomes *eo tegmine pedum*, and *pix, id mercimonium...quo flamma alitur*; but the most striking example is his *per quae egeritur humus aut exciditur caespes* to describe the legionary's entrenching tools.[2]
>
> Mr. Bruce M. Metzger's recent note[3] on Greek and Latin parallels to our English proverb fails to bring out one interesting fact: "to call a spade a spade" is not only equivalent to, but derived from, "ten skaphen skaphen legein," and the mistranslation preserves a blunder by one of the most famous classical scholars of the Renaissance, Desiderius Erasmus. In his collection of *Apothegms*[4] the great Dutchman quotes Plutarch's version[5] of the proverb, and renders "skaphe" by *ligo*, "hoe" or "mattock." The mistake is forgiveable, as "skaphe" seems rather elusive in its meanings. It is of course connected with the verb "skaptein", "to dig"; but as Metzger remarks, the noun signifies "anything dug or scooped out" rather than "the tool with which one digs"; that is "skapheon".
>
> Erasmus' *Apothegms* appeared in 1531; his mistake was conveyed into English in 1542 by the translation[6] of Nicholas Udall or Uvedall, with "spade" for *ligo*. This is his quaint rendering of the sentence: "Philippus aunswered, that the Macedonians wer feloes of no fyne witte in their termes, but altogether grosse, clubbyshe, and rusticall, as they whiche had not the witte to calle a spade by any other name then a spade." Various Elizabethans took up the phrase, and it has become so

embedded in the language that no one would think of trying to correct it now.

[1] The Better-Speech Institute of America. The proprietors are said to be prospering fabulously. I quote from *Time* XXXI (Jan. 24, 1938), 26.
[2] Cf. *Ann.* I, 41; XV, 38; and I, 65.
[3] *Classical Journal* XXXIII (1938), 229.
[4] Cf. *Apophthegmata lepideque dicta principum, philosophorum ac diversi generis hominum ex Graecis pariter ac Latinis auctoribus selecta*, in *Opera Omnia* IV, 194.
[5] Cf. *Moralia* II, 178(b).
[6] Cf. *Apophthegmes, that is to saie, prompte, quicke, wittie and sentencious saiyings, of certain Emperours, Kynges, Capitaines, Philosophiers and Oratours...first gathered and compiled in Latine by the ryght famous clerke Maister Erasmus of Roterdame, and now translated into Englyshe by Nicolas Udall. Excusum typis Ricardi Grafton*, 1542; page 167. Udall, Headmaster of Eton College, was the *plagosus Orbilius* of his day; Thomas Tusser laments that he received fifty-three stripes "for fault but small or none at all." He is also remembered as the author of the comedy *Ralph Roister Doister*.
John Paul Heironimus, "On Calling a Spade 'An Agricultural Implement' in Latin," *The Classical Journal*, 33 (1938), 426-427.

Forty years after these two notes in *The Classical Journal*, I published a small note in 1978 concerning the appearance of "to call a spade a spade" in modern German as a loan translation from the English. About 450 years after Erasmus it is slowly gaining some currency in the German language, but it is very doubtful that it will ever replace the traditional German equivalents of "das Ding (Kind) beim rechten Namen nennen" (to call a thing (child) by its proper name). But it is fascinating to see once again how the importance of the Anglo-American language and culture throughout the world is also disseminating proverbs and proverbial expressions, in this case a phrase that goes back to classical antiquity:

Vor einigen Monaten war in der *Zeit* in einer von Rudolf Walter Leonhardt verfaßten Buchbesprechung folgendes zu lesen: "Alles, was der Literaturfreund an dem Literatur-Kritiker [Marcel] Reich-Ranicki zu schätzen weiß, findet er in diesem Buch wieder. Da ist ein sachkundiger

Mann, der eine Fülle von Fakten abrufbereit im Gedächtnis gespeichert hat, der sich nie drückt und einen Spaten immer einen Spaten nennt" (Nr. 6; 3. Februar 1978, S. 43). Verdutzt fragt sich der Leser, was es mit diesem Ausdruck "einen Spaten einen Spaten nennen" auf sich hat. Keine der vielen Redensartensammlungen hilft weiter, auch Lutz Röhrichs *Lexikon der sprichwörtlichen Redensarten*, 2 Bde. (Freiburg, Herder, 1973) läßt ihn im Stich, und das aus gutem Grund [heute nicht mehr, da Röhrich meine Forschungsergebnisse dieses kurzen Beitrags in der erweiterten Auflage seines Lexikons verarbeitet hat; vgl. *Das große Lexikon der sprichwörtlichen Redensarten*, 3 Bde. (Freiburg: Herder, 1991-1992), Bd. 3, S. 1496]. Es handelt sich nämlich um eine sehr beliebte englische Redensart, die der anglophile Journalist Leonhardt Wort für Wort aus dem Englischen übersetzt hat: "to call a spade a spade". Übrigens ist diese Redensart auch nicht in alten und neuen deutschen Wörterbüchern verzeichnet, dafür aber doch in den englisch-deutschen oder deutsch-englischen Wörterbüchern und Redensartenbüchern. So verzeichnen z.B. Karl Engeroff und Cicely Lovelace-Käufer in ihrem *English-German Dictionary of Idioms* (5. Aufl., München: Hueber, 1975) unter dem Stichwort *spade* folgendes: "to call a spade a spade = das Ding (Kind) beim rechten Nemen nennen" (S. 240). Und auch in Ronald Taylors und Walter Gottschalks *German-English Dictionary of Idioms* (4. Aufl., München: Hueber, 1973) steht unter *Kind* das gleiche: "das Kind beim rechten Namen nennen = to call a spade a spade" (S. 277).

Damit ist zwar die Bedeutung der Redenart "to call a spade a spade" geklärt, aber noch nicht ihr Ursprung, der sich bis weit in die griechische Antike zurückverfolgen läßt. Nachdem die Redensart schon im 19. Jahrhundert und Anfang des 20. Jahrhunderts in der englischen Zeitschrift *Notes and Queries* (N & Q) verschiedentlich kurz besprochen worden war[1], wurden dann in den dreißiger Jahren drei längere philologische Quellenuntersuchungen veröffentlicht[2], die eine große Menge griechischer und lateinischer Belegtexte von Plutarch bis Erasmus von Rotterdam zusammenstellen.

Für die englische Sprache ist die Fassung "Ficus ficus, ligonem ligonem vocat" aus Erasmus' *Apophthegmata* (1531) wichtig, da Nicholas Udall den *ligo* (=Rodehacke, Haue) in seiner englischen Ausgabe von 1542 als *spade* wiedergegeben hat: "...to call a spade by any other name than a spade." Danach läßt sich die Redensart in der englischen Literatur bis zum heutigen Tag verfolgen, und sie gehört besonders im Amerikanischen zu den populärsten. [...] Die Verdeutschung "einen Spaten einen Spaten nennen" ist wohl zu forciert, als daß sie Redensarten wie "das Kind beim (rechten) Namen nennen" oder "kein Blatt vor den Mund nehmen" wird ersetzen können.

[1][Bibliographische Angaben der kurzen Beiträge aus *Notes and Queries*, die hier in diesem Kapitel abgedruckt sind].

[2][Bibliographische Angaben der drei längeren Beiträge von J.M. Edmons, Bruce M. Metzger und John Paul Heironimus, die ebenfalls hier abgedruckt vorliegen].

[3]Vgl. die vielen Belege bei Burton Stevenson, *The Macmillan Book of Proverbs, Maxims, and Famous Phrases*, 7. Aufl. (New York: Macmillan, 1968), S. 2194.

Wolfgang Mieder, "Einen Spaten einen Spaten nennen," *Der Sprachdienst*, 22 (1978), 121-122.

But whether the old "spade"-phrase will eventually reach proverbial status in the German language is not of major concern to us here. This short excursus concludes this review of the scholarly treatises of the classical phrase of calling a thing or matter by its proper name that became current in English via Erasmus of Rotterdam as "to call a spade a spade." A number of English variants from the past have already been mentioned, but they will be repeated in more meaningful contexts and with more inclusive bibliographical information in later chapters. Many early and more modern contextualized citations in literature and the mass media will, of course, be discussed as well, and the ninth chapter will provide a discussion of the controversial nature of the "spade"-phrase today in light of political correctness. Altogether it is the goal of this study to present a very detailed survey of the origin, history, and meaning of the phrase. As a case study it might well serve as a model for other equally fascinating investigations of individual proverbs and proverbial expressions.

Postscript

It is with much excitement and sincere appreciation that I add this postscript to my review of previous studies regarding the origin, history, and above all meaning of the "spade"-phrase. The following "suggestions" were sent to me by my colleague and friend Professor Alan Dundes after he had carefully scrutinized my manuscript in his role as editor of the *Peter Lang International Folkloristics Series*. While his interpretive comments and psychological insights are of great significance, they also indicate how important it is that folklorists work together in order to solve such fascinating issues as for example the complete understanding of the proverbial expression "to call a spade a spade." In addition, these remarks clearly show the respect that we have for each other's scholarly work and the friendship that has helped us along with our various research projects. Were it not for the sharing of ideas in the spirit of scholarship and friendship, our life as scholars would be marked by loneliness. Instead, we gladly share our knowledge and thereby delight in the fruits of our labors.

But here are the crucial comments which Professor Alan Dundes sent to me on January 10, 2002:

There are two clues to the answer to the puzzle [why the spade was especially chosen to become part of the phrase]. The "mistranslation" theory is not really satisfactory. One clue is that the earliest texts indicate that only "blunt" people call a spade a spade (p. 36). "I'm but a boor and call a spade a spade." (p. 37). The context makes it clear that whatever the tricky Greek word was, it must have had some obscene referent. Otherwise the phrase makes no sense. Edmund Gordon points to the same thing when he says that "calling a spade a spade" represents "freedom" (p. 145) of language in speaking of sex and physiological functions. In other words, whatever the original "spade" was, refined and cultured people would not use that word to refer to it. Only a vulgar, boorish, uneducated person would use the word. Now the English word "spade" doesn't really carry that sense at all, but presumably the original Greek (and Latin) words did. That's one clue.

The second clue is the association with "fig". Early on, the phrase involved "a fig is a fig and a spade is a spade." But exactly why should the spade be combined with "fig"? In the context stated above (that only vulgar people would use such a term), the "fig" takes on added significance. "Fig" is a fairly standard symbol of either male or female genitals. Adam and Eve supposedly covered their genitals with "fig" leaves. The "fig" is the basis of the famous "fica" gesture (in which the thumb is placed between the second and third fingers) to ward off the evil eye among other things. See J. Leite de Vasconcellos, *A Figa: Estudio de Etnografia Comparativa* (Porto: Araujo Sobrinho, 1925) for discussion. For illustrations of the gesture, see Desmond Morris, et al., *Gestures: Their Origins and Distribution* (New York: Stein and Day, 1979), pp. 147-159. For discussion of German fig symbolism, see Baron Siegmar von Schultze-Galléra (pseudonym Dr. Aigremont), *Volkserotik und Pflanzenwelt*, 2 vols. (Halle: Trensinger, 1907–1910), vol. 1, pp. 74–78. The point is that "fig" seems to be related to "ficken" which in turn is related to our Anglo-Saxon four letter word. The symbolism of fig is not new. See Vincenz Buckheit, "Feigensymbolik im antiken Epigramm," *Rheinisches Museum für Philologie*, 103 (1960), 200–209.

What all this suggests to me is that calling a fig a fig is some kind of reference either to a vulva or a penis, rather than using some kind of polite euphemism. In other words, "fig" had an explicit sexual reference such that it would not be used in polite society or in public. If that is so, then presumably the original word from which "spade" was translated must have a comparable meaning. It was evidently some kind of digging implement or perhaps a hollow container. I was intrigued by the proposal you mention that spade referred to "jakes" [p. 17]. That explanation may well be incorrect, but it might have some slight merit after all.

In ancient times, before the advent of modern plumbing, individuals had to take a "digging" tool outside with them to dig a hole in which to defecate. Josephus in his *The Jewish War* includes in his description of the Essenes the following ethnographic detail. Speaking of the Essenes' observance of the sabbath, "and they abstain from seventh-day work more rigidly than any other Jews, for not only do they prepare their meals the previous day so as to avoid lighting a fire on the Sabbath, but they do not venture to remove any utensil or to go and ease themselves. On other days they dig a hole a foot deep with their trenching-tool (for such is the hatchet they give to the novices) and draping their cloak round them so as not to affront the rays of the god, they squat over it; then they put the excavated soil back in the hole." (Josephus, *The Jewish War* [London: Penguin Books, 1970], p. 136). A passage in *Deuteronomy* (23:12–14) seems to confirm this account: "Thou shalt have a place also without the camp, whither thou shalt go forth abroad: and thou shalt have a paddle upon thy weapon; and it shall be when thou wilt ease thyself abroad, thou shalt dig therewith, and shalt turn back and cover that which cometh from thee."

The point of all this is that if the original "spade" was basically the "digging" stick carried by individuals to use in connection with their daily defecation, one could see why it might not be polite to refer to this tool. If the original word was actually a container of some kind, it would be as though it were a "chamber pot" and would similarly not be referred to in polite society. Calling such a "spade" a "spade" (instead of using some acceptable euphemism) would make sense of the metaphor. And even though the original word has now been lost in (mis)translation, the general sense of the expression has survived intact. That is, to call a toilet stick a toilet stick (just as referring to a sexual part by its folk name [fig]) is to be blunt and direct, if at the same time a bit vulgar. Admittedly, all this is pure speculation on my part, but at least offers some kind of rationale for the folk metaphor.

These are the "speculations" by Alan Dundes who brings his vast knowledge of folklore and Freudian psychology to bear on the "spade"-phrase. But his thoughts do not seem particularly far-fetched to me. Since he refers to German matters as well, let me add here that the German language does in fact have the term "Spatengang" (to go to defecate with spade in hand to bury the feces); see Heinz Küpper, *Illustriertes Lexikon der deutschen Umgangssprache*, 8 vols. (Stuttgart: Ernst Klett, 1982-1984), vol. 7, p. 2665. But there is also the German expression "der erste Spatenstich" (the first thrust [prick, puncture, stab] with a spade) with the meaning of "defloration"; see Ernest Borneman, *Sex im Volksmund. Der obszöne Wortschatz der Deutschen* (Reinbek: Rowohlt, 1971), section 22.13. In this latter case the "spade" is clearly a metaphor for the penis.

Now then, if we return one more time to Erasmus of Rotterdam and his so-called "mistranslation", we can venture the following final "speculation": Erasmus knew his Bible extremely well, and he definitely was aware of the *Deuteronomy* passage dealing with defecation cited by Alan Dundes above. He also was a great Greek scholar, and when he chose to translate the Greek word most likely intentionally by "ligo" (spade), he might have had the Bible reference in mind as an allusion. Referring to a spade used after defecation would certainly have been a blunt, boorish or even vulgar thing to say. However, might he not also have been thinking of the penis? After all, he cites the "ficus"-phrase first and was obviously aware of its traditional sexual meaning. The spade can then represent the penis (the digging tool) that will enter the vulva (fig). In other words, it really is not stretching the Freudian imagination too far to argue that Erasmus of Rotterdam is actually speaking of the vulva (fig) and the penis (ligo), albeit in a rather indirect fashion. However, that is, of course, what proverbs in particular and folklore in general are all about.

There is one last hurdle to cross with this interpretation. It would be sealed if and when someone can find a Latin reference where "ligo" (spade) refers to the penis. It is my conjecture, and I am certain that my friend Alan Dundes would agree, that this metaphor exists. Someone just has to find it in the vast Latin writings that contain so many treasures, including our "Ficus ficus, ligonem ligonem vocat."

II.

From Aristophanes to Erasmus of Rotterdam

From the previous chapter it has become clear that the earliest written reference of the proverbial expression "to call a spade a spade" is to be found in classical Greek literature. Several fragmentary texts containing the phrase used by a number of Greek authors were cited, both in the Greek original and for the most part also with English translations. In this second chapter these early sources are presented in chronological order in English translation only. Greek scholars will have no difficulties locating the texts in the original. language There is no need to cite the Greek texts here since the purpose of this study is to show how the phrase entered the English language and how it has fared from the sixteenth century to the modern age.

Everything known about the expression points to Aristophanes (445?–385) as the earliest written source. But in the pertinent scene of his satirical comedy *Clouds* (423) no "spade" appears at all. Instead the two characters Strepsiades and Pasias speak of a "kneading trough." This small verbal exchange has given translators quite some difficulty, as can be seen from the following three examples. In 1812, R. Cumberland rendered it like this:

Streps. Where is this dun of mine? Come hither, friend,
How do you call this thing?
    Pasias. A kneading trough,
Or as we say, a cardopus —
    Streps. Go to!
Dost think I'll pay my money to a blockhead,
That calls this kneading-trough a *cardopus*?
I tell you, man, it is a *cardopa* —
Go, go you will not get a doit from me,
You and your *cardopus*.
    Pasias. Will you not pay me?
    Streps. Assure yourself I will not — Hence, begone!
Will you not beat your march, and quit my doors?
    Pasias. I'm gone, but take this with you, if I live
I'll sue you in the Prytaneum before night.
    Streps. You'll lose your suit, and your twelve pounds besides.
I'm sorry for your loss, but who can help it?

You may ev'n thank your cardopus for that.
> *Comedies of Aristophanes. Viz: The Clouds, Plutus, The Frogs, The Birds*, translated by R. Cumberland (London: Lackington, Allen, and Co., 1812), p. 92.

One hundred fifty years later, William Arrowsmith offered a more modern translation, replacing the "kneading trough" or "cardopus" with a simple "basket":

STREPSIADES
Reappearing from the house; in his hands he holds a large basket.
Now where's that creditor of mine?
Holding up the basket in front of Pasias.
— All right, what's this?
PASIAS
That? A basket.
STREPSIADES
A *basket*?
And a stupid ignoramus like you has the nerve to come around badgering me for money? By god, I wouldn't give a cent to a man who can't even tell a basket from a baskette.
PASIAS
Then you won't pay me back?
STREPSIADES
Not if *I* know it.
Look here,
you Colossus of Lard, why don't you quietly melt away?
Beat it, Fatboy!
He threatens to beat him with his baskette.
PASIAS.
I'm going. Yessiree. And by god,
if I don't post my bond with the magistrates right now,
my name's not Pasias.
Nossiree.
STREPSIADES
Tch tch. Poor Pasias.
You'll just lose your bond on top of all your other losses.
And, personally speaking, I wouldn't want to see you suffer
just because your grammar's bad.
Beating Pasias over the head with his baskette.
Remember?

Baskette!
> Aristophanes, *The Clouds*, translated by William Arrowsmith (Ann Arbor, Michigan: University of Michigan Press, 1962), p. 90.

As the third translator, Kenneth McLeish most likely was aware of the previous translation attempt when he also speaks of a basket in his English version of 1979:

> STREPSIADES *comes out again, carrying a basket.*
> STREPSIADES
> Where's Moneybags? Ah, there. Now then: what's this?
> PASIAS
> What's what? Oh ... a basket.
> STREPSIADES
> A basket!
> And you have the nerve to ask for money!
> I wouldn't give tuppence to a man
> Who can't tell a basket from a basketess.
> PASIAS (*slowly*)
> You ... wouldn't ... give ... tuppence ...?
> STREPSIADES
> Not likely. So,
> *Lard-belly*, you'd better just melt away.
> Slide off my doorstep.
> *Pasias*
> Right! You've done it now!
> I'll have you in court if it's the last thing I do!
> *He storms out with his* FRIEND. STREPSIADES *jeers.*
> STREPSIADES
> You're throwing good money after bad. That's a pity,
> On top of everything else. I mean,
> If you can't tell a basket from a basketess ...
>> *Aristophanes: Clouds, Women in Power, Knights*, translated by Kenneth McLeish (Cambridge: Cambridge University Press, 1979), pp. 55–56.

These three translations differ considerably from each other. When Erasmus translated parts of this scene into Latin, he retained the idea of a kneading-trough and cites it as a variant of the phrase "to call a spade a spade."

36 "Call a Spade a Spade"

A better source than Aristophanes for this expression is a fragment from Menander (343-291), yet another Greek writer of comedies. One of his fragments from unidentified plays reads as follows:

"Demonstration" is my name; Truth and Outspokenness
Are friends of mine, and Freedom is my first cousin.
The only mortals I'm an enemy to are those
Who fear my tongue. I know everything; and what I know
About your secrets, I unfold in clear detail.
To me, a fig's a fig; I call a spade a spade.
  Menander: Plays and Fragments, translated by Philip Vellacott (Harmondsworth, Middlesex: Penguin, 1973), p. 296.

There is only one major problem with this text. The Greek original has "to call a trough a trough," but the modern translator rendered it freely with Erasmus' erroneous rendition of "to call a spade a spade." It is important to note that Menander's text is thus not the direct origin of the much newer "spade"-phrase! And Erasmus made yet a second mistake in assuming that Meander's fragment actually belonged to Aristophanes.

But there is another "tub"-source that must have preceded the one from Menander. The Athenian statesman and orator Demosthenes (384-322) gives a detailed account of how Philip of Macedonia razed the Greek city of Olynthus in the year 348. In his account on "Olynthus" he includes the following paragraph that was to be repeated numerous times in other versions of this particular incident. And it is these words of Philip that later were of great influence on Erasmus of Rotterdam:

Euthycrates and Lasthenes received the recompense of their treason, though not exactly in the way they had expected. Philip maintained them at his court, but only as servile dependents and parasites. The Macedonian courtiers held them in contempt, the soldiers reviled them for their baseness. On one occasion they complained to Philip. "Never mind," said he; "the Macedonians are a blunt people; they call a spade a spade."
  The Olynthiac and Other Public Orations of Demosthenes, translated by Charles Rann Kennedy (London: Bell & Daldy, 1871), p. 249.

Once again it is necessary to point out that the translator is using the "spade"-phrase that does not appear in the original. Demosthenes also could not have known it, since it begins only with Erasmus. He obviously used the earlier "trough" original.

Erasmus in his short treatise on the Greek expression does not refer to Demosthenes, and he also does not mention Plutarch (46?–120?), who includes the account regarding Philip of Macedonia in his *Sayings of Kings and Commanders* that is part of his larger work entitled *Moralia*:

> When the men associated with Lasthenes, the Olynthian, complained with indignation because some of Philip's associates called them traitors, he said that the Macedonians are by nature a rough and rustic people who call a spade a spade.
> *Plutarch's Moralia*, ed. Frank Cole Babbitt, 15 vols. (Cambridge, Massachusetts: Harvard University Press, 1968), vol. 3, p. 47 (178b, no. 15).

With this we come to the Greek rhetorician and satirist Lucian (117–180), who in his work on "How to Write History" (c. 170) not only employs the "trough"-phrase but increases its rhetorical effectiveness by preceding it with a similar "fig"-variant, just as Menander had done before him. Lucian uses both phrases to make the point that historians should write the plain and objective facts by telling things exactly the way they happened. That is, of course, exactly the way the expression is used to this very day:

> That, then, is the sort of man the historian should be: fearless, incorruptible, free, a friend of free expression and the truth, intent, as the comic poet says [Lucian thinks of Aristophanes, but it is Menander], on calling a fig a fig and a trough a trough, giving nothing to hatred or to friendship, sparing no one, showing neither pity nor shame nor obsequiousness, an impartial judge, well disposed to all men up to the point of not giving one side more than its due, in his books a stranger and a man without country, independent, subject to no sovereign, not reckoning what this or that man will think, but stating the facts.
> *Lucian*, with an English translation by K. Kilburn, 8 vols. (Cambridge, Massachusetts: Harvard University Press, 1959), vol. 6, p. 57.

Lucian also used the expression in his play *Jupiter tragoedus*, where he has Heracles say to Zeus:

> Then hear me frankly, Zeus, for as the comic poet puts it,
> "I'm but a boor and call a spade a spade."

If that is the way things stand here with you, I shall say good-bye forever to the honours here and the odour of sacrifice and the blood of victims and go down to Hell, where with my bow uncased I can at least frighten the ghosts of the animals I have slain.

    Lucian, with an English translation by A.M. Harmon, 8 vols. (Cambridge, Massachusetts: Harvard University Press, 1968), vol. 2, p. 139.

Finally, it should also be mentioned that Cicero (106-43), famed Roman statesman and orator, cites the phrase in Greek in one of his numerous Latin letters from the year 45 B.C. This is, of course, a clear indication that the expression had "jumped" from Greek currency to a new life in the Roman world, something that Erasmus appears not to have known:

Here is your Stoic disquisition in a nutshell: "The wise man will call a spade a spade." What a lot of talk arising from a single word of yours! I am gratified that, in arguing with me, there is no word you dare not use. As for me, I maintain, and ever shall maintain, as has always been my habit, the modest reserve of Plato; so I have used veiled language in writing to you of what the Stoics deal with in the most outspoken way.

    Cicero. *The Letters to His Friends*, with an English translation by W. Glynn Williams, 3 vols. (Cambridge, Massachusetts: Harvard University Press, 1965), vol. 2, p. 271.

This contextualized reference once again makes perfectly clear what the proverbial expression meant to the ancients and what it still means today: to speak directly and factually by avoiding indirect of veiled language. Note should, however, be taken again of the fact that the modern translators use the "spade"-phrase when rendering the Greek texts into English. The Greeks used "trough" in its various meanings, and "spade" as such becomes used only with Erasmus of Rotterdam in the sixteenth century.

    These then are the most important Greek and Latin texts that contain early variants of the English proverbial expression "to call a spade a spade." Clearly the classical double phrase of "to call a fig a fig, and a trough a trough" would not have entered the English language, albeit in truncated and altered form, had not Erasmus of Rotterdam included it in his famous *Adagia* collection which he published in a number of largely expanded versions between 1500 and 1536, with many later editions to follow in Latin as well as translations into numerous languages. While the first edition of 1500 registered 818 adages (i.e., proverbs and proverbial expressions), the richly annotated last edition of 1536 contained 4151 entries. It is utterly amazing what detailed information Erasmus was able to assemble in these pages. Every expression is explained in great detail with many references to classical literature. Some entries might be but a paragraph long, but there are also those which are monographs of dozens of pages. Erasmus of Rotterdam had quite a bit to say also about the ancient proverbial phrase under discussion here. In fact, one gets the feeling from the following paragraph of 1515 that he knows almost everything about it. And yet, it is also here where he makes his famous (intentional?) translation mistake from "trough" to "spade". Here is the English translation of Erasmus' explanation of the phrase with the detailed notes as provided by R.A.B. Mynors:

Ficus ficus, ligonem ligonem vocat
He calls figs figs and a spade a spade (II iii 5)

"Ta suka suka, ten skaphen skaphen legon" [all Greek texts have been transliterated and are cited in quotation marks],* Calling the figs figs, calling a spade a spade, is an iambic line from the comedies of Aristophanes[1] [actually Menander] adapted for use as an adage. It suits a man who speaks the truth in a simple and countrified style, who tells of things as they are, and does not wrap them up in ornamental verbiage. The technical writers on rhetoric describe figures of speech which enable one to clothe obscenities in seemly language, to make rude things sound gentle and proud things modest, and to say biting things so as to win approval. Men of more homely mother-wit[2] speak more crudely and more plainly, and call things by their true names. Lucian[3] in the *Jupiter tragoedus*: 'For I'm a rustic fellow, as it says in the comedy, and call a spade a spade.' Again,[4] in his *How History Should Be Written*, he thinks a writer should be uncommitted and incorruptible, reporting things as they really happened, and calling figs figs and a spade a spade. It is also found in another form:[5] I call figs figs and a dough-trough a dough-trough. Aristophanes[6] in the *Clouds*: 'I'd never give a man a ha'penny / Who called a *kardopos* a *kardopê*.' *Kardopos* means a trough for making bread in. The poet makes Socrates a great quibbler, maintaining that one ought not to use the form *kardopon*, as used by Cleonymus, but *kardopên*, as (says he) 'you speak of Sostraten.'

*The line quoted by Erasmus comes from an unidentified Greek comedy, and is cited by Lucian *Quomodo historia conscribenda sit*

41, whence he no doubt took it. It is now commonly ascribed to Menander (frag 717). *skaphê*, the Greek noun in the second half of the line, is connected with *skaptein*, to dig, and means a dug-out vessel, a wash-tub or kneading-trough, and also a boat. In *1508* this was rendered by the Latin derivative *scapha*, a skiff of small boat; but in *1515*, misled apparently by the connection with digging, Erasmus altered this to *ligo*, a spade, and thus produced our proverb 'to call a spade a spade,' (Tilley [*A Dictionary of the Proverbs in England in the Sixteenth and Seventeenth Centuries*] S 699), which seems to have no ancient equivalent in either language. (He [Erasmus] has been faced with the same problem in II ii 49 ["Falces postulabum / Sickles I asked for"]).

[1] Aristophanes] It is not clear where Erasmus found this ascription; perhaps it was his own interpretation of 'in the comedy' in Lucian.

[2] homely mother-wit] Literally 'with a stupid Minerva' (I i 37).

[3] Lucian] *Jupiter tragoedus* 32; it is also referred to in Plutarch's 'Sayings of Kings' (*Moralia* 178A), but this is not used in the *Adagia*, being one of the chief sources of the *Apophthegmata* [1531]. In this form the saying is ascribed by Johannes Tzetzes, the twelfth-century Byzantine scholar, to Aristophanes (frag 901b; Kock 3 p 726); but this is not now accepted, and it remains anonymous as frag adesp 227.

[4] Again] Lucian *Quomodo historia conscribenda sit* 41.

[5] another form] Apostolius 16.10.

[6] Aristophanes] In his *Clouds*, the elderly Strepsiades attends the classes of Socrates (who is parodied as a master logician and expert in language) to be taught some argument which will save him from his creditors. At a much later stage in the play, he is given a comic lecture on the problem of words which, like *kardopos* a kneading-trough, though masculine in form are feminine in grammatical gender, for the feminine form would be *kardopê*. Erasmus, quoting from memory, has confused the two scenes, producing two lines of Greek based on *Clouds* 118 and 670-80; and he has then married up the illogical Greek habit of calling what 'ought to be' a *kardopê* a *kardopos*, in defiance of the grammatical gender, with the honest man's practice of calling a *kardopos* a *kardopos*, 'a spade a spade,' where the gender is quite irrelevant. The result, on a small scale, is chaos; and this is not very well cleared up by the last sentence, added in 1523, in which the attack which Aristophanes chooses to make in passing on Cleonymus, a contemporary whom he disliked,

has been misunderstood. (Sostrate is a woman's name, female in sense and feminine in gender.)
Collected Works of Erasmus. Vol. 33: *Adages II i 1 to II vi 100*, translated and annotated by R.A.B. Mynors (Toronto: University of Toronto Press, 1991), pp. 132–133 and p. 384 (notes). This English translation with but three shortened notes is reprinted in William Barker (ed.), *The Adages of Erasmus* (Toronto: University of Toronto Press, 2001), pp. 170–171.

Obviously William Barker as the editor of these selected adages of Erasmus felt that the proverbial expression "to call a spade a spade" was of general interest enough still today to include it in this truncated modern edition. In his introduction he even included the following specific comments:

A very small class of proverb[s] appears in English directly out of Erasmus' own, sometimes erroneous, interpretation of ancient texts. "Pandora's box" and "To call a spade a spade" are two results of Erasmus' misinterpretation of the ancient sources. "Pandora's box" was actually "Pandora's jar" until Erasmus translated *pithos* as *pyxis*. The Latin expression for "To call a spade a spade" was something along the lines of "To call a skiff a skiff"; Erasmus thought that the Latin *scapha* meant "spade" not "small boat" and changed *scapha* to *ligo*. It shows the powerful influence of the *Adages* that two such expressions, essentially invented by Erasmus in a work of Latin scholarship some five hundred years ago, should have lasted until the present day.
William Barker (ed.), *The Adages of Erasmus* (Toronto: University of Toronto Press, 2001), p. xxxix (introduction).

Barker's comment is a valid one, of course, but he does not seem to be aware of the fact that Erasmus clearly liked his version of the phrase, using it two more times in his voluminous writings after his first citation in the expanded *Adagia* edition of 1515. Once he employed it in its traditional "trough, boat" wording in 1523, but then in 1531, he returned to his own coinage of "spade," and it is in this form that the phrase became anglicized.

As part of his *Colloquies* that appeared in Basel in 1523, Erasmus published a four-page text entitled "Pseudocheus and Philetymus: The Dedicated Liar and the Man of Honor." As he has these men argue about the secrets of "smart" businessmen who know how to manipulate customers through lies, the honest one of the two uses the proverbial expression to argue for being truthful and factual. However, interestingly enough, Erasmus does not use his own "ligo" (spade) in this case but "scapha" (a small boat; skiff), once again indicating the difficulty of translating the Greek original:

PSEUDO. [...] I sow dissension, with my lies, between men who are far apart.
PHIL. What's the use of that?
PSEUDO. A double use. First, if a promise I've made in another's name, and in whose name accepted a commission, is not carried out — for I sell airy promises of this kind at a high price — I pretend this or that man was to blame for things going wrong.
PHIL. What if he denies it?
PSEUDO. He's far away, say in Basel; I do the promising in England. Next, it happens that once the quarrel's been started, neither man believes the other if any blame is laid on me. — That's an example of the art [of deceitful business dealings] for you.
PHIL. But we simple souls, who call a fig a fig and a spade a spade, are accustomed to call this art theft.[1]
PSEUDO. How little the fellow understands civil law! Are you allowed to bring an action for theft against one who keeps for himself what's deposited with him, or repudiates a debt, or has cheated by some such device?
PHIL. You ought to be allowed to.
PSEUDO. Just mark the skill of professionals. By these methods there's greater profit, or certainly just as much and there's less risk.
PHIL. Bad luck to you with your tricks and lies! I don't care to bid you farewell.
PSEUDO. Snarl away in your filthy rags of righteousness. Meantime I'll live enjoyably with my thefts and lies under the patronage of Ulysses and Mercury.

[1]The Latin original has: "At istam artem nos crassiores solemus vocare furtum, qui ficum vocamus ficum , et scapham scapham." Cited from *Opera omnia Desiderii Erasmi Roterdami*, ed. L.-E. Halkin, F. Bierlaire, and R. Hoven (Amsterdam: North-Holland Publishing Company, 1972), ordinis primi, tomvs tertivs (*Colloqvia*), p. 323.
The Colloquies of Erasmus, translated by Craig R. Thompson (Chicago: University of Chicago Press, 1965), p. 137.

This is quite a reality check about ill business practices, based in part on Erasmus' own experiences with the deceitful and underhanded methods of doing business by the bookseller and printer's agent Francis Berckman from Antwerp.

But it is the third citation of the "spade"-expression in the works of Erasmus that also had a lasting influence on the English language. In 1531 Erasmus had published his influential *Apophthegmata* in Basel, based to a large degree on Plutarch's "Sayings of Kings" in his *Moralia*. It is there where Erasmus picked up the use of the "trough"-phrase used by Philip of Macedonia (citing it in its Greek original and calling it a famous proverb), but he once again preferred to use his very own variant "to call a spade a spade" as well:

Quum hi qui apud Lasthenem erant quererentur, indigneque ferrent quod quidam ex Philippi comitatu dicerent ipsos proditores, Philippus respondit, *Macedones esse ingenio parum dextro, sed plane rusticanos, qui ligonem nihil aliud nossent vocare quam ligonem*. Alludens ad illud proverbium celebre, "ta suka suka, ten skaphen skaphen legon." Innuit autem, illos re vera esse proditores. Rusticana veritas quamque rem suis nominibus appellat.

Cited from *Opera omnia Desiderii Erasmi Roterdami* (Curâ & impensis Petri Vander, 1703; rpt. London: Gregg Press, 1962), qvartvs tomvs (*Apophthegmatum libri*), p. 194, no. XIV).

Eight years after the Latin publication of the *Apophthegmata*, Richard Taverner in 1539 published a small book with liberally edited excerpts form Erasmus' *Adagia* in English translation:, and it is here where the classical phrase made the jump via Erasmus and Taverner into the English lnaguage:

Veritas simplex oratio.
Trouthes tale is simple, he that meaneth good fayth, goeth not aboute to glose hys communcacio wyth paunted wordes, Plaine and homely men call a fygge, a fygge, & a spade a spade. Rhetorike and colorynge of spech proueth many tymes a mans maker to be naught.

Proverbes or adagies with newe addicions gathered out of the Chiliades of Erasmus by Richard Tauerner. Imprinted at London in Fletstrete at the synge of Whyte Harte, 1539. Rpt. as Desiderius Erasmus, *Proverbes or Adagies*. London 1539 (New York: Da Capo Press, 1969), p. 14[b].

It is important to note that Taverner clearly cites Erasmus' *Adagia* as his source. However, he did not do so in a second book entitled *The Garden of Wysdom* that he published in the same year of 1539, even though he is basing his text on Erasmus' *Apophthegmata* this time. This book about famous sayings by princes, philosophers, and others has a small chapter on Philip of Macedonia, and it is here where Taverner once again cites Erasmus' proverb in English translation, doubtlessly taking it directly from the humanist scholar:

There were some of his foreyn subgicttes whom he [Philip of Macedonia] hadde founde not very turstie, which complayned and toke the matter heuely, that his seruantes called them traytours. To whom Philip made this answere. Truly my contrye men the Macedonians be very homly men and rudely brought vppe, whiche can call a mattok nothyng els but a mattoke, and a spade a spade. Meaning that in very dede they were traytours. Uplandyshe and homely persons can not qualifie, but call euery thyng by the proper name.
The garden of wysdome wherin ye maye gather moste pleasaunt flowres, that is to say, proper wytty and quycke sayenges of princes, philosophers, and dyuers other sortes of men. Drawen forth of good authours, as well Grekes as Latyns, by Richard Tauerner. 1539. Solde in Lomberdstrete at the signe of the Lamb by John Daruye, p. Ciiii[a–b].

The concept of plagiarism did not exist in the sixteenth century the way we understand it today, but it would have been proper to refer to Erasmus of Rotterdam in the title (as Taverner had done in his other book) or at least in his one-page statement "Richarde Tauerner to the gentle readers" (p. Ai[b]). But be that as it may, Taverner's two translations of Erasmus' collections of proverbs and apophthegms brought the "spade"-phrase into the English language.

When Nicholas Udall translated the *Apophthegmata* more extensively three years later with clear reference to Erasmus of Rotterdam under the anglicized title *Apophthegmes*, the "spade"-phrase became solidified in the English language once and for all. It must not be forgotten that these early English "wisdom" books were circulated widely among those readers for whom Erasmus' Latin was not easily accessible:

When those persones that wer at Lasthenes greued, and tooke highly or fumyshly, that certain of the traine of Philippus called theim traitours, Philippus answered, that the Macedonians wer feloes of no fyne witte in their termes, but alltogether grosse, clubbyshe, and rusticall, as the whiche had not the witte to calle a spade by any other name than a spade. Alludyng to that the common used prouerbe of the grekes, callyng figgues, figgues: and a bote a bote. As for his menyng was, that thei wer traitours in veraye deede. And the fair flatte truthe, that the vplandyshe, or homely and plain clubbes of the countree dooen vse, nameth eche thyng by the right names.

Apophthegmes, that is to saie, prompte, quicke, wittie and sentencious saiynges, of certain Emperours, Kynges, Capttaines, Philosophiers and Oratours, as well Grekes, as Romaines, bothe veraye pleasaunt & profitable to reade, partely for all manner of persones, & especially Gentlemen. First gathered and compiled by the ryght famous clerke Master Erasmus of Roterodame. And now translated into Englyshe by Nicolas Udall. Excusum typis Ricardi Grafton. 1542. Rpt. as Desiderius Erasmus, *Apophthegmes*. London 1542 (New York: Da Capo Press, 1969), p. 167 (The II. Booke; Philippvs).

It is interesting to note that Erasmus does a superb historical and philological job in this paragraph. He recounts, albeit in laconic fashion, the incident when Philip of Macedonia used the double expression of "to call a fig a fig, and a trough a trough." Since the Greek word for "trough" can also mean "small boat; skiff," Udall chose to translate it as such. Erasmus obviously would not have objected to this, since he himself had used the Latin "scapho" to translate the Greek "trough" in his *Colloquies* cited above. But this time Erasmus also makes sure that he gets his own "ligo" formulation into the account to start with, and Udall follows through by translating it correctly as "spade." The result is the clear formulation "to calle a spade by any other name than a spade," that means, as Erasmus explains at the end, to name plainly "eche thyng by the right names" (Taverner has: "call euery thyng by the proper name"). In fact, then, this small account in English translation includes not only the metaphorical proverbial expression "to call a spade a spade" but also its more prosaic variant "to call a thing by its proper name." This latter innocuous phrase can well be used as a substitution for the former by those who argue that the "spade"-variant needs to be purged from the language because of its modern interpretation as a stereotypical slur against African Americans.

One thing can be said with certainty: Erasmus of Rotterdam, the great humanist link between classical antiquity and the modern European world, transplanted the proverbial expression "to call a spade a spade" via Richard Taverner's short English remnant out of his *Adagia* and adaptation of his *Apophthegmata* as well as the more complete translation of his *Apophthegmata* by Nicholas Udall into the English language. There it took a strong hold in relatively short time, and it was spread in due time to the various Englishes of the world. That the "spade"-phrase has fallen into discredit in the American version of the English language is due to special cultural and linguistic developments in the United States. The fact that the proverbial expression is now beginning to be questioned in other English-speaking parts of the world as well is, of course, due to the linguistic and cultural influence of this country. But this matter will be discussed in more detail in the ninth chapter of this study.

III.

The Expression in Dictionaries of Quotations

It is rather rare that the origin of a proverb or proverbial expression can be traced back to a particular person, and it is by no means certain whether Aristophanes did in fact originate the phrase "to call a trough a trough." Chances are that he might already be employing a common phrase in oral use. But be that as it may, the historical chain of written references begins with Aristophanes, and his name, at least in the scholarly world of lexicography, is attached to it. The same is true for Menander, who by now is known as the first employer of the longer variant "to call a fig a fig, and a trough a trough." But the authors of quotation dictionaries are quite aware of the apperance of the phrase in the writing of other Greek and Roman authors, and many of them include the special and important note that Erasmus of Rotterdam is the definite source of the modern European variant "to call a spade a spade." In any case, the fact that the phrase has this long history and that it is connected with famous names has led scholars to include it in dictionaries of quotations. But there is, of course, the other side of the coin. The phrase has long become proverbial, and most English speakers have no idea from where and from whom it came down to them. Consequently, we also have a long and impressive history of paremiographers including the phrase in collections of proverbs and proverbial expressions. But that fascinating aspect of the documentation of the phrase will be discussed in the next chapter.

The point to keep in mind in the diachronic study of any particular expression is simply this: Cast your net as wide as possible, and definitely include dictionaries of quotations and proverbs in the search. But even this is not enough to conduct a detailed and exhaustive search. Clearly language dictionaries of all types (dialect, euphemism, slang, etc.) must also be consulted, and, as can be imagined, the search can take on enormous proportions if it deals with a proverb or proverbial expression that is found in numerous cultures and their respective cultures. Studying any individual phrase thus becomes a fascinating investigation that is informed by such fields as anthropology, ethnography, folklore, history, language, literature, mass media, philology, sociology, etc. Many traditional phrases have in fact been surveyed in this fashion, as can be seen from the many entries in my *International Bibliography of Explanatory Essays on Individual Proverbs and*

Proverbial Expressions (Bern: Peter Lang, 1977). Some of these studies are involved monographs of up to several hundred pages!

But let us return to our muttons, as it were. What follows is a chronological survey of the treatment of the proverbial expression "to call a spade a spade" in quotation dictionaries. Obviously there would be more books of this type that could have been checked. The purpose of this chapter is not to be absolutely exhaustive but rather to give a representative overview of this area. Included are highy scholarly dictionaries as well as those that serve a more popular market. What will become clear is that dictionary makers do a good job in copying from each other over time, and yet, once in a while some new information, especially newer references, are added to attest to the continued use of the phrase. As in any detective work, though, one is never sure what any of the dictionaries might contain. This then leads to the important maxim that a serious phrase sleuth must check in as many quotation dictionaries as possible, ever mindful of the Bible proverb "Seek, and ye shall find" (Matthew 7,7).

In the middle of the nineteenth century John Bartlett published the first edition of his celebrated collection of *Familiar Quotations* (Boston: Little, Brown, and Company, 1858), but it took until the fifth edition of 1868 that the proverbial expression "to call a spade a spade" showed up in an appendix to the volume. Even though the phrase is listed with references to Plutarch and Aristophanes (most likely an indication that Bartlett knew about the scholarly discussion in the pages of *Notes and Queries*, as discussed in the first chapter of this study), the entry is listed under the "spade"-variant and not "trough," as one might have expected in light of the history of the expression. Clearly John Bartlett and his American compatriots were long used to the phrase as "to call a spade a spade," since it had already established itself as a common proverbial expression. The many references to it in proverb collections discussed in the following chapter bear witness to this. In any case, all quotation dictionaries list the phrase under its popular and well-known "spade"-variant.

Here now is the first occurrence in Bartlett's *Familiar Quotations*, followed by a list of entries from other quotation dictionaries. It will be seen that slowly but surely the lexicographers go beyond the classical sources and begin to register ever more references from literary sources of the English language:

1. John Bartlett, *Familiar Quotations* (Boston: Little, Brown, and Company, 1868), p. 583.

To call a spade a spade.
   Plutarch, *Reg. et Imp. Apoph. Philip.* xv.
"Ta suka suka, ten skaphen de skaphen onomazon" [all Greek texts have been transliterated and are cited in quotation marks].
   Aristophanes, as quoted in Lucian, *Quom. Hist. sit conscrib.* 41.

2. James Allan Mair, *A Handbook of Proverbs, Mottoes, Quotations and Phrases* (London: George Routledge, 1874), p. 213.

[identical to Bartlett's reference above; clearly copied from it].

3. J.C. Grocott, *Familiar Quotations* (London: George Routledge, 1879), p. 421.

SPADE. — "Never mind," said Philip; "the Macedonians are a blunt people; they call a spade a spade."
   Kennedy's Demosthenes, Vol. I. Page 249.

4. William S. Walsh, *The International Encyclopedia of Prose and Poetical Quotations* (Philadelphia: John C. Winston, 1908), p. 746.

"These Macedonians," said he, "are a rude and clownish people, that call a spade a spade."
   Plutarch. *Apothegms of Great Commanders, Phillip.*
Ficus ficus, ligonem ligonem vocat.
A fig's a fig, a spade a spade he calls.
   Erasmus. *Adagiorum Chiliades, Veritas.*
I'll give you leave to call me anything, if you don't call me "spade."
   Swift. *Polite Conversation.* Dialogue ii. [this has nothing to do with the "spade"-phrase, since here the word "spade" most likely refers to "eunuch," as will be explained in the fifth chapter].
Je ne puis rien nommer si ce n'est par son nom;
J'appelle un chat un chat, et Rollet un fripon.
I can call nothing by name if that is not his name.
I call a cat a cat, and Rollet a rogue.
   Boileau, *Satires.* i. 51. [Rollet was an attorney].

5. Kate Louise Roberts, *Hoyt's New Cyclopedia of Practical Quotations* (New York: Funk & Wagnalls, 1922), p. 541 (nos. 12-13); p. 542 (nos. 8-9 and 19); and p. 543 (no. 20).

50 *"Call a Spade a Spade"*

Je ne puis rien nommer si ce n'est par son nom;
J'appelle un chat un chat, et Rollet un fripon.
I can call nothing by name if that is not his name.
I call a cat a cat, and Rollet a rogue.
> Boileau, *Satires*. I. 51. [Rollet was an attorney].

Call a spade a spade.
> Burton — *Anatomy of Melancholy. Democritis Hunior to the Reader.* P. 11. Scalinger — *Note on the Priapeia Sive Diversorum Poetarum.* Baxter — *Narrative of the Most Memorable Passages of Life and Times*. (1696) Dr. Arbithnot — *Dissertations on the Art of Selling Bargains*. Philip of Macedon. See Plutarch's *Life of Philip*.

Ficum vocamus ficum, et scapham scapham.
We call a fig a fig, and a skiff a skiff.
> Erasmus — *Colloquy. Philetymus et Pseudocheus*. Also in *Dilucalum Philyphnus*. In his *Adagia* he refers to Aristophanes as user of a like phrase. Quoted by Lucian — *Quom. Hist. sit. conscribend*. 41. Found also in Plutarch — *Apopthegms* [sic]. P. 178 (Ed. 1624) Old use of the same idea in Taverner — *Garden of Wysdom*. Pt. I. Ch. VI. (Ed. 1539)

I cannot say the crow is white,
But needs must call a spade a spade.
> Humphrey Gifford — *A Woman's Face is Full of Wiles*.

Ramp up me genius, be not retrograde,
But boldly nominate a spade a spade.
> Jonson — *Poetaster*. Act V. 3.

I'll give you leave to call me anything, if you don't call me "spade."
> Swift — *Polite Conversation*. Dialogue II. [this has nothing to do with the "spade"-phrase, since here the word "spade" most likely refers to "eunuch," as will be explained in the fifth chapter].

6. W. Gurney Benham, *Putnam's Complete Book of Quotations, Proverbs and Household Words* (New York: G.P. Putnam's Sons, 1926), p. 144b and p. 746b.

I cannot say the crow is white,
But needs must call a spade a spade.
> Humphrey Gifford — *A Woman's Face is Full of Wiles*.

Calling figs figs, and a skiff a skiff.
> — Aristophanes, quoted by Lucian, *Quomodo His. sit Conscrib*. See also Lucian, *Jov. Trag.*, 32. Also in Plutarch's *Apophthegm*.

Ficum vocamus ficum, et scapham scapham.
We call a fig a fig, and a skiff a skiff.
— Erasmus. *Colloquy, Philetimus et Pseudocheus.*
Ficus ficus, ligonem ligonem vocat.
We call figs figs, and a hoe a hoe. — (Latin.)
[implied is clearly that this is a Latin proverb, but Benham does not appear to know that it goes back to Erasmus].
J'appelle un chat un chat, et Rollet un fripon.
Boileau. *Satire* I (1660).

7. [No editor given], *The Oxford Dictionary of Quotations* (Oxford: Oxford University Press, 1941), p. 162b, p. 215b, and p. 418b.

I cannot say the crow is white,
But needs must call a spade a spade.
Humphrey Gifford, *Song, A Woman's face is Full of Wiles.* Ault, *Elizabethan Lyrics.*
Ramp up me genius, be not retrograde,
But boldly nominate a spade a spade.
Jonson — *Poetaster,* v. i.
I'll give you leave to call me anything, if you don't call me "spade."
Swift, *Polite Conversation.* Dialogue 2. [This has nothing to do with the "spade"-phrase, since here the word "spade" most likely refers to "eunuch," as will be explained in the fifth chapter].

8. H.L. Mencken, *A New Dictionary of Quotations on Historical Principles from Ancient and Modern Sources* (New York: Alfred A. Knopf, 1942 [1960]), pp. 919-920.

The Macedonians ... had not the wit to call a spade by any other name than a spade.
Nicholas Udall: Tr. of Desiderius Erasmus: *Apothegms*, 1542.
We call figs figs, and a hoe a hoe. (Ficus ficus, ligonem ligonem vocat.)
Latin proverb [Mencken too fails to recognize Erasmus as the source of this proverb].

9. Burton Stevenson, *The Macmillan Book of Proverbs, Maxims, and Famous Phrases* (New York: Macmillan, 1948 [7th printing 1968]), p. 2194 (no. 1).

"Call a Spade a Spade"

Spades are Spades
That which is a trough he calls a trough.
("hostis kaleseie kardopon ten kardopen.")
> Aristophanes, *The Clouds*, I, 1251. (423 B.C.)
> Cited by Erasmus, *Adagia*, ii, iii, 5.

The Macedonians are by nature a rough and rustic people who call a tub a tub. ("ten skaphen skaphen legontas.")
> Philip of Macedon, to some envoys who complained that certain members of his train had called them traitors. (c. 350 B.C.) As given by Plutarch, *Sayings of Kings and Commanders*. Sec. 178B. Cited by Erasmus, *Adagia*, ii, iii, 5, who gives the Latin as, "Ficus ficus, ligonem ligonem vocat" (To call a fig a fig and a spade a spade). This is the first appearance of a "spade" in the proverb, and may have been due to a mistake on the part of Erasmus in confusing "skaphe", which means a tub, or boat, or bowl, or any sort of hollow vessel [also trough] which has been dug or scooped out, with some derivative from the stem of "skaptein", to dig, which may also mean the instrument with which the digging is done, i.e. a spade. But more probably it was a deliberate substitution on the part of Erasmus, who knew his Greek, and his account of the incident would seem to substantiate this. He says, "When those persons who were with Lathenes were aggrieved because certain members of Philip's train called them traitors, Philip answered that the Macedonians were altogether gross and rustical, and had not the wit to call a spade by any other name than a spade, alluding to the common proverb of the Greeks, calling figs figs, and a tub a tub, and meaning that they were traitors in very deed." And then Erasmus cites the proverb in another form, "Ficus ficus voco, panarium panarium" (To call a fig a fig and a bread-basket a bread-basket).

Confutation is my name, the friend of truth and candor. ... I call a fig a fig, a tub a tub. ("ta suka suka, ten skaphen skaphen legon.")
> Menander, *Fragments*. No. 545K. (c. 300 B.C.) This is the usual form of the Greek proverb, derived from Aristophanes. So frequently used that only a few examples will be cited.

Here is your Stoic disquisition in a nutshell, "The wise man will call a spade a spade." ("ho sophos euthurrhemonesei.")
> Cicero, *Ad Familiares*. Bk. ix, epis. xxii. (46 B.C.)

Calling a fig a fig and a tub a tub. ("ta suka suka. ten skaphen de skaphen onomason.")
> Lucian, *Writing History*. Sec. 41A. (c. A.D. 170)

Whiche call ... a mattok nothing els but a mattok, and a spade a spade.

Taverner, *Garden of Wysdome*. Sig. C4. (1539)
We are plain people and call figs, figs: prunes, prunes: & pears, pears. (Nous sommes simples gens, et appellons les figues, figues: les prunes, prunes: & les poires, poires.)
    Rabelais, *Pantagruel*. Bk. iv, ch. 54. (1548)
Brought up like a rude Macedon, and taught to call a spade a spade.
    Stephen Gosson, *Ephemerides*. (1579)
I cannot say the crow is white,
But needes must call a spade a spade.
    Humfrey Gifford, *A Woman's Face is Full of Wiles*. (1580)
He may, being a plain man, call a spade a spade.
    William Kemp, *Nine Daies Wonder*. (1600)
Ramp up my genius, be not retrograde;
But boldly nominate a spade a spade.
    Ben Jonson, *Poetaster*. Act v, sc. 3 (1602)
I think it good plain English, without fraud,
To call a spade a spade, a bawd a bawd.
    John Taylor, *A Kicksy Winsey*. (1619) [The play is actually *A Bawd*].
A loose, plain, rude writer, I call a spade a spade.
    Robert Burton, *The Anatomy of Melancholy: Democritus to the Reader*. (1621)
Gods people shall not spare to call a spade a spade, a niggard a niggard.
    John Trapp, *Mellificium Theologicum*. (1647)
This is not the Time of Day
For truth to be so obvious made,
We must not call a Spade a Spade.
    Edward Ward, *Hudibras Redivivus*, i, 7. (1706)
I love to call a spade a spade.
    Swift, *Polite Conversation*. Dial. iii. (1738)
There's no imaginative humbug about me. I call a spade a spade.
    Dickens, *Hard Times*. Bk. i, ch. 6 (1854)
I talked with her with daring frankness, frequently calling a spade a spade instead of coldly symbolizing it as a snow shovel.
    Mark Twain, *In Eruption*, p. 315. (1908) This is Twain's account of his talk with Elinor Glyn about her novel, *Three Weeks*.
Most people nowadays call it "a bloody shovel."
    Partridge, *Dictionary of Clichés: Call*. (1941)

10. J.M. and M.J. Cohen, *The Penguin Dictionary of Quotations* (Middlesex, England: Penguin Books, 1960 [1985]), pp. 416–417 (no. 27).

CECILY: When I see a spade I call it a spade.
GWENDOLEN: I am glad to say I have never seen a spade. It is obvious that our social spheres have been widely different.
    Oscar Wilde, *The Importance of Being Earnest*, II. [The response probably refers to a eunuch and not to the tool as such].

11. Bergen Evans, *Dictionary of Quotations* (New York: Avenel Books, 1968 [1978]), p. 650 (no. 4).

SPADE
A loose, plain, rude writer, I call a spade a spade. [Robert Burton: *The Anatomy of Melancholy*, "Democritus to the Reader" (1621)]
    The saying goes back to a story which Plutarch tells of Philip of Macdon, the father of Alexander the Great. Certain ambassadors whom Philip did not trust complained to him that they had been called traitors by some of his entrourage. Philip said they must excuse his followers; the Macedonians were notorious clods who hadn't any more sense than to call a tub a tub. The substitution of *spade* for *tub* was the doing of Erasmus in his relation of the incident in his *Adagia* (1500 [actually 1515]).
    There have been a number of objects whose simple designation has been proverbial, among different nations, for plain speaking. The Greeks said "to call a fig a fig" (in some way, now forgotten, a fig was indecent) and, as above, "a tub a tub." The phrase as now used — *to call a spade a spade* — is a contradiction of what it asserts. No one objects to calling a spade a spade; it is coarser and less inoffensive things that are glossed over with euphemisms.

12. J.M. and M.J. Cohen, *The Penguin Dictionary of Modern Quotations* (Middlesex, England: Penguin Books, 1980), p. 125.

A spade is never so merely a spade as the word
Spade would imply.
    Christopher Fry, *Venus Observed*, Act II.

13. George Seldes, *The Great Thoughts* (New York: Ballantine Books, 1985), p. 251.

The historian should be fearless and incorruptible; a man of independence, loving frankness and truth; one who, as the poet says, calls a fig a fig and a spade a spade. He should yield to neither hatred nor affection, but should be unsparing and unpitying. He should be neither shy nor deprecating, but an impartial judge, giving each side all it deserves but no more. He should know in his writings no country and no city; he should bow to no authority and acknowledge no king. He should never consider what this or that man will think, but should state the facts as they really occurred.
Lucian (120-200 A.D.) Greek satirist, *How History Should Be Written* (c. 170).

14. E.D. Hirsch, Joseph F. Kett, and James Trefil, *The Dictionary of Cultural Literacy* (Boston: Houghton Mifflin, 1988), p. 61.

call a spade a spade To speak directly and bluntly; to avoid EUPHEMISM: "The prosecutor said, 'Let's call a spade a spade; you didn't borrow the money, you stole it.'"
]This dictionary is not a quotation dictionary as such, but it lists cultural traditions like quotations, proverbs, etc.]

15. Tony Augarde, *The Oxford Dictionary of Modern Quotations* (Oxford: Oxford University Press, 1991), p. 87.

I hope
I've done nothing so monosyllabic as to cheat,
A spade is never so merely a spade as the word
Spade would imply.
Christopher Fry, *Venus Observed* (1950) act 2, sc. 1.

16. John Bartlett, *Familar Quotations*, ed. Justin Kaplan. 16th ed. (Boston: Little, Brown and Company, 1992), p. 81 (no. 11).

I call a fig a fig, a spade a spade.
Menander (c. 342-292 B.C.), *Unidentified fragment* 545.
The Macedonians are a rude and clownish people that call a spade a spade.

Plutarch, *Apothegms, Philip of Macedon*.

I think it good plain English, without fraud, To call a spade a spade, a bawd a bawd.
John Taylor [1580-1653], *A Kicksey Winsey*. [The play is actually *A Bawd*].

17. Suzy Platt, *Respectfully Quoted. A Dictionary of Quotations from the Library of Congress* (Washington, D.C.: Congressional Quarterly Inc., 1992), p. 329 (no. 1748).

The historian should be fearless and incorruptible; a man of independence, loving frankness and truth; one who, as the poet says, calls a fig a fig and a spade a spade. He should yield to neither hatred nor affection, but should be unsparing an unpitying. He should be neither shy nor deprecating, but an impartial judge, giving each side all it deserves but no more. He should know in his writings no country and no city; he should bow to no authority and acknowledge no king. He should never consider what this or that man will think, but should state the facts as they really occurred.

Lucian, *How History Should Be Written (De Historia Conscribenda)*.
— *The Great Thoughts*, ed. George Seldes, p. 251 (1985). [See no. 13 above].

18. A. Norman Jeffares and Martin Gray, *Collins Dictionary of Quotations* (New York: HarperCollins, 1995), p. 364 (no. 12) and p. 749 (no. 95).

Ramp up my genious, be not retrograde;
But boldly nominate a spade a spade.
Ben Jonson, *The Poetaster* (1601), V. i.
Cecily: When I see a spade I call it a spade.
Gwendolen: I am glad to say I have never seen a spade. It is obvious that our social spheres have been widely different.
Oscar Wilde, *The Importance of Being Earnest* (1895), III. [The response probably refers to a eunuch and not to the tool as such].

19. Ned Sherrin, *The Oxford Dictionary of Humorous Quotations* (Oxford: Oxford University Press, 1995), p. 167 (no. 34).

I hope

I've done nothing so monosyllabic as to cheat,
A spade is never so merely a spade as the word
Spade would imply.
    Christopher Fry, *Venus Observed* (1950).

20. Elizabeth Knowles, *The Oxford Dictionary of Phrase, Saying, and Quotation* (Oxford: Oxford University Press, 1997), p. 240 (no. 28).

call a spade a spade speak plainly or bluntly; not use euphemisms.
    [Knowles clearly feels that this is but a proverbial phrase and thus gives no references whatsoever].

21. Nigel Rees, *Cassell Companion to Quotations* (London: Cassell, 1997), p. 322 (no. 9) and p. 432 (no. 5).

Ramp up my genius, be not retrograde;
But boldly nominate a spade a spade.
    Ben Jonson, *The Poetaster*, Act 5, Sc. 1 (1601).
Macedonians had not the wit to call a spade by any other name than a spade.
    Plutarch, *Apophthegmata* — as translated from Greek to Latin by Erasmus. What was rather a trough, basin, bowl, or boat in the original Greek ended up as a 'spade' and passed into English giving us the expression 'to call a spade a spade', meaning 'to speak bluntly, to call things by their proper names without resorting to euphemisms'. The phrase was into the language by 1580.

22. Elizabeth Knowles, *The Oxford Dictionary of Quotations*, 5th ed. (Oxford: Oxford University Press, 1999), p. 170 (no. 4), p. 419 (no. 23), p. 817 (no. 23).

A loose, plain, rude writer ... I call a spade a spade.
    Robert Burton, *The Anatomy of Melancholy* (1621-51) 'Democritus to the Reader.'
Ramp up my genius, be not retrograde;
But boldly nominate a spade a spade.
    Ben Jonson, *The Poetaster* (1601) act 5, sc. 1.
CECILY: When I see a spade I call it a spade.
GWENDOLEN: I am glad to say I have never seen a spade.

Oscar Wilde, *The Importance of Being Earnest* (1895) act 3. [The response probably refers to a eunuch and not to the tool as such].

As can be seen especially from the most recent quotation dictionaries, their editors are ever more of the opinion that the phrase "to call a spade a spade" has become so proverbial that it barely deserves to be included any longer. The editors of the two standard works on quotations in English, the American *Bartlett's Familiar Quotations* and the British *Oxford Dictionary of Quotations*, have narrowed down the number of historical references considerably. The best reference work, and not only for the "spade"-phrase, is without doubt still today Burton Stevenson's voluminous *The Macmillan Book of Proverbs, Maxims, and Famous Phrases* (New York: Macmillan, 1948 [7th printing 1968]). It belongs into the library of any serious phrase sleuth, and it should be reprinted for the new generation of quotation and phrase enthusiasts, be they hobbyists or scholars.

Many quotation dictionaries on my shelves do not contain the phrase "to call a spade a spade" any longer. For example, its proverbial nature has brought an end to its inclusion in the following large and important dictionaries of recent vintage:

Andrews, Robert. *Dictionary of Quotations* (London: Routledge & Kegan Paul, 1987). 343 pp.

Andrews, Robert. *The Columbia Dictionary of Quotations* (New York: Columbia University Press, 1993). 1092 pp.

Carruth, Gorton, and Eugene Ehrlich, *The Harper Book of American Quotations* (New York: Harper & Row, 1988). 821 pp.

Colombo, John Robert. *The Dictionary of Canadian Quotations* (Toronto: Stoddard, 1991). 671 pp.

Daintith, John, Hazel Egerton, Rosalind Fergusson, Anne Stibbs, and Edmund Wright, *The Macmillan Dictionary of Quotations* (New York: Macmillan, 1987), 790 pp.

Donadio, Stephen, Joan Smith, Susan Mesner, and Rebecca Davison, *The New York Public Library Book of Twentieth-Century American Quotations* (New York: Warner Books, 1992), 622 pp.

Miner, Margaret, and Hugh Rawson, *The New International Dictionary of Quotations* (New York: Dutton, 1993). 480 pp.

Simpson, James B. *Contemporary Quotations. A Treasury of Notable Quotes Since 1950* (New York: Galahad Books, 1964). 500 pp.

Tripp, Rhoda Thomas, *The International Thesaurus of Quotations* (New York: Thomas Y. Crowell, 1970), 1088 pp.

But as the entries of the twenty-two quotation dictionaries reviewed above amply show, there is much valuable material to be found in them regarding the "spade"-phrase and its origin in classical antiquity and literary dissemination through the centuries to the modern age. But what has also become clear is that the lexicographical treatment of the phrase varies widely indeed, and no single dictionary, not even that edited by Burton Stevenson in 1948, is perfect or contains every reference listed in the twenty-two volumes. While the early quotation collections still include classical references in their original Greek or Latin, newer dictionaries do not bother with foreign languages much any more — another sign of the decrease in cultural literacy. Another obvious frustration with almost all of the dictionaries is the inprecise way of listing bibliographical references. Some entries provide at least book chapters or list acts and scenes in the case of plays. But page numbers and editions being cited are hardly ever given, making it a very time-consuming task to locate the "spade"-phrase or any other quotation in a meaningful context. The fact that dictionaries simply don't have the space to cite the texts in context is, of course, yet another, albeit understandable, shortcoming of such compilations.

But be that as it may, the many references cited in this chapter for the expression "to call a spade a spade" add up to an impressive history, even though there appears to be quite a bit of "copying" from each other. The following chapter will show that historical proverb collections will add many references of the phrase to this list. All of them, once they have been located in their written contexts, will eventually add up to an inclusive account of the history and above all the shades of meanings of the proverbial expression "to call a spade a spade." The proper study of any proverb or phrase must be based on a large textual basis in meaningful contexts. Identification of isolated texts can only be the first step towards the interpretation of the meaning in actual contexts.

IV.

The Phrase in Proverb and Idiom Collections

As with the treatment of the proverbial expression "to call a spade a spade" in quotation dictionaries, the way the phrase is registered in almost fifty proverb, phrase, and idiom dictionaries published between 1670 and 2001 is in fact very diverse. While some of them list the phrase with just one explanatory sentence, others add at least an example of the expression being used in context to it. Then there are those entries that refer to equivalent expressions as "to say (tell) it as it is," "to call a thing by its proper name," or "not to beat about (around) the bush." Of course, many lexicographers and paremiographers also include comments regarding the Greek origin of the phrase, and quite often they include at least one or several references from English and American literary works.

Not one of these collections and dictionaries includes all possible references of the phrase, of course. But with the exception of some volumes which are intended merely for the popular market, most of them provide materials that help to trace the origin and history of the phrase. Since one can never be certain what pertinent information might be hidden in any of these compilations, it behooves the serious scholar to look at all of them, taking the proverb "The more, the merrier (better)" as a guiding research principle.

There is no doubt that Burton Stevenson's massive *The Macmillan Book of Proverbs, Maxims, and Famous Phrases* (New York: Macmillan, 1948 [7th printing 1968]) presents the most complete and accurate record. It was already mentioned in the previous chapter on "The Expression in Dictionaries of Quotations," but the entire entry from his superb dictionary is repeated in this chapter. Stevenson's tome is clearly a dictionary that covers both quotations and proverbial language. Above all, the compiler took a serious scholarly approach to every phrase that he registered in this gargantuan volume. It is a shame that so few scholars make use of this most inclusive phrasal dictionary of the English language. Since it appeared in 1948, it is obviously outdated in regard to modern quotations and proverbs. Other books surveyed in this chapter pick up the missing pieces, but Stevenson's compendium is a definite must for serious diachronic work in phraseology. The book should be reprinted and, if at all possible, be brought up to date without dropping any entries. The problem would be the size of such an updated version, since the book contains 2957 double-column pages in small print!

As expected, Stevenson gives quite precise bibliographical references, even though some of the abbreviations can present problems at times. But such concerns vanish quickly when one compares this volume with most of the others. The titles of the works cited are often shortened beyond recognition, dates are missing, and above all, many lexicographers fail to include page numbers. It is one thing to state that the "spade"-phrase appears in the works of John Knox, for example, but it is quite another to find the precise citation in the actual context of the writings of the reformer. I have spent weeks trying to track down all the literary references that have been mentioned with hardly any contextual information in the dozens of quotation and proverb dictionaries presented in this study. These contextualized excerpts with many others that I have found through my own work will be presented in chronological order in the sixth chapter on "Literary Texts from the 16th to the 20th Century." Lexicographers and paremiographers definitely need to give more precise references in their collections, even though this information will take up valuable space.

Another matter that becomes quite obvious when perusing the forty-nine entries presented in this chapter is that for the most part the compilers copy from each other, sometimes *verbatim*. They also contain erroneous information, especially when it is claimed again and again that the expression "to call a spade a spade" in this form was already cited in Greek antiquity. This is simply not true, since it has long been established that it was Erasmus who initiated this variant of the Greek phrase "To call a fig a fig, and a trough a trough." And even Erasmus cited it, of course, in Latin as "Ficus ficus, ligonem ligonem vocat." And he did not accomplish this feat with the original publication of his *Adagia* in the year 1500, but rather in the much expanded edition of 1515. If the Greek history of the phrase is mentioned at all, this information is quite superficial and at times incorrect, again with the exception of Stevenson's dictionary.

It is also noticeable that paremiographers are slow with adding new materials to their collections. This can be seen from the very similar entries in the three editions of *The Oxford Dictionary of English Proverbs* from 1935, 1948, and 1970. On the other hand, we are very fortunate indeed to have Bartlett Jere Whiting's invaluable *Modern Proverbs and Proverbial Sayings* (Cambridge, Massachusetts: Harvard University Press, 1989), in which this magisterial paremiographer has registered thirty-three references from literary works published between 1905 and

1978. The entire dictionary is the best source we have for the appearance of proverbs and proverbial expressions in writings of the twentieth century. One small quibble might be added just the same: At times the actual citations are so short that it is not necessarily clear whether the word "spade" might not by chance refer to Blacks. After all, it is during the second half of the twentieth century that the word takes on this slang meaning. It is for this reason that I "hunted" all of the references down. If a case is to be made that the old phrase has now become a racial slur, then we need texts in contexts to substantiate this claim.

In addition to all of these inconsistencies and shortcomings, it should also be noted that the lexicographers differ widely regarding the choice of key-word for the phrase. This means that it is either listed under "call" or "spade." Personally, I would prefer to see the "spade"-phrase be catalogued under its noun referring to the garden implement. This is perhaps a small point, but it must be kept in mind whenever one is checking on a particular quotation or phrase. It is always best to check at least under two key-words to make sure that no information is missed.

The following dictionaries and collections vary greatly in importance and usefulness, but together they provide a composite picture of the origin, history, dissemination, and meaning of the proverbial expression "to call a spade a spade." There is no doubt that as many quotation and proverb dictionaries as possible must be checked in order to assemble the story behind a particular proverb or proverbial phrase.

1. John Ray, *A Collection of English Proverbs* (Cambridge: W. Morden, 1670), p. 193. Also reprinted in Henry G. Bohn, *Hand-Book of Proverbs. Comprising an Entire Republication of Ray's Collection of English Proverbs, with His Additions from Foreign Languages* (London: Bell & Daldy, 1870), p. 178.

To call a *spade* a spade.

2. W. Carew Hazlitt, *English Proverbs and Proverbial Phrases* (London: Smith 1869; rpt. London: Reeves and Turner, 1907; rpt. again Detroit, Michigan: Gale Research Company, 1969), p. 466.

To call a spade a spade.
Collier's *Old Ballads from Early Printed Copies*, 1840, p. 57.

3. Kwong Ki Chiu, *A Dictionary of English Phrases* (New York: A.S. Barnes, 1881; rpt. Detroit, Michigan: Gale Research Company, 1971), p. 297.

Call a spade a spade, to
   To be plain-spoken; to call things by their right names.
Why not *call a spade a spade*?
   Why shall we not call things by their right names?
The editor denounced the duel as a murderous combat, and not an affair of honor; he believes in *calling a spade a spade*.
   The editor denounced the duel as a murderous combat, and not an affair of honor; he believes in calling things by their right names.

4. A. Wallace, *Popular Sayings Dissected* (London: T. Fisher Unwin, 1894), p. 22.

Call a spade a spade
   An expression with which we are nowadays brought into daily contact through the advertisement of a certain extract of coffee ("Call a spade a spade and Bransom's coffee extract the perfection of coffee"), has a very much longer pedigree than coffee itself or the name of Bransom, for the expression is found in Aristophanes. The meaning is of course obvious, viz. — Call a thing by its right name; sternly, rigorously, accurately, accord its fair due. [See also the tenth chapter on "The Phrase in Advertisements and Cartoons"].

5. Vincent Stuckey Lean, *Collectanea*, 5 vols. (Bristol: J.W. Arrowsmith, 1902–1904; rpt. Detroit, Michigan: Gale Research Company, 1969; rpt. again Bristol: Thoemmes Press, 2000), vol. 3, p. 292.

Call a spade a spade. A term of reproach (Eunuch).
   B. and F., *Capt.*, iii. 5.
Cf. To call a Dog a Dog.
   Alternative title of Lely's *Pap with a Hatchet* 1589.
Philippus answered that the Macedonians were feloes of no fine wit in their terms but altogether gross, clubbish and rustical, as the which had not the wit to call a spade by any other name than a spade. Alluding to that the common used proverb of the Greeks calling figs figs, and a boat a boat.
   Udall, *Er. Ap.*, 189.

To call a spade a spade, a sycophant
A flattering knave.
    Taylor (W.P. = John Taylor, the Water Poet), *Motto Ded*.
Ramp up thy genius, be not retrograde,
But boldly nominate a spade, a spade.
    Ben Jonson, *Poetaster* (Against Marston and Dekker.)

6. Robert Nares, *A Glossary of Words, Phrases, Names, and Allusions in the Works of English Authors Particularly of Shakespeare and His Contemporaries* (London: George Routledge, 1905; rpt. Detroit, Michigan: Gale Research Company, 1966), p. 818.

SPADE. *To call a spade a spade*,
    was a popular phrase for to be plain-spoken. Why the spade was especially chosen to enter this figurative expression is not clear.
There are some few that will their judgement season
With mature understanding, and with reason:
And *call a spade a spade*, a sicophant,
A flatt'ring knave, and those are those I want.
    Taylor's Works, 1630.
Small eloquence men must expect from me,
My scholarship will name things as they be.
I thinke it good, plaine English, without fraud,
To *call a spade a spade*, a bawd a bawd.
    Ibid.
Hush, says my friend, mind what you say;
You know this is not time of day
For truth to be so obvious made,
We must not *call a spade a spade*
    Hudibras Redivivus, 1706.

7. Albert M. Hyamson, *A Dictionary of English Phrases* (New York: E.P. Dutton, 1922; rpt. Detroit, Michigan: Gale Research Company, 1970), p. 324.

Spade a spade, To call a:
    to speak bluntly and frankly without verbal embroidery.
Philip II of Macedon (382–336 B.C.) described his subjects as people who call a spade a spade.
    [Gosson, *Ephemerides of Phials* (1579)]

Spadish language:
  plain, blunt language. From 'to call a spade a spade.'

8. Frank H. Vizetelly and Leander J. de Bekker, *A Desk-Book of Idioms and Idiomatic Phrases in English Speech and Literature* (New York: Grosset & Dunlap, 1923), p. 404.

spade a spade, to call a.
  To speak in plain terms; use frank speech.
I drink no wine at all, which so much improves our modern wits: a loose, plain, blunt, rude writer, I *call a spade a spade*; I respect matter, not words.
  Burton *Anatomy of Melancholy* preface.

9. G.L. Apperson, *English Proverbs and Proverbial Phrases. A Historical Dictionary* (London: J.M. Dent, 1929; rpt. Detroit, Michigan: Gale Research Company, 1929), p. 592.

Spade a spade, To call a.
"ta suka suka, ten skaphen de skaphen onomason" [all Greek texts have been transliterated and are cite in quotation marks]. —
  Lucian, *Hist. Conscr.* 41
Whiche can call ... a spade a spade.
  1539: Taverner, *Garden of Wysdome*, sig. C$_4$.
That he, may, being a plain man, call a spade a spade.
  1600: Kemp, *Nine Daies Wonder*, in Arber, *Garner*, vii. 34 (1883).
Faith we do call a spade a spade, in Cornwall.
  1632: Jonson, *Magn. Lady*, I. *ad fin.*
[no text cited]
  1668: Shadwell, *Sullen Lovers*, IV. i.
Who call a fig a fig, and a spade a spade.
  1725: Bailey, tr. Erasmus' *Colloq.*, 181.
There's no imaginative sentimental humbug about me. I call a spade a spade.
  1854: Dickens, *Hard Times*, bk. i. ch. vi.

10. Anonymous, *Origin of Things Familiar. Sketches on the Origin of Common Things, Prevalent Beliefs, Everyday Words and Phrases, Familiar Signs and Symbols and Current Customs* (Cincinnati, Ohio: United Book Corporation, 1934), p. 28.

Call a Spade a Spade
This expression is not of modern origin. Burton, in his preface to "Anatomy of Melancholy," says: "I drink no wine at all which so much improves our modern wits; a loose, plain, rude writer, I call a spade a spade. I respect matter, not words." The phrase is also used by Richard Baxter in his narrative of 1696.

11. William George Smith, *The Oxford Dictionary of English Proverbs*, 1st ed. (Oxford: Clarendon Press, 1935), p. 502.

To call a spade a spade.
To call things by their real names, without any euphemism.
L. *Ficus ficus, ligonem ligonem vocat.*
Philippus aunswered, that the Macedonians wer feloes of no fyne witte in their termes, but altogether grosse, ... whiche had not the witte to calle a spade by any other name then a spade.
1542: Udall, *Erasm. Apoph.* 167.
Gods people shall not spare to call a spade a spade, a niggard a niggard.
1647: Trapp, *Marrow Gd., Authors* in *Comm. Ep.* 641.
Lady A. You know, I'm old Telltruth; I love to call a spade a spade.
1738: Swift, *Pol. Conversat.* iii. Wks. (1856) II. 351.
Chinese prosody is of an extremely complicated character ... it being an almost unpardonable fault to call a spade a spade.
1882: H.A. Giles, *Historic China* 55.
We call a nettle but a nettle, and The faults of fools but folly.
1607-8: Shakespeare, *Coriol.* II. i. 209.

12. Eric Partridge, *A Dictionary of Clichés* (London: Routledge & Kegan Paul, 1940 [5th ed. 1978]), p. 38.

call a spade a spade, to.
To call a thing by its right, esp. by its plain English name: current in English since C. 16 ('I cannot say the crow is white, | But needs must call a spade a spade', Humphrey Gifford, +1600); but a cliché only in C. 19-20. The prototype is in Aristophanes, but the operative original is the Latin *ficus ficus, ligonem ligonem vocat*, 'he calls figs *figs*, and a hoe a *hoe*' (Benham). Most people nowadays call it 'a bloody shovel'.

13. Charles Earle Funk, *A Hog on Ice and Other Curious Expressions* (New York: Harper & Row, 1948; rpt. New York: Warner Paperback Library, 1972; rpt. again New York: Harper Colophon Books, 1985), p. 184.

to call a spade a spade
   It means to call a thing by its right name, to avoid euphemism or beating about the bush. The saying is so old that what we have is just a translation of the original Greek. Perhaps it was old when Plutarch, in the first century A.D., used it in writing of the life of Philip of Macedon. But, although the expression is now firmly fixed in the English language, it is quite possible that the Greeks of Plutarch's time did not have the garden implement in mind in their use of the expression. The Greek words for "spade" and for "boat" or "bowl" were very similar, and it seems that the better translation would have been, "to call a boat a boat." Lucian, Greek writer of the second century, used the same saying, which Erasmus in the sixteenth century translated into Latin to read, "to call a fig a fig, and a boat a boat."

14. William George Smith, *The Oxford Dictionary of English Proverbs*, revised by Sir Paul Harvey, 2nd ed. (Oxford: Clarendon Press, 1948), p. 75.

Call a spade a spade, To.
   To call things by their real names, without any euphemism.
   Erasmus, *Ad. Ficus ficus, ligonem ligonem vocat.*
[no text cited]
   1519: Rastell, *The Four Elements* (Dodsley's *Old Plays* ed. Hazlitt i. 49.
Philippus aunswered, that the Macedonians wer feloes of no fyne witte in their termes, but altogether grosse, ... whiche had not the witte to calle a spade by any other name then a spade.
   1542: Udall, *Erasm. Apoph.* 167.
Gods people shall not spare to call a spade a spade, a niggard a niggard.
   1647: Trapp, *Marrow Gd., Authors* in *Comm. Ep.* 641.
Lady A. You know, I'm old Telltruth; I love to call a spade a spade.
   1738: Swift, (Dial. iii) 351.
Chinese prosody is of an extremely complicated character ... it being an almost unpardonable fault to call a spade a spade.

1882: H.A. Giles, *Historic Cina* 55.
We call a nettle but a nettle, and The faults of fools but folly.
1607–8: Shakespeare, *Coriol*. II. i. 209.

15. Burton Stevenson, *The Macmillan Book of Proverbs, Maxims, and Famous Phrases* (New York: Macmillan, 1948 [7th printing 1968]), p. 2194 (no. 1).

Spades are Spades
That which is a trough he calls a trough.
("hostis kaleseie kardopon ten kardopen.")
    Aristophanes, *The Clouds*, I, 1251. (423 B.C.)
    Cited by Erasmus, *Adagia*, ii, iii, 5.
The Macedonians are by nature a rough and rustic people who call a tub a tub. ("ten skaphen skaphen legontas.")
    Philip of Macedon, to some envoys who complained that certain members of his train had called them traitors. (c. 350 B.C.) As given by Plutarch, *Sayings of Kings and Commanders*. Sec. 178B. Cited by Erasmus, *Adagia*, ii, iii, 5, who gives the Latin as, "Ficus ficus, ligonem ligonem vocat" (To call a fig a fig and a spade a spade). This is the first appearance of a "spade" in the proverb, and may have been due to a mistake on the part of Erasmus in confusing "skaphe", which means a tub, or boat, or bowl, or any sort of hollow vessel [also trough] which has been dug or scooped out, with some derivative from the stem of "skaptein", to dig, which may also mean the instrument with which the digging is done, i.e. a spade. But more probably it was a deliberate substitution on the part of Erasmus, who knew his Greek, and his account of the incident would seem to substantiate this. He says, "When those persons who were with Lathenes were aggrieved because certain members of Philip's train called them traitors, Philip answered that the Macedonians were altogether gross and rustic, and had not the wit to call a spade by any other name than a spade, alluding to the common proverb of the Greeks, calling figs figs, and a tub a tub, and meaning that they were traitors in very deed." And then Erasmus cites the proverb in another form, "Ficus ficus voco, panarium panarium" (To call a fig a fig and a bread-basket a bread-basket).
Confutation is my name, the friend of truth and candor. ... I call a fig a fig, a tub a tub. ("ta suka suka, ten skaphen skaphen legon.")

> Menander, *Fragments*. No. 545K. (c. 300 B.C.) This is the usual form of the Greek proverb, derived from Aristophanes. So frequently used that only a few examples will be cited.

Here is your Stoic disquisition in a nutshell, "The wise man will call a spade a spade." ("ho sophos euthurrhemonesei.")

> Cicero, *Ad Familiares*. Bk. ix, epis. xxii. (46 B.C.)

Calling a fig a fig and a tub a tub. ("ta suka suka. ten skaphen de skaphen onomason.")

> Lucian, *Writing History*. Sec. 41A. (c. A.D. 170)

Whiche call ... a mattok nothing els but a mattok, and a spade a spade.

> Taverner, *Garden of Wysdome*. Sig. C4. (1539)

We are plain people and call figs, figs: prunes, prunes: & pears, pears. (Nous sommes simples gens, et appellons les figues, figues: les prunes, prunes: & les poires, poires.)

> Rabelais, *Pantagruel*. Bk. iv, ch. 54. (1548)

Brought up like a rude Macedon, and taught to call a spade a spade.

> Stephen Gosson, *Ephemerides*. (1579)

I cannot say the crow is white,
But needes must call a spade a spade.

> Humfrey Gifford, *A Woman's Face is Full of Wiles*. (1580)

He may, being a plain man, call a spade a spade.

> William Kemp, *Nine Daies Wonder*. (1600)

Ramp up my genius, be not retrograde;
But boldly nominate a spade a spade.

> Ben Jonson, *Poetaster*. Act v, sc. 3 (1602)

I think it good plain English, without fraud,
To call a spade a spade, a bawd a bawd.

> John Taylor, *A Kicksy Winsey*. (1619) [The play is actually *A Bawd*].

A loose, plain, rude writer, I call a spade a spade.

> Robert Burton, *The Anatomy of Melancholy: Democritus to the Reader*. (1602)

Gods people shall not spare to call a spade a spade, a niggard a niggard.

> John Trapp, *Mellificium Theologicum*. (1647)

This is not the Time of Day
For truth to be so obvious made,
We must not call a Spade a Spade.

> Edward Ward, *Hudibras Redivivus*, i, 7. (1706)

I love to call a spade a spade.

> Swift, *Polite Conversation*. Dial. iii. (1738)

There's no imaginative humbug about me. I call a spade a spade.

Dickens, *Hard Times*. Bk. i, ch. 6 (1854)
I talked with her with daring frankness, frequently calling a spade a spade instead of coldly symbolizing it as a snow shovel.
   Mark Twain, *In Eruption*, p. 315. (1908) This is Twain's account of his talk with Elinor Glynn about her novel, *Three Weeks*.
Most people nowadays call it "a bloody shovel."
   Partridge, *Dictionary of Clichés: Call.* (1941)

16. Morris Palmer Tilley, *A Dictionary of the Proverbs in England in the Sixteenth and Seventeenth Centuries* (Ann Arbor, Michigan: University of Michigan Press, 1950), p. 622 (S699).

To call a SPADE a spade
   Eras. *Adagia*, 485$_E$: Ficus ficus, ligonem ligonem vocat.
Plaine and homely men call a fygge, a fygge, and a spade a spade.
   1539: Tav., f. 14$_v$.
I cannot say the crow is white But needes must call a spade a spade.
   1580: H. Gifford, *Delectable Dream: Gilloflowers*, p. 113.
I am plain; I must needs call a spade a spade.
   1588: [Marprelate] *Epitome: Marpr. Tracts*, p. 118.
Be not retrograde: But boldly nominate a spade, a spade.
   1602: Jonson, *Poetaster* V iii 275.
I am a plaine Macedonian, I must need call a Spade a Spade.
   [c1616] 1630: *Pathomachia* IV ii, p. 39.
We call a Spade a Spade.
   1668: T. Shadwell, *Sullen Lovers* IV, p. 68.
[no text cited]
   1670: Ray, p. 193.
I love to call a spade a spade.
   1738: Swift, *Pol. Conv.* III, p. 463.
We call a nettle but a nettle and The faults of fools but folly.
   1608: Shakespeare, *C.* II i 207.

17. Archer Taylor and Bartlett Jere Whiting, *A Dictionary of American Proverbs and Proverbial Phrases, 1820–1880* (Cambridge, Massachusetts: Harvard University Press, 1958), p. 346.

Spade
He called things by their right names; and when he wanted a spade, he did not ask for a hoe.

1845: Cooper, *Chainbearer* 145; *Redskins* p. viii calling a "spade a spade."
[no text cited]
1928: Maurice Chideckel, *Strictly Private* 115.

18. William and Mary Morris, *Dictionary of Word and Phrase Origins* (New York: Harper & Row, 1962 [2nd ed. 1988]), p. 331.

spade a spade, to call a
   The first *spade-caller* is lost in antiquity, for the coiner of the Latin proverb "*Ficus ficus, ligonem ligonem vocat*" is unknown [no, it was Erasmus!], though Menander and Plutarch are both credited with it. As long ago as the early part of the sixteenth century, John Knox, Scottish Protestant reformer, gave an English version: "I have learned to call all wickedness by its own terms: a fig a fig, and a *spade a spade*."
   Words you use when you don't want *to call a spade a spade* are "euphemisms." The heyday of the euphemism in our language and culture was undoubtedly the Victorian era. When the names of many items of wearing apparel were inadmissible in polite society, the mention of shirt, trousers or — worse yet — breeches was a symptom of utmost depravity. As one versifier noted:
   I've heard that breeches, petticoat and smock,
   Give to thy modest mind a grievous shock
   And that thy brain (so lucky its device)
   Christened them "inexpressibles," so nice.
In those days, of course, the word "leg" was entirely inadmissible in polite society and even piano "limbs" were decorated with frilled trousers — or "inexpressibles."

19. Sanki Ichikawa, Takuji Mine, Ryoichi Inui, Kenzo Kihara, and Shiro Takaha, *The Kenkyusha Dictionary of Current English Idioms* (Tokyo: Kenkyusha, 1964), p. 628.

call a spade a spade
   call a thing by its real name; speak plainly or bluntly.
Why should people not be content to '*call a spade a spade*'? Their motives for using slang can seldom be analysed convincingly, but in general they seek three things in various degrees and proportions: novelty, vivacity, and intimacy.

S. Potter, *Our Language*, "Slang and Dialect."
There are others, and they are numberless as the sands, who are mortally afraid to *call a spade a spade*, because that would be the natural word, and to be natural, in their eyes, would be common, and by this declension they would fall into the pit of vulgarity.
V. Grove, *The Language Bar*, vi.
Even the most violently patriotic and militaristic are reluctant to *call a spade by its own name*. To conceal their intentions even from themselves, they make use of picturesque metaphors.
A Huxley, *The Olive Tree*, "Words and Behaviour."
Sometimes I get so fed up with all the mumbojumbo and abracadabra and making of holy mysteries about simple things that I like to *call a spade a shovel*.
N. Balchin, *Mine Own Executioner*, ii.
He had always been responsive to what they had begun to call 'Nature,' genuinely, almost religiously responsive, though he had never lost his habit of *calling a sunset a sunset and a view a view*, however deeply they might move him.
J. Galsworthy, *Indian Summer of a Forsyte*, i.

20. Ronald Ridout and Clifford Witting, *English Proverbs Explained* (London: Pan Books, 1967), p. 36 (no. 67).

Call a spade a spade
Speak plainly and to the point, saying exactly what you mean and using the simplest terms. In Arnold Bennett's novel, *The Card*, published in 1911, Mrs. Machin says: 'Ye can call it influenza if ye like. There was no influenza in my young days. We called a cold a cold.'

21. C. Edward Wall and Edward Przebienda, *Words and Phrases Index. A Guide to Antedatings, New Words, New Compounds, New Meanings, and Other Published Scholarship Supplementing the Oxford English Dictionary, Dictionary of Americanisms, Dictionary of American English, and Other Major Dictionaries of the English Language*, 4 vols. (Ann Arbor, Michigan: Pierian Press, 1969–1970), vol. 2, p. 53 and p. 249.

Call a spade a spade
American Speech, vol. 2, May 1927, p. 350.
Notes and Queries, vol. 206, July 1961, p. 263.

call a spade a spade, To
   American Speech, vol. 29, Oct. 1954, p. 210.
spade a spade, Call a
   [repetition of the three previous entries of p. 53 here on p. 249]

22. Ivor H. Evans, *Brewer's Dictionary of Phrase and Fable*, centenary edition (New York: Harper & Row, 1970), p. 1022.

To call a spade a spade.
   To be outspoken, blunt, even to the point of rudeness; to call things by their proper names without any "beating about the bush."

23. F.P. Wilson, *The Oxford Dictionary of English Proverbs*, 3rd ed. (Oxford: Clarendon Press, 1970), p. 98.

Call a spade a spade, To.
   Erasmus, *Ad. Ficus ficus, ligonem ligonem vocat.*
Say plainly, Give me a spade.
   1519: Rastell, *Four Elements* Hazl.-Dods. i. 49.
Plaine and homely, men call a fygge, a fygge, and a spade a spade.
   1539: Taverner [*Proverbes or adagies with newe addicions gathered out of the Chiliades of Erasmus*] 14^v.
Philippus aunswered, that the Macedonians wer feloes of no fyne witte in their termes, but altogether grosse, ... whiche had not the witte to calle a spade by any other name then a spade.
   1542: Udall, *Erasm. Apoph.* 167.
Gods people shall not spare to call a spade a spade, a niggard a niggard.
   1647: Trapp, *Marrow Gd., Authors* in *Comm. Ep.* 641.
You know, I'm old Telltruth; I love to call a spade a spade.
   1738: Swift, Dial. III. E.L. 320.
Chesham does not like to call s spade a spade. He calls it a horticultural utensil.
   1862: Thackeray, *Philip* ch. 23.
Chinese prosody is of an extremely complicated character ... it being an almost unpardonable fault to call a spade a spade.
   1882: H.A. Giles, *Historic Cina* 55.

24. Maxine Tull Boatner and John Edward Gates, *A Dictionary of American Idioms*, revised edition ed. Adam Makkai (Woodbury, New York: Barron's Educational Series, 1975), p. 44.

call a spade a spade
　To call a person or thing a name that is true but not polite; speak bluntly; use the plainest language. — A Cliché. *A boy took some money from Dick's desk and said he borrowed it, but I told him he stole it, I believe in calling a spade a spade.* (I believe in calling things by their true names, and taking money without permission is stealing.)

25. Bartlett Jere Whiting, *Early American Proverbs and Proverbial Phrases* (Cambridge, Massachusetts: Harvard University Press, 1977), p. 150 and p. 408.

To call a *Fig* a fig
I must have the privilege of calling a fig, — a Fig; an egg, — an Egg.
　　1774: Seabury, *Letters* 71.

To call a *Spade* a spade
We must call a spade a spade.
　　1692: Bulkeley, *Will* 90.
We don't call a spade, a spade, as you sinners do here. [The speaker is a Yankee servant in England.]
　　1785: J. Atkinson, *Match for a Widow* (London, 1788) 32.
I expressed an honest indignation by calling a Spade a *spade*.
　　1788: H. Williamson in Iredell, *Correspondence* 2.237.
According to the vulgar proverb, call a spade a spade.
　　1795: *Tablet* 45.
They could call a spade a spade.
　　1804: Brackenridge, *Modern* 341.
Dick maintains, in the teeth of all argument, that a spade is a spade.
　　1807: *Salmagundi* 30.

26. E.M. Kirkpatrick and C.M. Schwarz, *Dictionary of Idioms* (Edinburgh: Chambers, 1982; rpt. Ware, Hertfordshire: Wordsworth, 1993), p. 345.

call a spade a spade
　To say plainly and clearly what one means, not softening anything by trying to use polite words: *The trouble with doctors is that they never call a spade a spade — I sometimes find it difficult to know*

what they mean. [From a 16C mistranslation of a passage in one of Plutarch's works.]

27. A.P. Cowie, R. Mackin, and I.R. McCaig, *Oxford Dictionary of Current Idiomatic English*, 2 vols. (Oxford: Oxford University Press, 1983), vol. 2, p. 89.

call a spade a spade
call sth by its own name and not by a euphemism; describe sth straightforwardly as being what it is, even if this should give offence. *There is, of course, a 'calling a spade a spade' arrogance which makes a few working-class people overdo the rougher elements in their speech when with others from a different class.* He believes in calling a spade a spade *and if he wants to empty his bladder he doesn't ask where he can wash his hands. I wouldn't live anywhere except London. But I like the Scots. They* call a spade a spade, *they say what they mean and they have a sense of humour.*

28. Laurence Urdang and Frank R. Abate, *Idioms and Phrases Index*, 3 vols. (Detroit, Michigan: Gale Research Company, 1983), vol. 3, p. 1330.

spade, call a spade a
   CDEI/*spade*; DAI; DEI 2/*323*; ISED/*call*; ISED/*spade*; PE; RHD/*spade*; WPI 1; WPI 2.
spade, to call a spade a
   BDPF/*spade*; DEP/*297.*
spade a spade, call a
   CDEI/*spade*; DAI; DEI 2/*323*; ISED/*call*; ISED/*spade*; PE; RHD/*spade*; WPI 1; WPI 2.
spade a spade, to call a
   BDPF/*spade*; DEP/*297.*
   [the acronyms refer to standard language or phrase dictionaries]

29. Robert W. Dent, *Proverbial Language in English Drama Exclusive of Shakespeare, 1495-1616. An Index* (Berkeley, California: University of California Press, 1984), p. 641 (S699).

To call a SPADE a spade

(From 1539; see [R.W. Dent] *Shakespeare's Proverbial Language* [(Berkeley, California: University of California Press, 1981), p. 215]
Ficus ficus, ligonem ligonem vocat.
Eras. *Adagia* 485E.
(boldly nominate)
1601 (1602): Jonson *Poetaster* 5.3.276.

30. Adam Makkai, *Handbook of Commonly Used American Idioms* (Woodbury, New York: Barron's Educational Series, 1984), p. 43.

[identical text as no. 24 above].

31. James Rogers, *The Dictionary of Clichés* (New York: Facts on File Publications, 1985), pp. 40–41.

Call a Spade a Spade.
Speak plainly; avoid euphemism; tell it like it is. The ancient Greeks had a similar expression. As the dramatist Menander put it: "I call a fig a fig, a spade a spade." Plutarch records: "The Macedonians are a rude and clownish people that call a spade a spade." It has been argued that the Greek word did not mean spade and was mistranslated, but in any case the "spade" has served well for a standard of plain speaking, since it is an ancient, simple and universally recognized implement. The other side of the coin is that someone who leans unduly on rotundity or euphemism is likely to be described as "calling a spade an agricultural implement."

32. Laurence Urdang, Walter W. Hunsinger, and Nancy La Roche, *Picturesque Expressions: A Thematic Dictionary* (Detroit, Michigan: Gale Research Company, 1985), p. 105 (no. 43,2).

call a spade a spade
To speak plainly or bluntly; to be straightforward and candid, sometimes to the point of rudeness; to call something by its real name. The ultimate source of this expression is Erasmus' translation of Plutarch's *Apophthegmata*. According to the *OED*, the phrase in question was mistranslated from the original Greek. The expression has been popular in English since Nicholas Udall's 1542 translation of the Erasmus version. An early example is in Humfrey Gifford's *A Posie of Gilloflowers* (1580);

I cannot say the crow is white,
But needs must call a spade a spade.

33. Daphne M. Gulland and David Hinds-Howell, *English Idioms* (New York: Penguin Books, 1986), p. 212 (no. 4).

to call a spade a spade
to speak plainly and bluntly, to tell the plain truth without bothering with polite phrases. 'In Yorkshire we don't use flowery language; we call a spade a spade.'

34. Richard A. Spears and Linda Schinke-Llano, *NTC's American Idioms Dictionary* (Lincolnwood, Illinois: National Textbook Company, 1987), p. 46.

call a spade a spade
to call something by its right name; to speak frankly about something, even if it is unpleasant. (A cliché.) *Well, I believe it's time to call a spade a spade. We are just avoiding the issue. Let's call a spade a spade. The man is a liar.*

35. Kam Chuan Aik, *Dictionary of Proverbs* (Singapore: Federal Publications, 1988), p. 24 (no. 55).

Call a spade a spade
Say exactly what you mean in plain language. Use simple and direct expressions instead of referring to something in a roundabout way. *I prefer to call a spade a spade. Shoplifting should be called theft.*
Related Proverbs:
Fine words dress ill deeds. Let your yea be yea; and your nay, nay. (New Testament, James). Discretion of speech is more than eloquence. If you have no honey in your pot, have some in your mouth.

36. Bartlett Jere Whiting, *Modern Proverbs and Proverbial Sayings* (Cambridge, Massachusetts: Harvard University Press, 1989), pp. 585-586 (S365).

To call a Spade a spade (varied)
Innocence that cannot endure the spoken name of a spade.

1905: J.B. Cabell, *Line* (NY 1926) 216.
Call a spade a spade, although it may be a shovel.
   1909: M.R. Rinehart, *Man in Lower Ten* (NY 1947) 284.
In these days ... we have become accustomed when talking of spades to use no circumlocution or periphrasis whatever.
   1925: E.B. Chancellor, *"Old Q"* (L) 139.
He called a Ford a Ford.
   1926: P.G. Wodehouse, *Small Bachelor* (NY) 10.
Never wanted the word for a spade.
   1927: W.D. Steele, *Man Who* (NY) 301.
[They] were ... not civilized enough to call a spade anything but a spade.
   1933: G. Holt, *Six Minutes* (L) 11.
A spade was never a spade in Kate Townsend's bagnio.
   1936: H. Asbury, *French* (NY) 371.
Outspoken sort. An old spade caller.
   1937: P.A. Taylor, *Figure* (NY) 65.
Maraday ... was unused to hearing her own sex call a spade by its proper name.
   1940: N. Morland, *Gun* (L) 179.
A ... style in which a spade was often a bloody shovel.
   1940: C.E. Vulliamy, *Calico Pie* (L) 64.
A spade, not a spade, and not even a bloody shovel, but a horticultural implement of unimproved design.
   1952: R.L. Green, *Mason* (L) 207.
A Puritanical reluctance to call a spade a spade.
   1955: J. Creasey, *Murder* (NY) 113.
He trots out a filthy expression, presumably in the interests of calling a spade a spade.
   1956: *Boston Herald* 1/23 14.
He is still not one to call a spade a garden implement.
   1956: *New York Times Book Review* 7/15 8.
And when Dekker doesn't call a spade a spade, he calls it a steam-shovel.
   1956: *Harvard Summer News* 7/19 2.
Sooner call a spade a bloody shovel than a trowel.
   1956: A.W. Upfield, *Battling* (L 1960) 74.
Loving couples, sir, to call a spade a spade, littered that island.
   1956: A. Menen, *Abode* (NY) 144.
Millions of readers like to have a spade of dirt called a spade of dirt.
   1957: *Time* 8/26 61.

With spade-calling confidence.
   1958: *Time* 5/26 20.
He went about calling a spade what it jolly well was.
   1958: *New York Times Book Review* 7/27 6.
Why call a spade a spade if a more descriptive moniker is handy?
   1958: *Boston Herald* 8/7 30.
I am a plain blunt man who calls a fig a fig and a spade a spade.
   1958: L.S. de Camp, *Elephant* (NY) 38.
In the ... warfare of Australian politics, spades are called bloody shovels.
   1960: *Time* 2/22 37.
Calling a spade a spade and a nightingale a nightingale.
   1960: N. Woodin, *Room* (L) 128.
Call a spade a spade and let the chips fall where they may.
   1963: K. Vonnegut, *Cat's* (NY) 159.
The velvet of Victorian genteelness which required that no spade could be known as a spade.
   1965: C.P. Smith, *Where the Light* (NY) 371.
Some people are afraid of a spade being called a spade, or don't want to know where there is such a thing as a spade.
   1966: N. Devas, *Two Flamboyant* (L) 81.
A coarse person ... fond of calling a spade a dirty spade, but blessed with a heart of gold.
   1967: C.O. Skinner, *Madame* (B) 74.
Her Saxon proclivity for calling a spade a spade.
   1969: A. Gilbert, *Missing* (NY) 51.
She wasn't the kind of girl to call a spade a — a what? Anyway, she called a lay a roll in the hay.
   1969: P. Highsmith, *Tremor* (NY) 83.
[He] called a spade a bloody shovel.
   1970: H. Acton, *Memoirs* (NY) 67.
He not only called a spade a spade but told what was on the spade.
   1974: W. Snow, *Codline* (Middletown, Conn.) 126.
Bob made a thing of calling a spade a spade by a more vulgar name.
   1978: C. MacLeod, *Rest You* (NY) 41.

37. Michael Macrone, *It's Greek to Me! Brush Up Your Classics* (New York: HarperCollins, 1991), p. 120.

To Call a Spade a Spade

I am the god Argument, friend of free speech and truth, enemy only to those who fear my frankness. I know all and speak what I know, whether it be good or evil; I call a fig a fig and a kneading-trough a kneading-trough.

   Menander, unidentified fragment.

Calling a spade a spade is the very epitome of straightforwardness, both in its form and in its meaning. But if not for a small slip of a Renaissance translator, we would be busily calling "a kneading-trough a kneading-trough." (A kneading-trough is a wooden tub built for that purpose.)

In this fragment, Menander's character Argument, god of frankness, turns a line from Aristophanes' play *The Clouds* ("What is a trough he calls a trough") into a much-quoted Greek proverb. The Greek satirist Lucian and the Latin rhetorician Cicero, for example, both quote Menander, and the amusing metaphor later showed up in several books of proverbs — such as Plutarch's *Apophthegms* — and even in elementary grammar books. (Plutarch also attributes the saying to Philip II of Macedon.)

Englishmen, however, were not so familiar with the fig, and "kneading-trough" lacks the brevity that makes for a good catch-phrase. "Spade" fits the bill on the counts of familiarity and brevity, but so do a lot of other words. We owe the choice of "spade" to the Dutch humanist Erasmus, who (perhaps knowingly) mistranslated Plutarch, substituting the Latin *ligo* ("hoe" or "spade") for the Greek "kneading-trough." (The two words are nearly identical in Greek.) And when Nicholas Udall translated Erasmus's version into English in 1542, he rendered it to "to call a spade ... a spade." By this tortuous path — from Aristophanes to Menander to Plutarch to Erasmus to Udall — was coined a phrase.

38. Christine Ammer, *Have a Nice Day — No Problem! A Dictionary of Clichés* (New York: Dutton, 1992), p. 48.

call a spade a spade, to.
   To speak frankly and bluntly, to be quite explicit. The term dates from the sixteenth century, but may go back even to Greek and Roman times. One translation of Cicero's *Ad Familiares* reads, "Here is your Stoic disquisition ... 'the wise man will call a spade a spade.'" There are numerous repetitions throughout the 1500s, such as Richard Taverner's ("Whiche call ... a mattock nothing els but a mattock, and a spade a spade," *Garden of Wysdome*, 1539), as

well as later (by Ben Jonson, Robert Burton, Jonathan Swift, Charles Dickens, and Mark Twain, among others). A cliché since the nineteenth century, it acquired a slightly more sinister meaning when "spade" became an offensive slang word for a black person.

39. Linda and Roger Flavell, *Dictionary of Idioms and Their Origins* (London: Kyle Cathie, 1992), pp. 174-175.

spade: to call a spade a spade
> to speak one's mind, to put things bluntly. The ancient Greeks had a popular proverb for plain speaking, 'to call figs figs, and a tub a tub'. Plutarch quoted the expression in an episode of *Sayings of Kings and Commanders* but, when the scholar Erasmus drew upon the work in 1500 [actually 1515] for his *Adagia* (a collection of Greek and Latin proverbs traced back to their origins), he substituted 'spade' for 'tub'. Erasmus' version stuck and *to call a spade a spade* has been in popular use ever since.

Sometimes I get so fed up with all the mumbojumbo and abracadabra and making of holy mysteries about simple things that I like to call a spade a shovel.
  Nigel Balchin, *Mine Own Executioner*, 1945.
There are others, and they are numberless as the sands, who are mortally afraid to call a spade a spade, because that would be the natural word, and to be natural, in their eyes, would be common, and by this declension they would fall into the pot of vulgarity.
  Valerie Grove, *The Language Bar*, 1980s.

40. Anne Bertram and Richard A. Spears, *NTC's Dictionary of Proverbs and Clichés* (Lincolnwood, Illinois: National Textbook Company, 1993), p. 55.

Call a spade a spade
> To speak directly to the point; to say exactly what you mean. JILL: *Do you know Helen? The rather heavyset girl who —* JANE: *Heavyset? Just call a spade a spade and say that she's fat! —* Elsie, who always insisted on calling a spade a spade, refused to refer to herself as a senior citizen. "I'm no senior citizen; I'm an old woman," she said.

41. P.R. Wilkinson, *Thesaurus of Traditional English Metaphors* (London: Routledge, 1993), p. 189.

Call a spade a spade
Speak bluntly but accurately, without euphemism or evasion.

42. Richard A. Spears, *NTC's American English Idioms and Phrases* (Lincolnwood, Illinois: National Textbook Company, 1995), p. 53.

call a spade a spade
[identical to no. 34 above].

43. Richard A. Spears, *Essential American Idioms* (Lincolnwood, Illinois: National Textbook Company, 1996), p. 37.

call a spade a spade
[identical to no. 34 above].

44. Gregory Y. Titelman, *Random House Dictionary of Popular Proverbs and Sayings* (New York: Random House, 1996), pp. 38–39.

Call a spade a spade.
Call things by their proper names and don't try to pretty them up via euphemisms. The phrase has been traced back to Greek and Roman times. The playwright Menander (about 342–292 B.C.) is quoted as saying, "I call a fig a fig, a spade a spade," though some people attribute the saying to Aristophanes (about 450–385 B.C.). Plutarch (A.D. 46–120) considered that "The Macedonians are a rude and clownish people that call a spade a spade." In common use since the sixteenth century. The English clergyman and scholar Robert Burton (1577–1640) wrote: "A loose, plain, rude writer ... I call a spade a spade." His contemporary, the poet John Taylor (1580–1653), said, "I think it good English, without fraud, / To call a spade a spade, a bawd a bawd." The phrase is listed in the 1989 collection of *Modern Proverbs and Proverbial Sayings* by Bartlett Jere Whiting and in the 1993 *NTC's Dictionary of Proverbs and Clichés* by Anne Bertram.
Cecily: When I see a spade I call it a spade.

Gwendolen: I am glad to say I have never seen a spade. It is obvious that our social spheres have been widely different.
    1895: Oscar Wilde, *The Importance of Being Earnest*.
Call a spade a spade, although it may be a shovel.
    1909: Mary Roberts Rinehart, *The Man in Lower Ten*.
He called a Ford a Ford.
    1926: P.G. Wodehouse, *Small Bachelor*.
And he took me down to what he called his "den" in order that we might, "... call a spade a spade, and let the chips fall where they may."
    1963: Kurt Vonnegut, Jr., *Cat's Cradle*.
"I am a straight-shooting politician who calls a spade a spade," he [Mr. Zakhem] said.
    1992: *New York Times*.
When discussing sex, why not call a spade a spade instead of couching it in antiquated euphemisms?
    1993: *New York Times Book Review*.
"We could've won two games if Drew had made a right decision," Parcells said, with more tolerance than complaint. "But he's a good solid young guy. He calls a spade a spade."
    1993: *New York Times*.

45. Christine Ammer, *The American Heritage Dictionary of Idioms* (Boston: Houghton Mifflin, 1997), p. 97 and p. 646.

call a spade a spade
    Speak frankly and bluntly, be explicit, as in *You can always trust Mary to call a spade a spade*. This term comes from a Greek saying, *call a bowl a bowl*, that was mistranslated into Latin by Erasmus and came into English in the 1500s. Also see TELL IT LIKE IT IS.
tell it like it is
    Speak the truth, no matter how unpleasant. For example, *We're obliged to tell it like it is to the stockholders*. [Slang; second half of 1900s]

46. Robert Hendrickson, *Encyclopedia of Word and Phrase Origins* (New York: Facts on File, 1997), p. 122.

call a spade a spade.

To be straightforward and call things by their right names, to avoid euphemisms or beating around the bush. The words are from the garden, not from the game of poker. So old is this expression that it wasn't original with Plutarch, who used it back in the first century when writing about Philip of Macedon, Alexander the Great's father. The saying has been credited to the Greek comic poet Menander, who described the life of ancient Athens so faithfully that he inspired a critic to exclaim, "O Menander and Life, which of you imitated the other?" If this is so, to "call a spade a spade" goes back to at least 300 B.C., and the faithful Menander could have been quoting a much older Greek proverb. The expression was introduced into English by Protestant reformer John Knox, who translated it from the Latin of Erasmus as: "I have learned to call wickedness by its own terms: A fig a fig, and a spade a spade." Erasmus had taken the phrase from Lucian, a Greek writer of the second century and translated it as "to call a fig a fig and a boat a boat," which is possible because the Greek words for boat and garden spade were very similar.

47. David Pickering, *Dictionary of Proverbs* (London: Cassell, 1997), p. 36.

call a spade a spade (English)
   Call things by their proper names, so that their real nature is revealed. William Rastell, *The Four Elements*, 1519 (also quoted by Erasmus).

48. Elizabeth Walter et al., *Cambridge International Dictionary of Idioms* (Cambridge: Cambridge University Press, 1998), p. 364.

call a spade a spade
   to tell the truth about something, even if it is not polite or pleasant. *You know me, I call a spade a spade and when I see someone behaving like an idiot, I tell them.*

49. Myron Korach and John B. Mordock, *Common Phrases and Where They Come From* (Guilford, Connecticut: The Lyons Press, 2001), pp. 7–8.

Call a Spade a Spade

When speaking bluntly and to the point without "mincing words," you are "calling a spade a spade." This is another expression that came to us from ancient Greece.

When Lasthenes, as ambassador of Olynthus, called on Philip II of Macedon, he remarked that on his way to the palace he'd heard the Macedonians refer to him (Lasthenes) as a traitor. Philip replied, "Ay, these Macedonians are a blunt people who call figs 'figs' and a spade a 'spade.'" Yet Philip's remark to Lasthenes did not originate with him; he'd borrowed it from Lucian's famous dialogue in which Lucian quoted from Aristophanes, an Athenian playwright most famous for the *Lysistrata*. Aristophanes was the first to give literary from to the ancient Greek saying, "Figs they call figs and a spade a spade."

As was said at the beginning of this chapter, all of these entries from proverb, phrase, and idiom dictionaries, help in the attempt of gathering enough references for the "spade"-phrase in order to establish its origin, history, dissemination, and meaning. It has also already been alluded to the fact that the word "spade" has at least four relevant meanings: It can refer to the garden implement, it may mean a eunuch, it can signify a playing card, and, at least in the slang of the United States, it may refer to Blacks. Of all the dictionaries checked, only Christine Ammer takes note of the slur against African Americans in *Have a Nice Day — No Problem! A Dictionary of Clichés* (New York: Dutton, 1992), p. 48: "[...] A cliché since the nineteenth century, it acquired a slightly more sinister meaning when 'spade' became an offensive slang word for a black person." It is quite appropriate that Ammer draws attention to this fact, since the phrase can and is at times perceived as a racial slur. And yet, why did Christine Ammer not maintain this information in her subsequent *The American Heritage Dictionary of Idioms* (Boston: Houghton Mifflin, 1997 [see no. 45 above])? It seems to me that this would have been the proper and valid thing to do as a compiler of a phrasal dictionary intended for the mass market. Keeping the reference regarding the questionable nature of the ancient phrase could have helped to bring about a greater awareness in the modern American society that the phrase is no longer as innocuous as one might have think.

V.

Spade = Shovel, Eunuch, Card, and "Black"

When investigating an individual proverb or proverbial expression, it does not suffice to consult only quotation and proverb dictionaries. Quite often such phrases are also included in normal language dictionaries, whose lexicographers are quite keen in registering the various meanings of individual words of the traditional expression in question. It should also be noted that dialect dictionaries often contain regional and linguistic variants that are of much importance for the history and dissemination of any formulaic phrase. In other words, it behooves the scholar to check numerous dictionaries in order to assemble as complete a diachronic and synchronic survey as possible, always paying particular attention to shifts of meaning.

This is also the case for the proverbial expression "to call a spade a spade" under discussion in this study. Interestingly enough, Nathan Bailey included it in his invaluable early *Dictionarium Britannicum or a More Compleat Universal Etymological English Dictionary* (1736). John Ettlinger and Ruby Day have gone through this massive dictionary and excerpted the proverbial materials in their collection *Old English Proverbs* (Metuchen, New Jersey: The Scarecrow Press, 1992). Thus we find the following entry: "*To call a SPADE a SPADE.* That is, to speak plain; to call a thing or action by its right name; not to mince the matter" (p. 104). The phrase is also mentioned in Carey Woofter's regional collection of "Dialect Words and Phrases from West-Central West Virginia," *American Speech*, 2 (1927), 347-367: "*call a spade a spade* (verb phrase), to speak plainly. 'My father always called a spade a spade'" (p. 350). But here are three additional modern standard dictionaries that also did not fail to include the popular expression:

call a spade a spade, to call something by the real name; speak plainly or bluntly: *To call a spade a spade, he's a crook.*
   Jess Stein and Laurence Urdang (eds.), *Random House Dictionary of the English Language* (New York: Random House, 1967), p. 1362.

call a spade a spade, to call a thing by its proper name, to speak plainly or bluntly.

Eugene Ehrlich, Stuart Berg Flexner, Gorton Carruth, and Joyce M. Hawkins (eds.), *Oxford American Dictionary* (New York: Oxford University Press, 1980), p. 654.

call a spade a spade This often-heard injunction against the use of *euphemisms* led a reader to inquire. perhaps jestingly, why the admonition did not read "call a shovel a shovel," on the ground that that implement is more widely used. True enough, but the fact is that "spade" has been in the English language longer than "shovel," so it was readily at hand when the time came to translate the expression from the original Latin "Ficum ficum, ligonem ligonem vocat" — "He calls a fig a fig and *a spade a spade.*"

William and Mary Morris (eds.), *Dictionary of Contemporary Usage* (New York: Harper & Row, 1985), p. 100.

It is of importance to note that the meaning of the phrase is always given as to call *something* and not *someone* by the real name, i.e., the spade does not refer to a person as such. It was only in the twentieth century, when the noun "spade" took on the slang meaning of "black person," that the expression began to be used in reference to an individual and consequently became a slur in certain limited contexts.

But let us now take a look at the impressive treatment of the expression in the first edition of the *Oxford English Dictionary* from 1919. The entries under the various meanings of "spade" take up about 5 tightly set columns, and what follows are merely the relevant passages:

Spade
[...]
1. A tool for digging, paring, or cutting ground, turf, etc., now usually consisting of a flattish rectangular iron blade socketed on a wooden handle which has a grip or cross-piece at the upper end, the whole being adapted for grasping with both hands while the blade is pressed into the ground with the foot.
[...]
2. Phr. *To call a spade a spade*, to call things by their real names, without any euphemism or mincing of matters; to use plain or blunt language; to be straightforward to the verge of rudeness.

In the ultimate source of the first quotation, Plutarch's *Apophthegmata* 178 B, the Greek words are "ten skaphen skaphen legontas" [all Greek texts have been transliterated and are cited in quotation marks].

Spade = Shovel, Eunuch, Card, and "Black"

There is no evidence that "skaphe" (a trough, basin, bowl, boat, etc.) had the sense of 'spade'; in rendering it by *ligo* Erasmus evidently confused it with "skapheion" or other derivatives from the stem of "skaptein" to dig. Lucian *De Hist. Conscr.* 41 gives a fuller form of the phrase, "ta suka suka, ten skaphen de skaphen onomason."

Philippus aunswered, that the Macedonians wer feloes of no fyne witte in their termes, but altogether grosse, clubbyshe, and rusticall, as they whiche had not witte to calle a spade by any other name then a spade.

    1542: Udall, *Erasm. Apoph.* 167.

I cannot say the crow is white, But needes must call a spade a spade.

    1580: Gifford, *Posie of Gilloflowers* Wks. (Grosart) 101.

I am plaine, I must needs call a Spade a Spade.

    1589: *Marprel. Epit.* A ij.

I am a plaine Macedonian, I must need call a Spade a Spade.

    1630: *Pathomachia* iv. ii. 34.

Gods people shall not spare to call a spade a spade, a niggard a niggard.

    1647: Trapp, *Marrow Gd. Authors* in *Comm. Ep.* 641.

This is not Time of Day For Truth to be so obvious made, We must not call a Spade, a Spade.

    1706: E. Ward, *Hud. Rediv.* I. vii. 11.

I am old Tell-Truth; I love to call a Spade a Spade.

    1731-8: Swift, *Polite Conv.* 199.

They are the most unsavory vagabonds in their ordinary colloquies; they make no hesitation to call a spade a spade.

    1837: W. Irving, *Capt. Bonneville* III. 115.

If it is absolutely necessary to call a spade a spade then it must be done in a whisper.

    1884: *Punch*, 15 Nov. 229/2.

b. In allusions to the above phrase.

As surely as a Spade is a Spade, and ought so to be called.

    1677: W. Hughes, *Man of Sin* III. iii. 57.

A Spade with me was always a Spade, and Coscia a blundering Knave.

    1728-31: *Lett. from Fog's Jrnl.* (1732) I. 258.

Everything goes by its proper name; a spade is a spade; and a bayonet a bayonet.

    1816: J.W. Croker in *C. Papers* (1884) I. iii. 98.

A spade is a spade, and it is worse than useless to say that it is something else.

    1859: Trollope, *West Indies* ix. 123.

[...]

James A.H. Murray, Henry Bradley, W.A. Craigie, and C.T. Onions (eds.), *A New English Dictionary on Historical Principles* (Oxford: Clarendon Press, 1919), vol. 9, part 1, pp. 498–499.

As can be seen from these references, the editors of this comprehensive dictionary have done a superb job in registering a number of occurrences of the phrase. If one had only checked for the expression in this standard multi-volume compendium, the information gained would actually be quite satisfactory.

Since, as will be shown later in this and subsequent chapters, some speakers believe that the phrase refers to the "spades" suit of playing cards, we are including here the etymology of that meaning of the word "spade." The *OED* does, however, not include any references where the "spade"-phrase is referring to the card game:

Spade
[...] [ad. It. *spade*, pl. of *spada* (Sp. and Pg. *espada*)] sword [...], used as a mark on playing-cards. [...]
1. One or the other of the black spade-shaped marks by which one of the four suits in a pack of playing-cards is distinguished; hence *pl.*, the cards belonging to or forming this suit.
James A.H. Murray, Henry Bradley, W.A. Craigie, and C.T. Onions (eds.), *A New English Dictionary on Historical Principles* (Oxford: Clarendon Press, 1919), vol. 9, part 1, p. 499.

But the *Oxford English Dictionary* lists "eunuch" as a third meaning of "spade," and some scholars have indeed associated the proverbial expression with "calling a eunuch a eunuch":

Spade
[...] *Obs.* [ad. L. *spado.*] A eunuch.
[...]
Spade
[...] *Obs.* [f. *spaid, spayed*, pa. pple. of *spay* (...)] *trans.* To spay.
James A.H. Murray, Henry Bradley, W.A. Craigie, and C.T. Onions (eds.), *A New English Dictionary on Historical Principles* (Oxford: Clarendon Press, 1919), vol. 9, part 1, p. 499.

The dictionary, however, once again cites no text that shows the actual phrase referring to eunuchs. And this first edition of the *Oxford English*

Dictionary also does not include the fourth major meaning of the "spade"-word. Clearly the new slang meaning of "Black; African Ameri-can" had not yet been registered by lexicographers. By all the information that we have from slang dictionaries this term did not become current in the United States in any case until after 1919, when this particular volume appeared in print.

But that changed seventy years later in the second edition of the *Oxford English Dictionary* (1989). Actually, for the most part the editors copied the information of the first edition, but there are two major additions. First of all they had noticed that particularly in Great Britain people quite often speak more emphatically of a "(bloody) shovel," as can be seen by three references from the twentieth century:

Spade
[...]
2.c. More forcefully, in colloq. phr. *to call a spade a (bloody) shovel*: to speak with great or unnecessary bluntness.
We did not think it hypocritical to draw over our vagaries the curtain of a decent silence. The spade was not invariably called a bloody shovel.
    1919: W.S. Maugham, *Moon & Sixpence* iii. 12.
Sometimes ... I get so fed up with all the mumbo-jumbo and abracadabra and making of holy mysteries about simple things that I like to call a spade a shovel.
    1945: N. Balchin, *Mine Own Executioner* ii. 34.
As a literary starting-off point, the determination to call a spade a bloody shovel has imposed a fundamental limitation ... Outspokenness ... is simply not enough.
    1978: Cadogan & Craig, *Women & Children First* ii. 48.
[...]
    J.A. Simpson and E.S.C. Weiner (eds.), *The Oxford English Dictionary*, 2nd ed. (Oxford: Clarendon Press, 1989), vol. 16, pp. 94-95.

But under the entry for "spade" referring to the black suit of cards, the editors of the second edition of the *Oxford English Dictionary* have now included the slang term that is a slur against Blacks or African Americans:

Spade
[...]

92 *"Call a Spade a Spade"*

3.a. A Black person, a Negro, esp. male: freq. in White use, as a term of contempt or casual reference. Formerly among U.S. Blacks, a very dark-skinned Negro. *slang* (orig. U.S.).
    J.A. Simpson and E.S.C. Weiner (eds.), *The Oxford English Dictionary*, 2nd ed. (Oxford: Clarendon Press, 1989), vol. 16, p. 96.

While the editors present several contextualized references employing the slur, they do not include a citation of the phrase "to call a spade a spade" referring to Blacks. Nevertheless, it is clear from this discussion that both editions of the *Oxford English Dictionary* should be checked in any search for individual proverbial expressions.
    When studying the various possible meanings of the "spade"-phrase over time, we should therefore be able to find at least some references that actually speak of a "(bloody) shovel" or which allude (in)directly to eunuchs, card games, and Blacks. For the first of these four groups I can present a considerable number of texts in contexts beyond the three listed in the *Oxford English Dictionary*. They are listed here, as in all enumerations in this study, in convenient chronological order to indicate the historical development of these linguistic and semantic variants. In the following list with "shovel," I am also including texts that use "hoe," "implement," "utensil," etc.:

Spade = Shovel

The Chainbearer had none of this mystified nonsense about him. He called things by their right names; and when he wanted a spade, he did not ask for a hoe. As a consequence, he was obeyed, command being just as indispensable to men, on a thousand occasions, as any other quality.
    1845: J. Fenimore Cooper, *The Chainbearer; or, The Littlepage Manuscripts*, 2 vols. (New York: Stringer and Townsend, 1852), vol. 1, p. 138 (chapter 10).

Mr. Chesham. — In my opinion a most ill-advised and intemperate article. That journal, the *Pall Mall Gazette*, indulges in a very needless acrimony, I think.
Mr. Lowndes. — Chesham does not like to call a spade a spade. He calls it a horticultural utensil. You have a great career before you, Chesham.

You have a wisdom and gravity beyond your years. You bore us slightly, but we all respect you — we do indeed.
    1862: William Makepeace Thackeray, *The Adventures of Philip*, 2 vols. (Boston: Houghton, Mifflin and Company, 1892), vol. 1, p. 443 (chapter 23).

His [Compton Reade] style recalls that of the admiral who, when remonstrated with for his profanity by the bishop, declared that he hated nonsense, and liked to call a spade a spade; but that to call it a damned shovel was neither as accurate nor as sensible as calling it an agricultural implement. Much of Mr. Compton Reade's ostentatious downrightness is slovenly rhetoric of the damned shovel order. That his hotheadedness is not wholly an affectation is, however, proved by the want of verisimilitude in many portions of the narrative.
    1885: George Bernard Shaw, "Two Novels of Modern Society," in Brian Tyson (ed.), *Bernard Shaw's Book Reviews, Originally Published in the "Pall Mall Gazette" from 1885 to 1888* (University Park, Pennsylvania: Pennsylvania State University Press, 1991), p. 27. See also George B. Bryan and Wolfgang Mieder, *The Proverbial Bernard Shaw. An Index to Proverbs in the Works of George Bernard Shaw* (Westport, Connecticut: Greenwood Press, 1994), p. 223.

A writer may no longer call a spade a spade; he must cautiously refer to it as an agricultural implement lest he shock the supersensitiveness of hedonists and call down upon his head the Anathema Maranatha of men infinitely worse than Oscar Wilde.
    1898: William Cowper Brann, *The Complete Works of Brann the Iconoclast* (New York: The Brann Publishers, 1919), vol. 1, p. 152 ("Victor Hugo's Immortality").

"What I've done to build up my pile I've done open and with all the cards on the table. I have called a spade a spade, and I haven't referred to it, vague-like, as an 'industr'l utensil.' I haven't took the Lord in as a silent partner on my deals. What I've took I've took, and I've said, 'Whatcher going to do about it?' I've won out by strength, and I ain't ashamed of my way of playing the game."
    1907: Albert Payson Terhune, *Caleb Conover, Railroader* (New York: The Authors and Newspapers Association, 1907), p. 188 (chapter 8).

"I changed my plans, you see," he said, bustling his newspaper aside for me. "It is no discredit to your intelligence, Mr. Blakeley, but you lack the professional eye, the analytical mind. You legal gentlemen call a spade a spade, although it may be a shovel."

"'A primrose by the river's brim
A yellow primrose was to him,
And nothing more!'"
I quoted as the train pulled out.

    1909: Mary Roberts Rinehart, *The Man in Lower Ten* (New York: Zebra Books, 1990), pp. 166-167 (chapter 22).

I do not believe that there was in that genteel Bohemia an intensive culture of chastity, but I do not remember so crude a promiscuity as seems to be practised in the present day. We did not think it hypocritical to draw over our vagaries the curtain of a decent silence. The spade was not invariably called a bloody shovel. Woman had not yet altogether come into her own.

    1919: W. Somerset Maugham, *The Moon and Sixpence* (New York: The Modern Library, 1935), pp. 17-18 (chapter 3).

Corbin introduced you to the manly Saxon element. He had a rollicking ribaldry of speech, a tooraloorum style, in which a spade was often a bloody shovel. He snorted with contempt at the mere indication of effeminacy, abnormality or weakness. He looked at every problem resolutely from his own angle; he could not imagine any other.

    1940: C.E. Vulliamy, *Calico Pie. An Autobiography* (London: Michael Joseph, 1940), p. 64.

Mason himself was a continuous admirer of Trollope, even in the nineties, when few people read his works, and considered *Phineas Finn* and *Phineas Redux* two of the best novels in the English language. Mason went on to suggest a dip into *Ravenshoe* — 'some book!' — for contemporary colour, and to lend him D'Horsay on *The Follies of the Day* — 'It's ridiculously written, isn't it?' he adds. 'All round-about and flowery. A spade, not a spade, and not even a bloody shovel, but a horticultural implement of ancient and unimproved design.'

    1952: Roger Lancelyn Green, *A.E.W. Mason* (London: Max Parrish, 1952), p. 207.

Dance looked slightly taken aback at encountering this crude view of the situation. Then he laughed again, tossed off his drink, and took another which the barman pushed towards him. He recovered at once from what appeared to be a momentary shock, and raised his glass in mock salute. 'I'd like people to call a spade a damned shovel,' he said. 'It usually is, unless you can't be bothered to dig up the past.'
    1955: Gladys Mitchell, *Watson's Choice* (New York: David McKay, 1966), p. 147.

This, of course, is but a sampling. Readers will find a *Devil in Paradise* a good deal less scatological than some of Mr. [Henry] Miller's earlier works, although he is still not one to call a spade a garden implement.
    1956: Robert Clurman, "In and Out of Books," *The New York Times Book Review* (July 15, 1956), p. 8.

[Thomas] Dekker was an unsurpassedly keen observer of contemporary London life, if not a peeping Tom; and he gave us here [in his play *The Shoemaker's Holiday*] a vivid picture of the artisan and aristocratic milieus. [...] There is no doubting Thomas's skill. No profound intellectual, Dekker still possessed consummate wit, and produced a busty, gusty, lusty farce of great warmth and vigor. Teeming with bawdy *doubles ententes*, it makes *Measure for Measure* read like a Sunday sermon. And when Dekker doesn't call a spade a spade, he calls it s steam-shovel.
    1956: Caldwell Titcomb, "*The Shoemaker's Holiday*," *Harvard Summer News* (July 19, 1956), p. 2.

"Where you staying [*sic*], if I might ask?"
"With Mr. Luton, out of town on the river."
"Oh, Luton! Fine old-timer, he is. Not many of his sort left. Good old battler. Sooner call a spade a bloody shovel than a trowel. See you again."
    1956: Arthur Upfield, *The Battling Prophet* (London: William Heinemann, 1970), p. 78 (chapter 9).

"At last Doc Evatt has done something for his party," growled an Australian Laborite M.P. In the raucous and rowdy warfare of Australian politics, spades are called bloody shovels, and Dr. Herbert Vere Evatt is sometimes called worse. Last week, at 65, Doc Evatt ended his

rambunctious political career by accepting appointment by the New South Wales Labor premier as chief justice of the state supreme court.
    1960: Anonymous, "Australia: To the Bench," *Time* (February 22, 1960), p. 37.

Early in life she must have decided that risky stories are a substitute for sex appeal and she had a rich repertory at her command. One suspected that this had endeared her to Harry Dearbergh, her former husband, a rough old Englishman with a cockney accent and a bulldog manner. Together they had kept open house, gradually eliminating the dowdies and the dullards. Bridge tables, a copious buffet and a bar were sufficient to coax the supercilious who smiled at the crudities of their Amphitryon, for Dearbergh called a spade a bloody shovel. When he caught sight of one of his guests cramming his pockets with Havana cigars he said: 'Now you put those right back where you found them and keep one for yourself.'
    1970: Harold Acton, *Memoirs of an Aesthete, 1939–1969* (New York: The Viking Press, 1970), p. 67. Published in England as *More Memoirs of an Aesthete* (London: Methuen, 1970), p. 67.

A spade may be defined as a cultivating tool which has the blade set more or less in the same plane as the shaft. A shovel may be similarly defined, but since its primary function is to lift, retain and throw or turn the soil, its blade is broad and dished and the shaft may be of considerable length. It is not always easy, however, to distinguish between a blade and a shovel, to "call a spade a spade". The Cornish spade is an implement with a broad, pointed blade and a long shaft, but the closely similar Welsh or Irish implement is called a shovel.
    1970: Alan Gailey and Alexander Fenton (eds.), *The Spade in Northern and Atlantic Europe* (Belfast: Ulster Folk Museum & The Institute of Irish Studies, Queen's University Belfast, 1970), p. 2.

After weeks of bitter fighting, the Dallas-based oil company avoided takeover by Mesa through a massive corporate restructuring. [...] But when pressed, [T. Boone] Pickens reluctantly admits the deal is technically a loss for his side. "I hate to use the word 'outfoxed,'" Pickens says. "But we didn't get the company. Call a spade a spade; don't call it a shovel. I always hate to lose, and we did lose here."
    1987: Diane Jennings, "T. Boone Pickens: Villain? Or Hero?" *The Dallas Morning News* (March 1, 1987), p. 1E.

He called it "another in a never-ending series of hypocritical whitewash coming from our industry. It is time for us," he declared, "to be honest and call a spade a spade rather than a manually operated garden implement."
    1990: Mort Hochstein, "How Far Should Operators Go to Regulate Drinking?" *Nation's Restaurant News* (January 1, 1990), p. 30.

But sometimes, as Malcolm [X] said, you need to talk right down to earth in a language everybody knows — even folks who say they don't know what those words mean. And I learned something about education and courage, too: What use is it to know a spade is not a shovel if you ain't got the stones to call a spade a spade?
    1992: David Bradley, "Malcolm's Pen: Brutal Truths," *The Kansas City Star* (November 15, 1992), p. J1.

call a spade a spade, to state things as they are; to be bluntly matter-of-fact.
call a spade a fucking shovel, offensive; to exaggerate.
    1996: James Lambert (ed.), *Macquarie Book of Slang* (Sydney: The Macquarie Library, 1996), p. 35.

Geraldine [Johnson] initiated and organized a highly successful community-wide effort to persuade then Mayor Art Agnos and the Redevelopment Agency to adopt a "first-time ever" policy that required majority participation and control by African-Americans in the development of the last parcel of vacant land in the Western Addition. She was an astute political analyst. She did not hesitate to take any one to court who attempts to trample on her, or the rights of others. She called a spade a "spade" and not an "agricultural tool." She could be very abrasive with anyone who even as a volunteer does not recognize the responsibility that attaches to volunteerism.
    1997: Anonymous, "Activist Geraldine Johnson Remembered," *The Sun Reporter* (November 20, 1997), p. S1.

The first black woman to represent South Africa in Britain pledged to let the winds of change blow through the colonial splendour of London's South Africa House, and to give the diplomatic cocktail circuit a wide berth. Cheryl Carolus, 40, who arrived in London last week to take up the post of High Commissioner, said: "It's a myth that diplomats lie through their teeth, but I will call a spade a spade and not a garden implement."

1998: Job Rabkin, "South Africa's Whirlwind Hits Town," *The Independent* (March 10, 1997), p. 11.

Over 80% of Ireland's Garda (police) force called in sick last Friday. [...] Finance Minister Charlie McCreevy angrily described the protest as "a lie," and insisted that the Government would not bow down to the demand of the protesting gardai. [...] "It's a plain lie to call in sick in such numbers and there's no point in calling it anything else. There's no point calling a shovel a spade when it's clearly a shovel."
1998: Anonymous, "Ireland Recovers from Bout of 'Blue Flu'," *Irish Voice* (May 12, 1998), p. 4.

[...] warned of the danger to the republic of those lunatics who liked to roll such words as 'communist' and 'agent' across their tongues. And yes, thank you for hearkening back to the glorious days of agrarian reformers, when the left first taught us to call a spade an agricultural implement or face the opprobrium of such geniuses as Our Boy Stevie.
1998: Robert Stacy McCain, "Inside Politics," *The Washington Times* (May 26, 1998), p. A7.

"When to Call a Spade a Spade"
Stephen Anderton ponders the status of the ceremonial tree-planting spade.
The next time you spot Prince Charles planting a tree on television, spare a thought for the spade. Spades can be celebrities, too. Spades can have shaken hands with more royalty than Sir Alastair Burnet. In the botanical garden on Malta a few years ago, I was lucky enough to be shown the official spade for planting ceremonial trees. The whole handle and shaft were covered in a hundred years' worth of little brass plaques, stating who had planted what with it, and when. It was heavy with overlapping armour plate, like the copper bottom of a tea clipper.
1998: Stephen Anderton, "When to Call a Spade a Spade," *The Times of London* (October 31, 1998), p. 10.

IMI is a Midlands engineer that tends to call a spade a spade. The market has punished it for this plainspeaking, assuming the valves and fittings it makes are terribly low-tech because they are grouped under prosaic names such as "Building Products". The shares stood at 532p last May. Now they are 252p. IMI has, however, twigged that if you call a spade a man-to-soil interface system, the market will like you more.

Hence, it is rebranding itself as a "controls" group — shades of Siebe, here — renaming divisions [...].
> 1999: Robert Cole, "IMI," *The Times* (London) (March 9, 1999), no pp.

[Coach Mac] McCallion is renowned for his expertise in forward play, and for "standing up for his players". As one ally of McCallion said last night: "Mac is always a straight shooter. He doesn't call a spade a spade. He calls it a bloody shovel. He sometimes finds himself off-side with officialdom because he invariably speaks his mind. He would provide NSW with that required edge to be consistent winners."
> 1999: Greg Growden, "No-Nonsense McCallion the Dark Horse in Race to Take over from Williams," *Sydney Morning Herald* (May 31, 1999), p. 30.

Next time you go to the garden shed you won't be able to call a spade a spade. It might have become a "manually operated soil inverting instrument." However, there are more interesting, even more entertaining, things to read. Support your local library.
> George Brookbank, "It's No Time to Sweat the Big Chores," *The Tucson Citizen* (June 1, 1999), p. T2.

"Indians in Corporate America: Calling a Spade a Bloody Shovel"
[...] In setting up a fund to help launch small companies, Hemant Shah is going down a road that he has long wanted to travel. When he left India in 1975, armed with a degree in pharmacy, his goal was to learn as much as possible about the pharmaceutical industry so that he could start a business in India. [...] Shah has not cut himself off from India, however. Ranbaxy Laboratories, India's largest pharmaceutical company, is one of his clients, and Shah is helping expand its operations in the United States.
> 1999: Mukul Pandya, "Indians in Corporate America: Calling a Spade a Bloody Shovel," *Little India*, 6, no. 3 (1999), 25.

The contemplative routine of the convent was being disrupted by the presence of workmen converting the electrical service from overhead lines to buried cables. Mother Superior called the electric company's complaint department to ask for help. "The profanity these men use constantly is unsuitable for our community. You must make them stop cursing so much," said the nun. "Very well, sister. But you must make allowances for their habits. Even when they are trying to be tactful, they will still tend to call a spade a spade," said the company spokeswoman. Mother Superior then observed, "I think the term they actually use is 'fucking shovel'."

2001: Luke Davis, "Sick Twisted Jokes," http://sickjokes.about. com/ comedy/sickjokes/library/w (May 5, 2001).

These contextualized examples make it perfectly clear that nobody has a black person in mind when using the expression "to call a spade a spade." The fact that the spade is associated with a shovel, garden implement, etc. shows that the expression is used in its traditional sense of speaking plainly. The context also shows that African Americans like Malcolm X use the phrase without any thoughts of it being a slur. Of interest are also the two references to calling "a spade a fucking shovel," obviously a coarse exaggeration of the otherwise innocuous phrase.

Spade = Eunuch

But let us now turn to the few references in which the proverbial expression is thought to refer to eunuchs, something that will no doubt surprise the modern user of the phrase. And yet, nobody less than Archer Taylor, the internationally renowned paremiologist of the twentieth century, had the following to say about this "imperfectly understood English proverbial phrase" in his *The Proverb* (Cambridge, Massachusetts: Harvard University Press, 1931; rpt. with an introduction by Wolfgang Mieder. Bern: Peter Lang, 1985): "The phrase *To call a spade a spade* may allude to a spayed dog, and possibly we can find support for this explanation in the synonymous Italian *to call a cat a cat* (Chiamar gatta gatta). On the other hand, the German *to show him what a rake is* (einem zeigen was eine Harke ist) suggests that 'spade' means a garden implement" (pp. 192-193). Taylor speaks of a spayed animal rather than a eunuch, but he certainly had this latter meaning in mind. When he cites the Italian equivalent, he seems to be unaware that it most likely is a loan translation from the French "appeler un chat un chat" that goes back to Nicolas Boileau in the seventeenth century, as has been pointed out by a number of quotation lexicographers. But as can be seen, Taylor is also thinking of spade as a garden implement in his conjectures about the possible origin of the "spade"-phrase. For once the master paremiologist is simply not certain about the precise reference of the metaphor.

Mitford M. Mathews, the well-known editor of *A Dictionary of Americanisms on Historical Principles* (Chicago: University of Chicago Press, 1951), recounts another fascinating conjecture along these lines. In his article "Of Matters Lexicographical" (1954), we find the following story:

> That evening I met on the street Robert J. Bonner, a distinguished classical scholar, who has since passed away. On this occasion Dr. Bonner, oddly enough, took me somewhat severely to task for not being able to point out the logic and reason shown in our well-known expression *to call a spade a spade*. I defended myself as best I could on short notice, explaining that I had nothing to do with originating the expression, that it is not of American origin, and reminded him that language has a way of crystallizing into forms that can hardly be explained logically.
>
> He then gave me the 'proper' background of the expression, and an account of how it arose. He said that the failure of people to appreciate the naturalness of the expression comes from the fact that it is slightly misspelled, that properly written it is *to call a spayed a spayed*. Farmers, he said, are accustomed to spay those hogs they do not wish to become breeders and so reduce them to impotency so far as making any contribution to the ongoing of their kind is concerned. From this custom the expression arose of calling *a spayed hog a spayed hog*. As time passed *hog* was dropped as entirely needless, no other animal being spayed, and then, by those not acquainted with the activities on farms, *spayed* was apprehended erroneously as *spade*, with the result that we now have a common expression which, the way it is written, is absurd. He regarded the original term as quite sensible and natural, springing as it did right out of the daily life of the folk.
>
> He had worked out this explanation without the drudgery of examining any works of reference. After he had thought it all up, he had consulted one of his younger colleagues whose father had been a farmer, and this young man had placed a stamp of instant approval on his elder's simple diagnosis of this old expression, because he knew for a fact that farmers do spay hogs.
>
> Like the Wedding-Guest when he turned from the bridegroom's door, I went away from this street scene 'like one that has been stunned,' amazed that such an absurd notion could have originated in the head of a man who must have spent long hours in the

company of some kinds of dictionaries at least. My amazement grew when I consulted the *OED* [*Oxford English Dictionary*] and found that the phrase in question has a classical background, owing its present form to a slight error made by Erasmus in grappling with a slithery Greek idiom at a time when scholars were not so fortunate as to have the ninth edition of Liddell and Scott at their elbow.

Never since this experience have I attributed unusual sagacity and sensitivity about words and etymologies to those who have cultivated a daily acquaintance with the classics.

Mitford M. Mathews, "Of Matters Lexicographical," *American Speech*, 29 (1954), 209–213 (here pp. 210–211).

This is a wonderful account of folk etymology! I might simply add that not a single reference has been found of the "spade"-phrase referring to spaying hogs. But there are dozens of such etiological tales floating about that try to explain the archaic metaphors of proverbial phrases. All of this is yet another proof that only painstaking scholarly work can in fact lead to the correct explanation of the origin and meaning of proverbs and proverbial expressions.

But how about some actual occurrences where the "spade"-phrase does refer to spaying or a spayed-one, i.e., a spade? Of all the contextualized references in the present study there is but *one* that would perhaps permit this interpretation. It is included in a number of quotation and proverb dictionaries (see chapters 3 and 4) with the claim that it is based on "to call a spade a spade." But here is what Jonathan Swift actually wrote in his *Polite Conversation* of 1738 that is filled with proverbial materials:

Miss. They say, a Fool will ask more Questions, than twenty wise Men can answer.
Col. Indeed, Miss, *Tom Neverout* has posed you.
Miss. Why, Colonel, every Dog has his Day. But, I believe, I shall never see a Goose again, without thinking on Mr. *Neverout*.
Lord Sm. Well said Miss; I'faith Girl, thou hast brought thy self off cleverly. *Tom*, what say you to that?
Col. Faith, *Tom* is nonplust; he looks plaguily down in the Mouth.
Miss. Why, my Lord, you see he's the provokingest Creature in Life: I believe, there is not such another in the varsal World.
Lady Answ. Oh Miss, the World's a wide Place.

Nev. Well, Miss, I'll give you Leave to call me any Thing, so you don't call me a Spade.
Eric Partridge (ed.), *Swift's Polite Conversation with Introduction, Notes and Extensive Commentary* (New York: Oxford University Press, 1963), p. 143 (Second Conversation).

This quotation from Jonathan Swift was purposely taken from the edition by the lexicographer and phraseologist Eric Partridge, who has provided this enlightening annotation: "'any Thing, so you don't call me a Spade': provided you don't call me a eunuch. This rare word, noted by the *OED* for 1680, comes from Latin *spado*" (p. 143). To be sure, the editors of both editions of the *OED* failed to cite this reference out of Swift under "spade" (eunuch). Partridge says nothing about this statement having anything to do with the "spade"-phrase, and it is questionable whether Swift was in fact citing it here. It is at best an allusion to the phrase which Swift, after all, knew very well. Later in his *Polite Conversation* he writes: "I am old Tell-truth, I love to call a Spade, a Spade" (Third Conversation, p. 167). One thing is for certain, the "spade"-phrase has very little to do with eunuchs, but it is an intriguing example of folk etymology.

Spade = Playing Card

It has already been established that the proverbial expression "to call a spade a spade" has nothing to do with playing cards in general and the suit of spades in particular. Yet again, that does not mean that this connection does not exist in the folk's mind. References are, as in the case of "spade" (eunuch), relatively rare:

spade. Always call a spade a spade, especially in a card game.
Evan Esar, *Esar's Comic Dictionary* (New York: Harvest House, 1943), p. 260.

Spade
There's no one more exasperating than a bridge partner who calls a spade two spades.
1968: Evan Esar, *20,000 Quips & Quotes* (New York: Barnes & Noble, 1995), pp. 754-755.

The informant [a student] thought the origin of the proverb was in card games where one card is made "wild", or is able to stand for any other card in the deck. Perhaps it was the custom to have, for example, the Two of Spades "wild", then the two would be called a King of Hearts, or Ace of Diamonds, or whatever. To say "Call a spade a spade" would be to ask that all cards be called as they actually are.

 Jane McKinnon, "Call a spade a spade" (March 1, 1969), cited from the Folklore Archive at the University of California at Berkeley.

The new/old law of securities transfer: calling a "spade" a "heart, diamond, club or the like."

 Martin J. Aronstein, "The New/Old Law of Securities Transfer," *Cardozo Law Review*, 12 (December 1990), 429–469 (here p. 429).

Bouchard's respect for Chrétien and Canada is about the equivalent of Parizeau's. The difference between Parizeau and Bouchard is that Parizeau shows a degree of respect for veracity. As he did this week, Parizeau calls a spade a spade. Bouchard calls a spade many things. Jack of clubs, queen of hearts, deuce of diamonds. Most of all joker. And everyone in Canada now knows who the joke is on. Jacques Parizeau.

 Lawrence Martin, "Bouchard Calls a Spade Many Things," *The Gazette* (November 28, 1998), p. B7.

Although I believe that it is wrong for government to encourage human weaknesses such as gambling, our state's leadership continues to travel down this road to easy tax money. So be it. But let's call a spade a spade, or a diamond a diamond, or a club a club, etc.

 Tom Miller, "Under the Dome: Call a Spade a Spade. [Gov. Cecil] Underwood Giving Casino Gambling Bill Some Positive Spin," *The Charleston Gazette* (March 22, 1999), p. 5A.

I Call a Spade a Spade
I was playing poker with the boys
And things were going well,
When through the crowd and all the noise
Comes our small town Jezebel.

She strutted over where I sat
And cocked her sassy head.
She tried to sit down in my lap.
And this is what she said:

"If you'll be my King of Diamonds,
I'll be your Queen of Hearts;
You're wastin' time at poker,
I can teach you more than cards!"

I pushed my chair against the wall
And quickly backed away;
She couldn't hold a candle
To my sweet, young fiancee.

"You're not my Queen of Hearts, m'am;
I'm taken, I'm afraid;
I'm not your King of Diamonds,
And I call a spade a spade!"

She was surprised I turned her down,
Her smile began to fade;
I didn't mean to shame her, but
I call a spade a spade.
    Beth B. Jacks, "Poems" (March 3, 2001), http://www.zoomnet.net/petecol/jacks_b.html

A few more statements regarding the belief that the expression originated from playing cards will be cited in chapter eleven that presents the results of four surveys based on questionnaires. They represent attempts by the folk to understand the "spade"-metaphor which appears to make as much sense referring to the card game as to a garden implement.

Spade = *"Black" (African American)*

There is no doubt that the word "spade," at least in the slang of American English, has taken on the meaning of a black person or African American. This can readily be seen from a short lexicographical history as presented in various dictionaries, showing that the slur originated in the 1920s in the United States with later occurrences also in Great Britain:

The English have relatively few aliens in their midst, and in consequence they have developed nothing comparable to our huge repertory of opprobrious names for them. [...] the American language offers: [...]

106 *"Call a Spade a Spade"*

For Negro: *nigger, coon, shine, jigabo, spade, Zulu, skunk, jig, jit, buffalo, boogie, dinge, smoke, moke* and *snowball.*
    H.L. Mencken, *The American Language* 4th ed. (New York: Alfred A. Knopf, 1936 [1960]), pp. 294-296.

NEGRO. Afric, Afro, black bean, blackbird, blackhead, blacky, boogie, brownskin, buggy, burr-head, charcoal, chocolate, chocolate drop, coon, cotton picker, crow, cuddy, cuffee, cuffey, dark cloud, darkey, darky, dinge, dingy, dink, dusky, ebony, eight-ball, 8-ball, God's image cut in ebony, ink, ink face, jap, jazz-bo, jig, jigaboo, jit, kink, licorice stick, moke, musk, muskrat, nig, nigger, possum, quashee, quashie, shade, shine, shot, skunk, smoke, spade, squasho, sun-burned Irishman, sunshine, thicklips, woolly head, zigaboo, zoolo, zulu. *Spec.* Aframerican, Africamerican, unbleached American, *an American Negro*; black diamond, *a Negro of good traits*; black diamond in the rough, *a Negro of crude exterior but intrinsic worth*; coal-chutes blackie, blue, snowball, spade, *a very dark Negro*; gee-chee, *a Negro from Charleston, S.C.*; Harlemaniac, *blend of "Harlem" and "maniac"*; blackamuffin, *blend of "blackamoor" and "ragamuffin"*; all God's chilluns, black ivory, the colored, the cullud, niggerdom, *Negroes collectively.*
    Lester V. Berrey and Melvin van den Bark, *The American Thesaurus of Slang* (New York: Thomas Y. Crowell, 1942), p. 360 ("spade" is also registered on p. 415 and p. 583).

The DAE (*Dictionary of American English*, 1938-44) does not list such vulgar synonyms for *Negro* as *ape, eight-ball, jazzbo, jigaboo* (with variants, *jibagoo, jig, zigabo, zigaboo, zig*), *jit, seal, shine, skunk, smoke, snowball, spade, squasho* and *Zulu*.
    H.L. Mencken, *The American Language. Supplement I* (New York: Alfred A. Knopf, 1945 [1961]), p. 636. Same reference in H.L. Mencken, *The American Language*, The Fourth Edition and the Two Supplements, abridged, with annotations and new material, by Raven I. McDavid (New York: Alfed A. Knopf, 1963 [1974]), p. 387.

[no reference!].
    Mitford M. Mathews, *A Dictionary of Americanisms on Historical Principles* (Chicago: University of Chicago Press, 1951), p. 1603 (here only "spade" referring to "a blade on the rotary wheel of a spader").

Spade = Shovel, Eunuch, Card, and "Black"

Spade: (1940's–50's) a Negro (probably picked up from white usage).
Clarence Major, *Dictionary of Afro-American Slang* (New York: International Publishers, 1970), p. 107.

spade. A Negro: low: from ca. 1920. Ex the colour of the card-suit. *Spades*. Coloured people, esp. Negroes and West Indians: low, e.g. 'Teddy boys': since ca. 1947. (*The Observer*, March 1, 1949.) In cards, a 'dark' suit: cf. 'as black as the ace of spades'.
Eric Partridge, *A Dictionary of Slang and Unconventional English*, 7th ed. (New York: Macmillan, 1970), p. 804 and p. 1422.

spade [derog.] A Negro, esp. a very dark-skinned Negro. 1931: "The plutes compromised with the blacks / the spades inhabited Harlem and let the / ofays have Wall Street to themselves." Bob Brown in *Amer. Mercury*, Dec., 407/2. 1956: "A 'spade' is a Negro." S. Longstreet, *The Real Jazz Old and New*, 147. *Common since c1920.*
Harold Wentworth and Stuart Berg Flexner, *Dictionary of American Slang* (New York: Thomas Y. Crowell, 1975), p. 505.

call a spade a spade to speak forthrightly. From an old Greek proverb.
spade a black person.
Anita Pearl, *Dictionary of Popular Slang* (Middle Village, New York: Jonathan David, 1980), p. 20 and p. 153.

spade 1. to castrate; to desex. See SPAY. [early 1600s–pres.] 2. a eunuch. See SPADA. 3. a derogatory nickname for a Negro. From the black color of the spade in playing cards. Not connected with senses 1 or 2. [British and U.S. slang, early 1900s–pres.].
Richard A. Spears, *Slang and Euphemism. A Dictionary of Oaths, Curses, Insults, Sexual Slang and Metaphor, Racial Slurs, Drug Talk, Homosexual Lingo, and Related Matters* (Middle Village, New York: Jonathan David, 1981), p. 368.

nigger A black person — blackbird, blood, blue, blue-gum, blue-skin, boogie, boot, bro, brother, burrhead, chocolate drop, chungo bunny, clink, cluck, coon, darky, dinge, eightball, geechee, groid, hardhead, Hershey bar, hod, inky-dink, jarhead, jig, jigaboo, jit, jungle bunny, kinky-head, mayate, nig, niggra, peola, schvartze, scuttle, shade, shad-mouth, shadow, skillet, smoke, spade, spook, zig, zigaboo. *All these terms will give deep offense if used by nonblacks.*

Robert L. Chapman, *Thesaurus of American Slang* (New York: Harper & Row, 1989), p. 172.

spade. A black person. "The four Turlocks hated Negroes and never hesitated in voicing their disgust. 'Goddamned spades killed my cousin Captain Matt — one of them gets out of line with me, he's dead" (James A. Michener, *Chesapeake*, 1978).
The allusion is to the card suit, and this kind of *spade* derives from the Italian *spada*, a broad sword, not the spade that is a shovel, though the two forms have the same Indo-European root, *sphe-*.

Hugh Rawson, *Wicked Words. A Treasury of Curses, Insults, Put-Downs, and Other Formerly Unprintable Terms from Anglo-Saxon Times to the Present* (New York: Crown Publishers, 1989), p. 369.

ace of spades an American black; a very dark American black. (The name for the "one" of spades in card playing). The term alludes to the blackness of spades. Intended and perceived as derogatory when used by whites. Not widely known. Male use. Also a term of address. From the expression "black as the ace of spades." *Freddy came in looking like the run-of-the-mill ace of spades, platform shoes, and the like. Who's that ace of spades coming around the corner?*
spade an American black. (Intended and perceived as derogatory and provocative). Also a term of address. From the blackness of the ace of spades in a deck of cards. User is considered to be racially bigoted.

Richard A. Spears, *Forbidden American English* (Lincolnwood, Illinois: Passport Books, 1990), p. 2 and p. 175.

spade offensive, orig US. A Black. 1928-. N. Saunders, "On Saturdays try Brixton market — nearly as big, more genuine, lots of spades" (1971).

John Ayto and John Simpson, *The Oxford Dictionary of Modern Slang* (Oxford: Oxford University Press, 1992), p. 233.

spade, A black person. ["... one quiet church went to extra ordinary lengths to rid itself of the 'dicty spade' who wore his learning on his sleeve." Darryl Pinckney, *High Cotton* (1922).]

Jordan L. Linfield and Joe Kay, *"Your Mother Wears Army Boots!" A Treasure Trove of Insults, Slurs and Putdowns* (New York: Avon Books, 1992), p. 243.

spade A reference to any African American; a derogatory term.
Geneva Smitherman, *Black Talk: Words and Phrases from the Hood to the Amen Corner* (Boston: Houghton Mifflin Company, 1994), p. 213. Also in the revised edition (Boston: Houghton Mifflin Company, 2000), p. 268.

spade a black. Derogatory white use, from the colour of the playing card, and now regarded as extremely offensive:
    And if that little spade said something
    different, she's lying. (Macdonald, 1976)
R.W. Holder, *Euphemisms* (Oxford: Oxford University Press, 1995), p. 346.

It would be a mistake, however, to hypothesize that only in America are Blacks subject to so many demeaning nicknames. Similar coinages, based on the word Black, can be found very far from the planatations or the newer ghettoes. Among the best-known is *spade* or *ace-of-spades* (from which it derives). Used at one time by American Blacks to indicate a person with very dark skin, it became popular in the UK [United Kingdom] in the 1960s, thanks to among others the author Colin MacInnes in his novels *Absolute Beginners* (1959) and *City of Spades* (1961); MacInnes also coined the nonce word *spadelet* to describe a Black infant. *Club*, another black suit, means the same. The rhyming slang *razor blade*, generally abbreviated to *razor*, or *luke* (from *Lucozade*, otherwise a soft drink) equals spade. *Super-spade*, an American coinage of the 1960s, was a Black person who was noticeably self-conscious about his/her race. It also punned on the comic hero Superman.
Jonathon Green, *Words Apart: The Language of Prejudice* (London: Kyle Cathie, 1996), p. 29.

Several things become clear from this enumeration of dictionary references. The slang term of "spade" meaning a black person or African American goes back to the 1920s and is definitely a derogatory designation, above all if used by whites as a slur against Blacks. But as so often with stereotypes, it might well be used positively among members of the minority group in question. This can be seen quite well from three additional references collected from student informants by folklore students from the University of California at Berkeley in the sixties, clearly predating the so-called "political correctness" movement in the United States:

spade: This word is used to refer to negroes of either sex and all ages. It is used by both Negroes and Caucasions [*sic*] freely. It is neither a negative or a positive word. Example: I went to see some spade friends last night in San Francisco.
    Judy Caldeira, "Spade" (February 19, 1968), cited from the Folklore Archive at the University of California at Berkeley.

spade: The term refers to a Negro, especially one who swings. The informant uses the Term in this context. "A spade came by looking for Mary today."
    Jeffrey Friedman, "Spade" (May 1, 1968), cited from the Folklore Archive at the University of California at Berkeley.

"I'm a Spade. So I dance like a Spade" [informant used this phrase]. The informant related that she and her Negro friends prefer to be called Spades, rather than Nigger or any other word denoting their race. She said she started referring to herself and her soul brothers and sisters as "Spades" about three years ago when she heard it used around Oakland. She mentioned that the term was used more frequently among dopers, Black Panthers, and other "degenerate" groups because she believed the term to come from "Black as the ace of spades"; she added that the ace of spades is bad!
    Diane Goserud, "Spade" (April 1, 1969), cited from the Folklore Archive at the University of California at Berkeley.

The ambivalence of the slang term "spade" as well as the phrase "(black as the) ace of spades" regarding their reference to Blacks is obvious. An interesting final example is the poem "My Ace of Spades" (1969) by the African American painter, trumpet player, and poet Ted Joans:

> *My Ace of Spades*
> MALCOLM X spoke to me & sounded you
>   Malcolm X said this to me, then told you that
>   Malcolm X whispered in my ears but screamed on you
>   Malcolm X praised me and thus condemned you
>   Malcolm X smiled at me and sneered at you
>   Malcolm X covered me and exposed you
>   Malcolm X made me PROUD and you all got scared

Malcolm X told me to hurry and you begin to worry
Malcolm X sung to me but growled at you
Malcolm X freed me and frightened you
Malcolm X told it like it *damn shor* is!
He said I gotta fight to be really FREE
  Malcolm X told both of us
    the truth, now didn't he?
Ted Joans, *Black Pow-Wow. Jazz Poems* (New York: Hill and Wang, 1969), p. 96.

Clearly Ted Joans does not intend to use the poem's title as a slur against Malcolm X. On the contrary, he means it very positively in obvious defiance of those bigoted people to whom it represents a slur against African Americans.

As we bring this chapter to a close, it is necessary to observe in summary that none of the lexicographers of various language and slang dictionaries bothered to mention that in more recent times the phrase "to call a spade a spade" has been interpreted as a slur against Blacks due to the association with the derogatory slang meaning of "spade." In fact, there are exactly two exceptions to this disturbing observation regarding the slowness of lexicographers to register new meanings of traditional phrases. In chapter 4 (no. 38) I already mentioned the following clarifying reference:

call a spade a spade, to. [...] A cliché since the nineteenth century, it acquired a slightly more sinister meaning when "spade" became an offensive slang word for a black person.
  Christine Ammer, *Have a Nice Day — No Problem! A Dictionary of Clichés* (New York: Dutton, 1992), p. 48.

I can now add at least this second dictionary reference that pointed to the newly perceived stereotypical meaning of the "spade"-phrase. It actually precedes the statement by Christine Ammer by one year, and is included in a highly specialized dictionary from the era of "political correctness":

call a spade a spade get to the point, speak plainly / straight from the shoulder / straight out, be up front / frank / on the up and up / above board. The expression is associated with a racial slur and should be avoided.

Rosalie Maggio, *The Bias-Free Word Finder. A Dictionary of Nondiscriminatory Language* (Boston: Beacon, 1991), p. 61.

There you have it, the two lone voices in the lexicographical and paremiographical wilderness! There can be no doubt that dictionary makers of all types lag far behind for the most part in registering new phrases as well as new meanings of old expressions. That is why it is so important that specialized dictionaries are published. Of course, it would behoove lexicographers of larger single or multi-volume dictionaries to pay attention to such findings. As will be shown in later chapters of this study, there is no denying the fact that to a considerable degree the traditional "spade"-phrase is understood as a racial slur today, especially in American English of the United States.

VI.

Literary Texts from the 16th to the 20th Century

The quotation, proverb, and language dictionaries discussed in chapters three to five provided an impressive number of literary references, albeit only if all of them were in fact checked. But even though, due to space limitations the lexicographers and paremiographers can only cite truncated snippets of each reference, and often there is a lack of precise bibliographical information. All of this makes it extremely difficult to track these references down so that they might be listed in a more complete literary context. Such contextualized citations are, however, of great importance if the clear meaning of the proverbial expression "to call a spade a spade" is to come to light. Without the actual context, it is impossible to tell whether a certain occurrence of the "spade"-phrase carries the meaning of speaking plainly or whether it is referring to eunuchs or playing cards, or whether it is being used as a slur against African Americans.

As would be expected, I have found additional literary uses of the expression, and it is with a bit of scholarly pride that I include them in the following chronological enumeration. It is, of course, clear that until about 1920 the phrase could only be used in its traditional meaning. It is, however, somewhat surprising that not a single modern reference out of literary works exhibits the racist use of the phrase as a slur against African Americans. On the other hand, one can interpret this fact quite positively. Obviously literary authors have shied away from using the phrase in this sense. As will be shown in chapters eight to ten, the mass media has been less reluctant in reporting occurrences of the slur.

The following texts in contexts have been grouped by centuries and are arranged chronologically in each section. To a considerable degree they have been found in the quotation, proverb, and language dictionaries mentioned above. However, there are also many more texts which I located through my own literary investigations and by means of modern database searches. With even more detailed work, especially as ever new databases are established, additional references will surely be found. However, they will hardly change the general picture presented here.

One additional point needs to be made before presenting the materials themselves. It relates to the earliest English literary reference in John Rastell's *The Nature of the Four Elements* (1519). In the second chapter we have already pointed out that the proverbial expression "to call a spade a spade" entered the English language by way of two translations of parts of Erasmus of Rotterdam's works by Richard Taverner (1539) and Nicholas Udall (1542). Erasmus had created the Latin "spade"-variant "ficus ficus, ligonem ligonem vocat" in the 1515 edition of his expanded *Adagia*, and it makes perfect sense that the two translators Taverner and Udall followed suit in their translations. But the question is where John Rastell came up with his much earlier statement from the year 1519:

> For is it not as good to say playnly
> Gyf me a spade
> As gyf me a spa ve va ve va ve vade?

And a second question follows at once: Does this reference really allude to the expression "to call a spade a spade?" The magisterial paremiographer Bartlett Jere Whiting must have thought so, for he included these three lines in his *Proverbs in the Earlier English Drama* (Cambridge, Massachusetts: Harvard University Press, 1938; rpt. New York: Octagon Books, 1969), p. 364. William George Smith in his second edition of *The Oxford Dictionary of English Proverbs* (1948) agreed and listed Rastell as the earliest reference of the phrase, albeit without citing these three lines. F.P. Wilson as the editor of the third edition once again concurred in 1970, keeping the 1519 reference to Rastell and adding the actual text to it. And yet, later paremiographers, notably Burton Stevenson, Morris Palmer Tilley, and Robert W. Dent chose *not* to include this text in *The Macmillan Book of Proverbs, Maxims, and Famous Phrases* (1948), *A Dictionary of the Proverbs in England in the Sixteenth and Seventeenth Century* (1950), and *Proverbial Language in English Drama Exclusive of Shakespeare, 1495–1616* (1984) respectively. Why not? Did they question the proverbiality of this reference as I am inclined to do? No matter what, it is at best an allusion to Erasmus' Latin phrase, certainly not a direct translation as in the case of Taverner and Udall. But in all fairness, there is a good chance that John Rastell knew Erasmus' *Adagia*. After all, he was a printer, barrister, playwright, and a brother-in-law of Sir Thomas More to boot. Clearly he was part of the circle of scholarly humanists, and he might have read if not actually possessed the *Adagia*. In that case his allusion to the Latin "spade"-phrase might have been a unique and spontaneous translation from memory. This would make him the first to have used the proverbial expression in the English language, even though it is at best nothing more than a questionable hint at it. And it certainly had no influence in spreading the phrase in the wording of "to call a spade a spade" in the English language. That credit belongs without a doubt to Richard Taverner and Nicholas Udall some twenty years later.

With this said, we can launch into a review of a fascinating list of contextualized references from Anglo-American literature over a period of almost five hundred years:

Sixteenth Century

Hu.   Then let vs some lusty balet syng
Yng. Nay syr by thy heuyn kyng
      For me thynkyth it seruyth for no thyng
      All suche peuysh prykyeryd song
Hu.   Pes man pryksong may not be dispysyd
      For ther with god is well plesyd
      Honowryd praysyd and seruyd
      In the churche oft tymes among
Yng. Is god well pleasyd trowst thou therby
      Nay nay for there is no reason why
      For is it not as good to say playnly
      Gyf me a spade
      As gyf me a spa ve va ve va ve vade
      But yf thou wylt haue a song that is good
      I haue one of robynhode
      The best that euer was made
Hu.   Then a feleshyp let vs here it
  1519: John Rastell, *The Nature of the Four Elements* (London: T.C. & E.C. Jack, 1908; rpt. New York: AMS Press, 1970), p. E[viib].

Here is a modernized version of the reference, with HU. standing for "Humanity" and IGN. for "Ignorance":

HU.   Then let us some lusty ballad sing.
IGN. Nay, sir, but the Heaven King!
      For methinketh it serveth for nothing.
      All such peevish prick-eared song!
HU.   Peace, man, prick-song may not be despised,
      For therewith God is well pleased,
      Honoured, praised, and served,
      In the church ofttimes among.

IGN. Is God well pleased, trow'st thou, therby?
      Nay, nay, for there is no reason why,
      For is it not as good to say plainly,
      Give me a spade,
      As give me a spa, ve, va, ve, va, ve, vade?
      But if thou wilt have a song that is good,
      I have one of Robin Hood,
      The best that ever was made.
HU.   Then, a' fellowship, let us hear it.
   1519: John Rastell, *Interlude of the Four Elements*; cited from W. Carew Hazlitt (ed.), *A Select Collection of Old English Texts, Originally Published by Robert Dodsley in the Year 1744*, 4th ed., 15 vols. (London: Reeves and Turner, 1874), vol. 1, pp. 48–49.

That I haue called hir ane onstinate idolatrice, one that consented to the murther of her owin husband, and ane that hes committed whordome and villanous adulterie, I glaidlie grant, and never myndis to deny; but railing and seditione thai ar neuer able to prove in me, till that first thei compell Esaij, Jeremie, and Ezechiel, St. Paull, and vtheris, to recant; off whome I haue learned, plainelie and bauldlie, to call wickitnes to be the awin termes — a feg, a feg, and a spead, a spead.
   1570: John Knox; cited from Richard Bannatyne (Secretary to John Knox), *Memorials of Transactions in Scotland, A.D. MDLXIX – A.D. MDLXXIII* (Edinburgh: Bannantyne Club, 1836), p. 97. See also Bartlett Jere Whiting, "Proverbs and Proverbial Sayings from Scottish Writings before 1600," *Mediaeval Studies* 11 (1949), 123–205; 13 (1951), 87–164 (here p. 129).

   Song
A woman's face is full of wiles,
Her tears are like the crocadill:
With outward cheer on thee she smiles,
When in her heart she thinks thee ill.

Her tongue still chats of this and that,
Than aspen leaf it wags more fast;
And as she talks she knows not what,
There issues many a truthless blast.

Thou far dost take thy mark amiss
If thou think faith in them to find;

The weathercock more constant is,
Which turns about with every wind.

O, how in pity they abound!
Their heart is mild, like marble stone:
If in thyself no hope be found
Be sure of them thou gettest none.

I know some pepper-nosëd dame
Will term me fool, and saucy jack,
That dare their credit so defame
And lay such slanders on their back:

What though on me they pour their spite?
I may not use the glozer's trade,
I cannot say the crow is white,
But needs must call a spade a spade.
    1580: Humphrey Gifford; cited from Norman Ault (ed.), *Elizabethan Lyrics from the Original Texts* (New York: Capricorn Books, 1960), pp. 84-85.

The Puritans are angry with me; I mean the Puritan preachers. And why? Because I am too open; because I jest. I jested because I dealt against a worshipful jester, Dr. [John] Bridges, whose writings and sermons tend to no other end than to make men laugh. I did think that Martin [Marprelate] should not have been blamed of the Puritans for telling the truth openly. For, may I not say that John of Canterbury is a petty pope, seeing he is so? You must then bear with my ingramness [ignorance]. I am plain; I must needs call a spade a spade; a pope a pope. I speak not against him, as he is a Councillor; but as he is an Archbishop, and so Pope of Lambeth.
    1588: Martin Marprelate; cited from William Pierce (ed.), *The Marprelate Tracts 1588, 1589* (London: James Clarke, 1911), p. 118.

Seventeenth Century

At the end of which time, if any be behind [in paying money], I will draw a Catalogue of all their names I ventured with. Those that have shewn themselves honest men; I will set before them this character, *H.* for Honesty. Before the other bench-whistlers shall stand *K.* for Ketlers or Keistrels, that will drive a good companion, without need in them, to contend for his own. But I hope I shall have no such need! If I have, your honourable protection shall thus far defend your poor servant, that he may, being a plain man, call a spade a spade.

    1600: William Kemp, *Kemp's Nine Days' Wonder* (London: Nicholas Ling, 1600); cited from Edward Arber (ed.), *An English Garner: In Gatherings from Our History and Literature*, 7 vols. (London: Arber, 1877–1883), vol. 7, p. 34.

Virg. [...]
Now read the evidence: but first demand
Of either prisoner, if that writ be theirs.
Tib. Shew this unto Crispinus. Is it yours?
Tuc. Say, ay. [*Aside*] — What! dost thou stand upon it, pimp?
Do not deny thine own Minerva, thy Pallas, the issue of thy brain.
Cris. Yes it is mine.
Tib. Shew that unto Demetrius. Is it yours?
Dem. It is.
Tuc. There's a father will not deny his own bastard now, I warrant thee.
Virg. Read them aloud.
Tib. Ramp up my genius, be not retrograde;
But boldly nominate a spade a spade
What, shall thy lubrical and glibbery muse
Live, as she were defunct, like punk in stews!
Tuc. Excellent!

    1602: Ben Jonson, *The Poetaster: or, His Arraignment*; cited from Felix E. Schelling (ed.), *The Complete Plays of Ben Jonson*, 2 vols. (New York: J.M. Dutton, 1962), vol. 1, p. 292. See also Karl Pfeffer, *Das elisabethanische Sprichwort in seiner Verwendung bei Ben Jonson* (Gießen: Richard Glagow, 1933), p. 142 (no. 286).

Men. Now, the gods crown thee!
Cor. And live you yet? — [*To Valerie*] O my sweet
lady, pardon.
Vol. I know not where to turn: — O, welcome home; —
And welcome, general; and ye're welcome all.
Men. A hundred thousand welcomes: — I could weep,
And I could laugh; I'm light and heavy; — welcome:
A curse begin at very root on's [*sic*] heart
That is not glad to see thee! — You are three

That Rome should dote on: yet, by the faith of men,
We're some old crab-trees here at home that will not
Be grafted to your relish. Yet welcome, warriors:
We call a nettle but a nettle, and
The faults of fools but folly.
Com. Ever right.
Cor. Menenius ever, ever.

    1607: William Shakespeare, *Coriolanus* (Act II, scene 1). See also Robert W. Dent, *Shakespeare's Proverbial Language. An Index* (Berkeley, California: University of California Press, 1981), p. 215 (S699). This is the closest that Shakespeare comes to the "spade"-phrase.

[I poured out whatever came into my mind], out of a confused company of notes, and writ with as small deliberation as I do ordinarily speak, without all affectation of big words, fustian phrases, jingling terms, tropes, strong lines, that like Acestes' arrows caught fire as they flew, strains of wit, brave heats, elogies, hyperbolical exornations, elegancies, etc., which many so much affect. I am *aquae potor* [a water-drinker], drink no wine at all, which so much improves our modern wits, a loose, plain rude writer, *ficum voco ficum et ligonem ligonem* [I call a fig a fig and a spade a spade], and as free, as loose, *idem calamo quod in mente* [what my mind thinks my pen writes], I call a spade a spade, *animis haec scribo, non auribus* [I write for the mind, not the ear], I respect matter, not words; remembering that of Cardan, *verba propter res, non res propter verba* [words should minister to matter, not vice versa], and seeking with Seneca, *quid scribam, non quemadmodum*, rather what than how to write: for as Philo thinks, "He that is conversant about matter neglects words, and those that excel in this art of speaking have no profound learning."

    1628: Robert Burton, "Democritus to the Reader," in R. Burton, *The Anatomy of Melancholy*, ed. Holbrook Jackson (London: J.M. Dent, 1972), pp. 31-32.

    Taylors Motto.
Dedicated to Every Body.
Yet not to euery Reader doe I write,
But onely vnto such as can Read right:
And with vnpartiall censures can declare,
As they find things, to iudge them as they are.

For this age, of Criticks are such store,
That of a B. will make a Battledore,
Swallow downe Camells, and Gnats will straine,
Make Mountaines of small Molehills, and againe
Extenuate faults, or else faults amplifie,
According as their carping censures flye.
Such are within the Motto of I haue,
But though the gallant Gulls be ne'r so braue,
And in their owne esteeme are deemed wise,
I hauve a mind their follies to despise.
There are some few that wil their iudgement season
With mature vnderstanding, and with reason:
And call a spade a spade, a Sicophant,
A flatt'ring Knaue, and those are those *I want*.
For those that seeme to read, and scarce can spell,
Who neither point, nor keepe their periods well:
Who doe a mans inuention so be-martyr,
So hanging, drawing, and so cut and quarter,
Making good lines contemptible threed-bare,
To keepe my booke from such as those *I care*.
    Adue.
        John Taylor.
    1630: John Taylor, *Taylors Motto*; cited from *Works of John Taylor the Water-Poet*, comprised in the Folio Edition of 1630 (Manchester: C. Simms, 1869), p. 43 (reprint p. 203). The "Motto" follows the play *A Kicksy Winsey*, but is not part of it as some lexicographers have claimed (see chapters 3 and 4).

Small eloquence men must expect from me,
My Schollership will name things as they be.
I thinke it good, plaine English, without fraud
To call a Spade a Spade, a Bawd a *Bawd*.
Two little Pamphlets I haue wrote before,
Which I was bold to call a *Thiefe*, and *Whore*,
Yet was my *Whore* so chaste, that shee had not,
From end to end, one foule offensiue spot,
Nor did my *Thiefe*, from any man purloyne,
Or liu'd by filching either goods or coyne.
    1630: John Taylor, *A Bawd*; cited from *Works of John Taylor the Water-Poet*, comprised in the Folio Edition of 1630 (Manchester: C.

Simms, 1869), p. 92 (reprint p. 252). This reference is from the play *A Bawd* and not *A Kicksy Winsey*, as several lexicographers have claimed (see chapters 3 and 4).

Dam. What is your name, sir, or your country?
Boy. John Try-gust my name; a Cornish youth, and the poet's servant.
Dam. West country breed I thought, you were so bold.
Boy. Or rather saucy; to find out your palate, master Damplay. Faith we do call a spade a spade, in Cornwall. If you dare damn our play in the wrong place, we shall take heart to tell you so!
Pro. Good boy.

1631: Ben Jonson, *The Magnetic Lady*; cited from Felix E. Schelling (ed.), *The Complete Plays of Ben Jonson*, 2 vols. (New York: J.M. Dutton, 1962), vol. 2, p. 520. See also Karl Pfeffer, *Das elisabethanische Sprichwort in seiner Verwendung bei Ben Jonson* (Gießen: Richard Glagow, 1933), p. 142 (no. 286).

Coun. Gent. These Gentlemen are as mad are [*sic*] March-Hares, Madam, as the saying is; but to our business, I had not the power as I was saying, to keep from you longer, Lady, not so much as a pissing while, d'y see! for Cat will to kind as the saying is.
Luce. Oh Sir, you complement, you are an absolute Countrey Courtier.
Coun. Gent. Who I? alas not I, in sober sadness, we that live in the Countrey are right down d'ye see, we call a Spade a Spade, as the saying is, for our part.
Luce. You doe well Sir, for hypocrisie is an abominable vice.
Coun. Gent. 'Tis indeed to be a Pharisy and carry two faces in a Hood, as the saying is.
Emil. Now I wish my t'other two Fools would come back and drive away this.
Luce. I perceive you are very good at Proverbs, Sir, don't you use to play at that sport with the Countrey Gentlewomen?
Count. Gent. O yes, I am an old dog at that, I am too hard for 'em all at it, d'ye see.

1668: Thomas Shadwell, *The Sullen Lovers: or, The Impertinents. A Comedy*; cited from Montague Summers (ed.), *The Complete Works of Thomas Shadwell*, 5 vols. (London: The Fortune Press, 1927), vol. 1, pp. 68-69.

It is in this case an excellent rule, *de vivis nil nisi verum, de mortuis nil nisi bonum*; and I wish we could exactly follow it in both parts: the former is in our power, and we shall keep close to it and speak nothing but the truth, and such truth as shall in great part carry its evidence along with it: the latter is not so in our power, because we cannot keep men alive, and their dying doth not alter the nature of their actions, whereof we are necessitated to speak; and if we speak the truth we must in this case speak plain. We do not reveal secrets, but plain matters of fact, things done openly before the sun and of publick concernment; and, therefore, let none be offended if, where the matter requires it, we use their own dialect. We must call a spade a spade, and rebellion by the name of rebellion, tho' some masters of rebellion may call us Tobiahs and Sanballats for so doing. It were better to hate and avoid the thing than to storm at the name.

1692: Gershom Bulkeley, *Will and Doom, or The Miseries of Connecticut by and under an Usurped and Arbitrary Power*; cited with an introduction by Charles J. Hoadly from *Collections of the Connecticut Historical Society* (Hartford, Connecticut: Connecticut Historical Society, 1895), vol. 3, pp. 89–90 (preface).

Eighteenth Century

By ancient Grannums we are told,
In Proverb true, as well as old,
That Birds, who are of the same Feather,
Delight to meet, and flock together:
So that the neighbouring Owls will follow
The Howlet, that they hear, but hollow;
Nay, if a Wolf but makes a Noise,
And elevates his howling Voice,
The rest will from their Dens come out;
And gather round the bawling Brute;
As Zealots, join with one another,
To hear the Howls of Holy Brother.
Hush, says my Friend, mind what you say;
You know this is not Time of Day
For Truth to be so obvious made,
We must not call a Spade, a Spade.

1708: Edward Ward, *Hudibras Redivivus: or, A Burlesque Poem on the Times*, 2 vols. (London: Booksellers of London, 1708), vol. 1, p. 11 (part 7, canto 10).

Lady Sm. Well, but do you hear, that Mrs. *Plump* is brought to Bed at last?
Miss. And pray, what has God sent her?
Lady Sm. Why, guess if you can.
Miss. A Boy, I suppose.
Lady Sm. No, you are out, guess again.
Miss. A Girl then.
Lady Sm. You have hit it; I believe you are a Witch.
Miss. O, Madam, the Gentlemen say, all fine Ladies are Witches; but I pretend to no such Thing.
Lady Ans. Well, she had good Luck to draw *Tom Plump* into Wedlock; she rises with her — [arse] upwards.
Miss. Fye, Madam, what do you mean?
Lady Sm. O, Miss, 'tis nothing what we say among ourselves.
Miss. Ay, Madam, but they say, Hedges have Eyes, and Walls have Ears.
Lady Ans. Well, Miss, I can't help it; you know I am an old Tell-truth, I love to call a Spade, a Spade.

1738: Jonathan Swift, *A Complete Collection of Genteel and Ingenious Conversation* (London: B. Motte, 1738); cited from Eric Partridge (ed.), *Swift's Polite Conversation* (London: Andre Deutsch, 1963), pp. 166-167 (Third Conversation).

But you [merchants from New York] must not expect any undue complaisance from *me*. — You must be content with plain English, from a plain countryman; I must have the privilege of calling a fig, — a Fig; an egg, — an Egg. If, upon examination, your conduct shall, in any instances, appear to be weak, you must bear to be told of it: — if wrong, to be censured: — if selfish, to be exposed: — if ridiculous, to be laughed at: — Do not be offended if I omit to say, that if your conduct shall appear honourable, that it shall be commended. Honourable and virtuous actions want no commendation, — they speak for themselves.

1774: Samuel Seabury, "The Congress Canvassed: or, An Examination into the Conduct of the Delegates, at Their Grand Convention, Held in Philadelphia, Sept. 1, 1774;" cited from S. Seabury, *Letters of a Westchester Farmer (1774-1775)*, ed. Clarence H. Vance

(White Plains, New York: Westchester County Historical Society, 1930; rpt. New York: Da Capo Press, 1970), pp. 71-72.

I wrote the Governor a letter concerning the conduct of some members, when the business referred to was first moved in Congress; and, with my usual want of prudent dissimulation, I expressed an honest indignation, by calling Spade a *spade*. The letter, it seems, has been read in Convention; and a correspondent, up the country, writes me that he fears it has hurt me greatly.
    1788: Hugh Williamson; cited from Griffith J. McRee (ed.), *Life and Correspondence of James Iredell, One of the Associate Justices of the Supreme Court of the United States*, 2 vols. (New York: Peter Smith, 1949), vol. 2, p. 237.

The world too, like St. Paul and his fellow christians, is "in jeopardy every hour," by the misapplication and abuse of words. There is a tribe, in every populous city, of *gentel* young men, called Bucks, whose ideas are so few in number, that they do not venture into service, without certain auxiliaries, called *cant phrases*, to support them. Now as we may aptly enough suppose, that all people of "household understanding" who, according to a vulgar proverb, call a spade a spade, are *foes* to the coxcombs, just mentioned; therefore these uncouth terms, like the grim looks of a Cossac, or the whiskers of a Hessian, are useful to annoy the enemy.
    1795: Anonymous, "The Farrago. No. XII," *The Tablet* (August 4, 1795), p. 45.

Nineteenth Century

There was no press at these places [ancient Athens and Rome], or in these times. The invention of printing is of a later date. But they had in lieu of pen and ink, what they called the style, hence the phrase style, vertere stylum, and they impressed their thoughts upon wax. They made use of ink in copying upon vellum and parchment. But notwithstanding the want of a press, they were not without satyric salt in their writings. Nor are we to suppose that they were altogether free from what we denominate scurrility. They could call a spade a spade. Aristophanes was a great blackguard. His Comedy of the Clouds is a sufficient specimen. Lucilius, amongst the Romans was a rough man. Cum lutulentus flueret, etc. Do we suppose that nature was not then the same as it is now?

1804: Hugh Henry Brackenridge, *Modern Chivalry*, ed. Claude M. Newlin (New York: American Book Company, 1937), p. 341 (part 2, chapter 2).

Dick [Paddle] is known to the world as being a most knowing genius, who can see as far as anybody — into a millstone, maintains, in the teeth of all argument, that a spade is a spade, and will labor a good half-hour by St. Paul's clock to establish a self-evident fact.

1807: William Irving, James Kirke Paulding, and Washington Irving, *Salmagundi*, 2 vols. (New York: G.P. Putnam's Sons, 1897), vol. 1, p. 37 (chapter 2).

Then there is no attempt at that misty pomp of language which you appear to think laudable. I believe there is not one inversion in the whole thing (at least, I repeat again, not one *intentional* inversion), and everything goes by its proper name; a spade is a spade; and a bayonet a bayonet, and if on one or two occasions the French are the Gauls, I am ashamed of it. I will now, since I am on the subject, tell you a fact — that 'Talavera' was written in consequence of a conversation at a literary table, at which I insisted that poetry ought not to be fiction, and that so powerful was the charm of simplicity and nature, that if two poems were to be written on the subject of the then recent triumph of Talavera, and that one was to deal in Mars and Bellona, helmets and shields, knights and heroes, and that the other (ceteris paribus) should call everything by its proper name, talk of Wellington and Bellona, bayonet and cap, cavalry and infantry, the latter would be the most popular.

1816: John Wilson Croker; cited from Louis J. Jennings, *The Correspondence and Diaries of the Late Honourable John Wilson Croker*, 3 vols. (London: John Murray, 1884), vol. 1, p. 98.

Wyeth would fain have slipped by this cavalcade unnoticed; but the river, at this place, was not more than ninety yards across; he was perceived, therefore, and hailed by the vagabond warriors, and we presume, in no very choice language; for, among their other accomplishments, the Crows are famed for possessing a Billingsgate vocabulary of unrivalled opulence, and for being by no means sparing of it whenever an occasion offers. Indeed, though Indians are generally very lofty, rhetorical, and figurative in their language at all great talks and high ceremonials, yet, if trappers and traders may be believed, they are the most unsavory vagabonds in their ordinary colloquies. They make no hesitation to call a spade a spade; and when they once undertake to call hard names, the famous pot and kettle, of vituperating memory, are not to be compared with them for scurrility of epithet.

    1837: Washington Irving, *Captain Bonneville*, 2 vols. (New York: G.P. Putnam's Sons, 1895), vol. 2, pp. 126–127 (chapter 12).

The county of Delaware has, of itself, nobly given the lie to the assertion, the honest portion of its inhabitants scattering the knaves to the four winds, the moment there was a fair occasion made for them to act. A single, energetic proclamation from Albany, calling a "spade a spade," and not affecting to gloss over the disguised robbery of these anti-renters, and laying just principles fairly before the public mind, would itself have crushed the evil in its germ. The people of New York, in their general capacity, are not the knaves their servants evidently suppose.

    1845: James Fenimore Cooper, *The Redskins; or, Indian and Injin: Being the Conclusion of the Littlepage Manuscripts*, 2 vols. (New York: Stringer and Townsend, 1852), vol. 1, p. x (preface).

"Yes, curse him [a person just deceased named Green]!" was the answer. "If they have a particularly hot corner 'away down below'[i.e., hell], I hope he's made its acquaintance before this."
"Most likely he's smelled brimstone," chuckled the judge.
"Smelled it! If old Clubfoot [i.e., the devil] hasn't treated him with a brimstone-bath long before this, he hasn't done his duty. If I thought as much, I'd vote for sending his majesty a remonstrance forthwith."
"Ha! ha!" laughed the judge. "You're warm on the subject."
"Ain't I? The blackleg scoundrel! Hell's too good for him."
"H-u-s-h! Don't let your indignation run into profanity," said Judge Lyman, trying to assume a serious air; but the muscles of his face but feebly obeyed his will's feeble effort.
"Profanity! Poh! I don't call that profanity. It's only speaking out in meeting, as they say, — it's only calling black, black — and white, white. You believe in a hell, don't you, judge?"

    1854: Timothy Shay Arthur, *Ten Nights in a Bar-Room, and What I Saw There*, ed. Donald A. Koch (Cambridge, Massachusetts: Harvard University Press, 1964), p. 187 (temperance movement).

"Very well," said Bounderby, "I was born in a ditch, and my mother ran away from me. Do I excuse her for it? No. Have I ever excused her for it? Not I. What do I call her for it? I call her probably the very worst woman that ever lived in the world, except my drunken grandmother.

There's no family pride about me, there's no imaginative sentimental humbug about me. I call a spade a spade; and I call the mother of Josiah Bounderby of Coketown, without any fear or any favour, what I should call her if she had been the mother of Dick Jones of Wapping. So, with this man. He is a runaway rogue and a vagabond, that's what he is, in English."

1854: Charles Dickens, *Hard Times for These Times* (Oxford: Oxford University Press, 1955), p. 32 (chapter 6). See also George B. Bryan and Wolfgang Mieder, *The Proverbial Charles Dickens. An Index to Proverbs in the Works of Charles Dickens* (New York: Peter Lang, 1997), p. 264.

In truth, there is not room for a machinery so complicated [a House of Assembly] in this island [Jamaica]. The handful of white men can no longer have it all their own way; and as for the negroes — let any warmest advocate of the "man and brother" position say whether he has come across three or four of the class who are fit to enact laws for their own guidance and the guidance of others. It pains me to write words which may seem to be opposed to humanity and a wide philanthropy; but a spade is a spade, and it is worse than useless to say it is something else.

1859: Anthony Trollope, *The West Indies and the Spanish Main* (London: Frank Cass, 1968), p. 123 (chapter 9).

Mr. Cheesacre was rather at a loss to know how he should begin. [...] He had so often told the widow [Mrs. Greenow] that care killed a cat, and that a live dog was better than a dead lion; and found so little efficacy in the proverbs, that he did not care to revert to them. He was aware that some more decided method of proceeding was now required. Little hints at love-making had been all very well in the earlier days of their acquaintance; but there must be something more than little hints before he could hope to bring the matter to a favourable conclusion. The widow herself had told him that he ought to talk about love; and he had taken two glasses of cherry-brandy, hoping that they might enable him to do so. He had put on a coat with brilliant buttons, and new knickerbockers, in order that he might be master of the occasion. He was resolved to call a spade a spade, and to speak boldly of his passion; but how was he to begin? There was the difficulty. He was now seated in a chair, and there he remained silent for a minute or two, while she smoothed her eyebrows with her handkerchief after her last slight ebullition of grief.

1864: Anthony Trollope, *Can You Forgive Her?* (New York: Berkeley Publishing Corporation, 1977), p. 446 (chapter 47).

"Rough dealing, awkward language," whine our fops:
The world's too squeamish now to bear plain words
Concerning deeds it acts with gust enough:
But, thanks to wine-lees and democracy,
We've still our stage where truth calls spade a spade!

1875: Robert Browning, "Aristophanes' Apology," in F.G. Kenyon (ed.), *The Works of Robert Browning*, 10 vols. (New York: Barnes & Noble, 1912), vol. 8, p. 15 (lines 406-410). See also Cornelia Marschall Smith, *Browning's Proverb Lore* (Waco, Texas: Baylor University, 1989), p. 91 (no. 403).

"I like her [Miss Wilton] very much," he [Milford] added.
"Oh, yes, I do too, but she's silly to be thinking of practicing law," said Lawson.
"Silly is a brutal word in such a connection; a word not usually applied to a lady by a gentleman," retorted Milford.
"Oh, bosh!" exclaimed Lawson, with a short laugh. "I have nothing in common with your finical sticklers for sugar-coated circumlocution; a spade is a spade."
"And a gentleman is always a gentleman," said Milford. "There is no room for mistake."

1886: [James] Maurice Thompson, *A Banker of Bankersville. A Novel* (New York: Cassell, 1886), pp. 104-105 (chapter 6). See also Jan Harold Brunvand, *A Dictionary of Proverbs and Proverbial Phrases from Books Published by Indiana Authors Before 1890* (Bloomington, Indiana: Indiana University Press, 1961), p. 131.

"Yesterday I cut an orchid, for my buttonhole. It was a marvellous spotted thing, as effective as the seven deadly sins. In a thoughtless moment I asked one of the gardeners what it was called. He told me it was a fine specimen of *Robinsoniana*, or something dreadful of that kind. It is a sad truth, but we have lost the faculty of giving lovely names to things. My own quarrel is with words. That is the reason I hate vulgar realism in literature. The man who could call a spade a spade should be compelled to use one. It is the only thing he is fit for."

1890: Oscar Wilde, *The Picture of Dorian Gray*; cited from Coulson Kernahan (ed.), *The Complete Works of Oscar Wilde*, 10 vols. (New York: William H. Wise, 1927), vol. 4, pp. 352–353.

Note that in poetic diction you must by no means "call a spade a spade." The statement of a plain fact is highly objectionable, and a roundabout expression has to be resorted to. For example, if a girl have red hair, describe it as "Glowing with the glory of the golden God of Day," or, if Nature has blest her with a "pug-nose," you should, like Tennyson, describe it as "Tip-tilted like the petal of a flower."

1894: Francis A. Fahy, "How to Become a Poet," in D.J. O'Donoghue (ed.), *The Humour of Ireland* (London: Walter Scott, 1894), pp. 358–367 (here p. 361).

CECILY. It would distress me more than I can tell you, dear Gwendolen, if it caused you any mental or physical anguish, but I feel bound to point out that since Ernest proposed to you he clearly has changed his mind.
GWENDOLEN (*meditatively*). If the poor fellow has been entrapped into any foolish promise I shall consider it my duty to rescue him at once, and with a firm hand.
CECILY. (*thoughtfully and sadly*). Whatever unfortunate entanglement my dear boy may have got into, I will never reproach him with it after we are married.
GWENDOLEN. Do you allude to me, Miss Cardew, as an entanglement? You are presumptuous. On an occasion of this kind it becomes more than a moral duty to speak one's mind. It becomes a pleasure.
CECILY. Do you suggest, Miss Fairfax, that I entrapped Ernest into an engagement? How dare you? This is no time for wearing the shallow mask of manner. When I see a spade I call it a spade.
GWENDOLEN. (*satirically*). I am glad to say that I have never seen a spade. It is obvious that our social spheres have been widely different.

1895: Oscar Wilde, *The Importance of Being Earnest. A Trivial Play for Serious People* (London: Methuen, 1985), p. 48 (Act 2).

The World Runs Round
[...]
One voice is heard
By the ocean's shore,
Speaking a word
Quiet and sane,
Amid the human rush and roar

Like a robin's song in the rain.
The red gold of the sun
Seems to stream in power
Already from behind the shower
When that song's begun.

It doth not insist, or claim;
You may hear, or go:
It clamors not for gain or fame,
Tranquilly and slow
It speaketh unafraid,
Calls the spade, spade,
With the large sense mature
Of him that hath both sat, and roved,
And with a solemn undercurrent pure,
As his that now hath lived and loved.

Brightened with glimpse and gleam
Of mother-wit —
There is more salt in it,
More germ and sperm
Of the great things to be,
Than louder notes men speak and sing.
[...]

>1899: Edward Rowland Sill, *Herminone and Other Poems* (Boston: Houghton, Mifflin and Company, 1899), pp. 16-17.

Twentieth Century

"Oh, defend me!" groaned the marquis. Once more he wiped his brow, as he crouched behind the white-lilac bush. "Why, the woman is a second Messalina!" he said. "Oh, the trollop! the wanton! Oh, holy Gregory! Yet I must be quiet — quiet as a sucking lamb, that I may strike afterward as a roaring lion. Is this your innocence, Mistress Ursula, that cannot endure the spoken name of a spade? Oh, splendor of God!" Thus he raged behind the white-lilac bush [...].

>1905: James Branch Cabell, *The Line of Love* (Freeport, New York: Books for Libraries Press, 1969), p. 216.

"The time has come when we must speak of a certain matter frankly," or, "At last the time has arrived when demoralization of the bar caused by a certain criminal lawyer must be dealt with as it is and without gloves." Once when Joe had saved a half-witted negro from "the extreme penalty" for murder, the Toscin had declared, with great originality: "This is just the kind of thing that causes mobs and justifies them. If we are to continue to permit the worst class of malefactors to escape the consequences of their crimes through the unwholesome dexterities and the shifty manipulations and technicalities of a certain lawyer, the time will come when an outraged citizenry may take the enforcement of the law in its own hands. Let us call a spade a spade. If Canaan's streets ever echo with the tread of a mob, the fault lies upon the head of Joseph Louden, who once more brought about a miscarriage of justice."

    1905: Booth Tarkington, *The Conquest of Canaan* (New York: Harper & Brothers, 1905), p. 138 (chapter 9).

Sorry I am that he [Mr. Chamberlain] is out of the battle, not only on personal but public grounds. His fiercest opponents would welcome his re-entry into the political arena, if only for the fact that we should then have a man to deal with and someone whose statement of the case for his side would be clear and bold, whose speeches would be worth reading and worth answering, instead of the melancholy marionettes whom the wire-pullers of the Tariff Reform League are accustomed to exhibit on provincial platforms. But I hope you will not let these pretexts or complaints move you or prevent you from calling a spade a spade, a tax a tax, a protective tariff a gigantic dodge to cheat the poor, or the Liberal Unionist party the most illiberal thing on record.

    1909: Winston S. Churchill; cited from Robert Rhodes James (ed.), *Winston S. Churchill. His Complete Speeches 1897-1963*, 8 vols. (London: Chelsea House, 1974), vol. 2, p. 1154 ("The Next Election," January 29, 1909). See also Wolfgang Mieder and George B. Bryan, *The Proverbial Winston S. Churchill. An Index to Proverbs in the Works of Sir Winston Churchill* (Westport, Connecticut: Greenwood Press, 1995), p. 372.

"Cornelia, will you ever forget the one when old Luther Burns got up and made a speech? He stated his opinions forcibly."
"Call a spade a spade, Captain. You mean he got red-mad and raked them all, fore and aft. They deserved it too — a pack of incapables. But what would you expect of a committee of men? That building committee held twenty-seven meetings, and at the end of the twenty-seventh meeting weren't no nearer having a church than when they begun."

1915: Lucy Maud Montgomery, *Anne's House of Dreams*; cited from *Anne of Green Gables. Three Volumes in One* (New York: Avenel Books, 1986), p. 524 (chapter 15).

He had always been responsive to what they had begun to call 'Nature,' genuinely, almost religiously responsive, though he had never lost his habit of calling a sunset a sunset and a view a view, however deeply they might move him. But nowadays Nature actually made him ache, he appreciated it so.

1922: John Galsworthy, *The Forsyte Saga*, 3 vols. (New York: Charles Scribner's Sons, 1931), vol. 1, p. 298 ("Indian Summer of a Forsyte").

When a man has earned a sobriquet so fearsome as that of 'Hellgate,' one may not unreasonably expect to find in the details of his career so much that is distinctly not *virginibus puerisque* that a record of his sayings and doings might well seem to be unfitted for general consumption, even in these days when we have become accustomed when talking of spades to use no circumlocution or periphrasis whatever. But, truth to tell, although there is no denying that the seventh Earl of Barrymore was a rake, one can never quite imagine him as being altogether so bad as his cognomen paints him.

1926: E. Beresford Chancellor, *"Old Q" and Barrymore* (New York: Brentano's, 1926), p. 139 ("The Earl of Barrymore," chapter 1).

"All wrong!" repeated Mr. Beamish.
And when Hamilton Beamish said 'All wrong!' it meant 'All wrong!' He was a man who thought clearly and judged boldly, without hedging or vacillation. He called a Ford a Ford.

1927: P.G. Wodehouse, *The Small Bachelor* (Middlesex, England: Penguin Books, 1987), p. 8.

The number of girls regularly on duty — each had one day off a week, which she usually spent at the theater or drinking in the cafés with her "fancy man" — varied from fifteen to twenty, and every one of them was a lady to her fingertips. Evening dress was the invariable rule, and bawdy talk and behavior were sternly prohibited; a spade was never a spade in Kate Townsend's bagnio. When a gentleman arrived he was met at the door by a uniformed Negro maid. If he was one of the steady clients, many of whom had charge accounts, he was ushered ceremoniously into the drawing-room, where he was expected to buy wine — at from ten to fifteen dollars a bottle — for the assembled company.

> 1936: Herbert Asbury, *The French Quarter. An Informal History of the New Orleans Underworld* (Garden City, New York: Garden City Publishing Co., 1936), p. 371.

"Yes. But what did he have a gun along with him for? Decoration, or use, or what?"
"Didn't Arthur tell you? Arthur tried to restrain him, and Slade was very rude, and told him to go away and lay on — oh, he was just as rude as you'd expect someone like him to be. He said — why, the things he said!"
"Yes, I know. Outspoken sort. An old spade caller. But what expl'nation did he give your husband?"
"Why, it really wasn't an explanation, at all, really. The man was either drunk, or crazy. He said he had a shotgun with him, and he intended to carry it with him as long as he felt like it, and certainly until he got the chance to shoot back at whoever had been shooting at *him* with a shotgun."

> 1937: Phoebe Atwood Taylor, *Figure Away* (Woodstock, Vermont: Foul Play Press, 1991), p. 65 (chapter 4).

gardening. People who write on gardening aren't the only ones who call a spade a spade.
hand. A diamond on the finger is worth more than a spade in the hand.

> 1943: Evan Esar, *Esar's Comic Dictionary* (New York: Harvest House, 1943), p. 116 and p. 128.

If I had signed the bill the people would have seen their prices going up, day by day. You would have realized soon that the bill which had been passed and called a price control law was not price control at all. What I have done is to call a spade a spade. I must now rely on the American people and upon a patriotic and cooperative Congress to protect us all from the great pressures now upon us, leading us to disastrous inflation unless we have the means to resist them.

> 1946: Harry S. Truman; cited from *Public Papers of the Presidents of the United States. Harry S. Truman. Containing the Public Messages, Speeches, and Statements of the President. January 1 to December 31, 1946* (Washington, D.C.: United States Government Printing Office, 1962), p. 331 ("Radio Address to the Nation on

Price Control," June 29, 1946). See also Wolfgang Mieder and George B. Bryan, *The Proverbial Harry S. Truman. An Index to Proverbs in the Works of Harry S. Truman* (New York: Peter Lang, 1997), p. 212.

When we talk about war, we use a language which conceals or embellishes its reality. Ignoring the facts, so far as we possibly can, we imply that battles are not fought by soldiers, but by things, principles, allegories, personified collectivities, or (at the most human) by opposing commanders, pitched against one another in single combat. For the same reason, when we have to describe the processes and the results of war, we employ a rich variety of euphemisms. Even the most violently patriotic and militaristic are reluctant to call a spade by its own name. To conceal their intentions even from themselves, they make use of picturesque metaphors. We find them, for example, clamouring for war planes numerous and powerful enough to go and 'destroy the hornets in their nests' — in other words, to go and throw thermite, high explosives and vesicants upon the inhabitants of neighbouring countries before they have time to come and do the same to us.

    1947: Aldous Huxley, "Words and Behaviour," in A. Huxley, *The Olive Tree and Other Essays* (London: Chatto & Windus, 1947), pp. 82-100 (here p. 87).

PERPETUA. Tell me why you've been cheating the Duke,
There's a good boy. What made you do it?
REEDBECK. I hope
I've done nothing so monosyllabic as to cheat.
A spade is never so merely a spade as the word
Spade would imply.
DOMINIC. One's helpless to help him.
PERPETUA. Poppadillo, suppose I put it this way:
What made you supercherify with chousery
The Duke?
REEDBECK. That might be said to — that perhaps
Is not an unfair expression. And I say in reply
The reason was the fading charm of the world.
The banquet of civilization is over —
PERPETUA. Shall we call it
The groaning board?
REEDBECK. You may call it what you will.

> 1950: Christopher Fry, *Venus Observed. A Play* (New York: Oxford University Press, 1950), p. 36 (Act 2, scene 1).

I'm leaving for Tennessee shortly to speak at the dedication of an air research center, named for Gen. Arnold. I'm going to tear the Russians and the Republicans apart — call a spade just what it is and tell Malik if Russia wants peace, peace is available and has been since 1945.

> 1951: Harry S. Truman; cited from Robert H. Ferrell (ed.), *Off the Record. The Private Papers of Harry S. Truman* (New York: Harper & Row, 1980), p. 214 (letter to Bess Truman of June 25, 1951). See also Wolfgang Mieder and George B. Bryan, *The Proverbial Harry S. Truman. An Index to Proverbs in the Works of Harry S. Truman* (New York: Peter Lang, 1997), p. 212.

"Yes. Yes," he repeated more briskly. "Well, we haven't heard everything Mallow can tell us, we've known that for some time. And whatever the reason —."
"Puzzling thing, that Ginn killed his woman," said Hardy, who sometimes revealed a Puritanical reluctance to call a spade a spade. "If Ginn knew she'd name him, and he thought Mallow had come to the police and also named him, he'd feel pretty vicious."
Roger said: "Yes, he would," very slowly.

> 1955: John Creasey, *Murder: One, Two, Three* (Roslyn, New York: Detective Book Club, 1960), p. 113 (chapter 15).

"According to the Riggses, and I have every reason to believe them, those heathen had no idea of what you might call the conventions, at all, sir. If they had any form of marriage, the Riggses never came across it. But as for what I shall call, respectfully, the joys of matrimony, the Riggses hardly came across anything else. It got so that Mrs. Riggs could scarcely go for a walk of an evening for fear of seeing something going on in the bushes that no respectable lady would wish to come upon. Loving couples, sir, to call a spade a spade, littered the island, the heathen having no morality worth speaking about, except an old man, who was a sort of king, and who settled any quarrels, and kept the children in order with a stick. Nobody else did."

> 1956: Aubrey Menen, *The Abode of Love. The Conception, Financing and Daily Routine of an English Harem in the Middle of the 19th Century Described in the Form of a Novel* (New York: Charles Scribner's Sons, 1956), pp. 143-144.

Vardanas sat down. I was vexed with him for putting me in the wrong with Eumenes. I hid my annoyance with an effort, as I am a plain blunt man who calls a fig a fig and a spade a spade. But the wise man does not defy necessity. I had thought so much about the project that I had counted my chickens before they were hatched. I saw my name in the history books as the hero who first brought an elephant to Europe.

 1958: L. Sprague de Camp, *An Elephant for Aristotle* (Garden City, New York: Doubleday, 1958), p. 38.

Whilst working for George I had the idea of writing some pastoral poems; *not* in dialect and *not* folksy: to do with country things, using country names and ideas certainly but I hoped the ultimate would be sophisticated twentieth-century poems. Calling a spade a spade and a nightingale a nightingale, yet with a rhetoric as highly imaged as the substance would stand. I felt I had the material at my fingertips — sometimes more than metaphorically speaking — and the whole idea excited me a lot.

 1960: Noel Woodin, *Room at the Bottom. A Novel* (London: Chatto & Windus, 1960), p. 128 (chapter 10).

Now, hoping to be hearty and persuasive, he said tinny things to me, things like, "I like the cut of your jib!" and "I want to talk cold turkey to you, man to man!"
And he took me down to what he called his "den" in order that we might, "... call a spade a spade, and let the chips fall where they may." So we went down steps cut into a cliff and into a natural cave that was beneath and behind the waterfall.

 1963: Kurt Vonnegut, *Cat's Cradle* (New York: Dell Publishing, 1971), p. 132 (chapter 87).

Spades Ain't Spades
You must not call a spade a spade;
It isn't nice to any more.
It now is termed a workman's aid,
For spade's a word kicked out the door.
And other words are on the run,
For instance, janitors no more.
It now is a custodian
Who vacuums or mops up the floor.
Assistant used to be the word,
But now if you'd be up-to-date,

And not thought of as quite absurd,
You use the word associate.
It used to be in olden days
We simply said we had a cold,
But now a virus is the craze;
It sounds more dignified, we're told.
It used to be when we got old
We were referred to as old men,
But times have changed — lo and behold,
I'm now a senior citizen!
I guess I've ranted on enough,
And maybe I my point have made —
To be considered up to snuff
You just don't call a spade a spade.
    1965: Tenney Call, *Rustic Rhymes by Old Scribe*, ed. Miriam Herwig (Randolph Center, Vermont: A Greenhills Book, 1979), no pp. given. Also in Wolfgang Mieder, *American Proverbs: A Study of Texts and Contexts* (Bern: Peter Lang, 1989), p. 191.

He laid a heavy hand on my shoulder. "She knows what she's talking about, Varvara does, and about this love business, where she comes from — they call a spade a spade — not like us. So just you remember what she's told you." He gave my shoulder a squeeze.
    1965: John Boynton Priestley, *Lost Empires, Being Richard Herncastle's Account of His Life on the Variety Stage from November 1913 to August 1914* (Boston: Little, Brown and Company, 1965), p. 156 (Book 2, chapter 3).

A second reason for the concealment of important facts about Robinson has been that many of his friends, including the members both of the New York executive group and the family group, wore the velvet of Victorian genteelness which required that no spade should be known as a spade, but should be disguised by some epithet assigned to it by current respectability. Up to date this blushing and pompous hypocrisy has successfully hidden the essentials of Robinson's personal life.
    1965: Chard Powers Smith, *Where the Light Falls. A Portrait of Edwin Arlington Robinson* (New York: Macmillan, 1965), p. 371 ("Comment on Sources").

Though I now grumble and criticise my lack of formal education, my upbringing did equip me better than some to deal with certain problems.

I developed a very nimble mind, unhampered by old railway lines of thought and procedure. I jumped conventional fences either because I did not see them, or despised the obstacle, and reached my objective that much quicker. Though I have since discovered that in doing so I trod on toes and bruised feelings. [...] At formal dinner parties my direct speech is a social danger; if the subject of conversation interests me, I will get it round my tongue and turn it inside out, only to find that some people are afraid of a spade being called a spade, or don't want to know there is such a thing as a spade.

>1966: Nicolette Devas, *Two Flamboyant Fathers* (London: Hamish Hamilton, 1985), pp. 80-81 ("The Studio Light").

The twenty-six-year-old actress took over complete management of her project [of a field hospital]. She also performed the duties of head nurse. [...] Her two steady workers were *mon p'tit dame* and an older Odéon actress named Madame Lambquin, a loud-mouthed, somewhat coarse person, fond of calling a spade a dirty spade but blessed with a heart of gold. There was one volunteer gentleman assistant who served as orderly, porter and general factotum and a military inspector who came daily to receive reports and, with the help of two stretcher bearers, perform the grim task of moving out the dead.

>1966: Cornelia Otis Skinner, *Madame Sarah* (Boston: Houghton Mifflin Company, 1966), p. 74 ("Sarah's Field Hospital").

Spade
The man who could call a spade a spade should be compelled to use one: it is the only thing he is fit for. — *Oscar Wilde*
Sometimes you have to call a spade a spade to get it back from your neighbor.
There's no one more exasperating than a bridge partner who calls a spade two spades.
Many a man who is candid enough to call a spade a spade is not courageous enough to call a liar a liar.
Many a man calls a spade a spade until he accidently trips over one.
The man who boasts he calls a spade a spade is usually giving someone a dirty dig.

>1968: Evan Esar, *20,000 Quips & Quotes* (New York: Barnes & Noble, 1995), pp. 754-755.

"If Angel wasn't abducted by one of these sex maniacs," Maggie went on (Crook liked her Saxon proclivity for calling a spade a spade), "what

is the motive? It's not as though Mumma's got any money, so they couldn't expect a ransom. She's lucky if she has something left on a Sunday morning to put in the dish at Mass."
    1969: Anthony Gilbert, *Missing from Her Home* (New York: Random House, 1969), p. 51.

He realized that he had had quite enough to drink, and his glass was still half full, but he'd ponder the letter anyway and maybe a flash of intuition would enable him to understand it better, to know what had really happened. Why was Ina so coy and devious, if she and John had slept together? She wasn't the kind of girl to call a spade a — what? Anyway, she called a lay a roll in the hay, or just called it going to bed with someone. She'd been quite frank with him about a couple of her affairs since her marriage.
    1969: Patricia Highsmith, *The Tremor of Forgery* (London: Heinemann, 1969), p. 81.

Let's Call a Spade a Spade
The "liquor-pushers" coined a phrase:
They say, "an alcoholic" —
(A term implying innocence
Like babies who have colic).
That alcohol's a habit-drug
They want us to ignore;
Shunning responsibility,
They claim that they deplore
This "illness" which their product
Is helping to create.
They cry: "Don't call folk 'drunkards'
That phrase is out of date."
This traffic and its victims
With habits that "benight" us
Really DO HAVE a new disease:
They have "DON'T-BLAME-ME-ITUS."
    1969: Florence Marshall Stellwagen, *Let's Call a Spade a Spade. A Book of Poems* (Dallas, Texas: Texas Alcohol Narcotics Education Press, 1969), pp. 5-7 (with four more verses).

The father, Adam Nathan Perry, interested me most of all. He was no longer living but his spirit was all over the place. He was the first American professor to teach political science as a college course. That was in 1865. He wrote a history of Williamstown and Williams College that was quite different from the usual town chronicles. He not only called a spade a spade but he told what was on the spade. The book shocked the old Williamstown families and they did their best to suppress it.

    1974: Wilbert Snow, *Codline's Child. The Autobiography of Wilbert Snow* (Middletown, Connecticut: Wesleyan University Press, 1974), p. 126 (chapter 8).

"Fine, Bob. I suppose you've heard the — er — terrible news?"
"We've heard Jemima Ames fell and cracked her nut, if that's what you mean." Bob made a thing of calling a spade by a more vulgar name. "As to whether it's terrible, I haven't made up my mind."

    1978: Charlotte MacLeod, *Rest You Merry* (New York: Avon Books, 1978), p. 55.

"Look here, mother," said he, "you must have a doctor."
"I shall have no doctor."
"You've got influenza, and it's a very tricky business — influenza is; you never know where you are with it."
"You can call it influenza," said Mrs. Machin. "There was no influenza in my young days. We called a cold a cold."
"Well," said Denry, "you aren't well, are you?"
"I never said I was," she answered grimly.

    1984: Arnold Bennett, *The Card. A Story of Adventure in the Five Towns* (London: J.M. Dent, 1984), p. 120 (chapter 8).

There is, to be sure, no way denying it that not all of these literary excerpts stem from well-known authors of the established canon. And yet, names like John Knox, Ben Jonson, Robert Burton, John Taylor, Jonathan Swift, Washington Irving, James Fenimore Cooper, Charles Dickens, Anthony Trollope, Robert Browning, Oscar Wilde, Winston S. Churchill, John Galsworthy, Harry S. Truman, Aldous Huxley, and Kurt Vonnegut are ample proof that the "spade"-phrase has found its way into prose, drama, and poetry of major Anglo-American writers. What is more, the proverbial expression "to call a spade a spade" is used in quite an innocuous fashion, simply expressing the fact that someone is voicing an opinion in a straight, blunt, and direct fashion, speaking plainly as it were.

    William Shakespeare's name is conspicuously absent from this list of names, yet he is included in the assembly of references above with the variant "We call a nettle but a nettle, and / The fault of fools but folly" (*Coriolanus*, II,1). It is surprising that Shakespeare did not employ the "spade"-expression, unless it was not yet solidly established outside of humanistic and educated circles at the turn from the sixteenth to the seventeenth century. After all, leaving aside the appearance of the proverbial phrase in the translations of Taverner and Udall, I have been able to find only four literary references in the English language from the sixteenth century.

Some authors have expanded the formulaic phrase for the sake of emphasis and/or satire, as for example:

"I must needs call a spade a spade; a pope a pope."
(1588: Martin Marprelate)

"We must call a spade a spade, and rebellion by the name of rebellion."
(1692: Gershom Bulkeley)

"Everything goes by its proper name; a spade is a spade; and a bayonet a bayonet."
(1816: John Wilson Croker)

"I hope you will not let these pretexts or complaints move you or prevent you from calling a spade a spade, a tax a tax."
(1909: Winston S. Churchill)

But there are also variants which most likely are based on the expression "to call a spade a spade":

"It's only calling black, black — and white, white."
(1854: Timothy Shay Arthur)

"He had never lost his habit of calling a sunset a sunset and a view a view, however deeply they might move him."
(1922: John Galsworthy)

"He called a Ford a Ford."
(1927: P.G. Wodehouse)

"There was no influenza in my young days. We called a cold a cold."

(1984: Arnold Bennett)

Interestingly enough, there are also two authors who stick very closely to Erasmus of Rotterdam's original two-fold formulation referring to figs and spades:

"I am [...] a loose, plain rude writer, *ficum voco ficum et ligonem ligonem.*"
(1628: Robert Burton)

"I am a plain blunt man who calls a fig a fig and a spade a spade."
(1958: L. Sprague de Camp)

These two references are separated by over three hundred years, and they represent the Latin and the English side of this particular proverbial coin. They also once again indicate that it is a matter of plain and clear speaking which is expressed by this traditional metaphor. This is convincingly expressed in the following statements:

"I am an old Tell-truth, I love to call a Spade, a Spade."
(1738: Jonathan Swift)

"A spade is never so merely a spade as the word / Spade would imply."
(1950: Christopher Fry)

"He not only called a spade a spade but he told what was on the spade."
(1974: Wilbert Snow)

Finally, there is even that ingenious term "spade caller," as when Phoebe Atwood Taylor characterizes someone in her novel *Figure Away* (1937) as an "Outspoken sort. An old spade caller." The longer context cited above makes it perfectly clear that this is not someone calling an African American names. Instead it is a definite reference to the traditional "spade"-phrase. But this truncated version is perhaps no longer kosher today, and it might best be replaced with its equivalent "straight shooter." In any case, before jumping to conclusions about racial slurs in communicative acts, both written and oral, the texts must always be analyzed in their socio- and psycholinguistic contexts.

VII.

Scholarly Use of the Proverbial Expression

Academic writing for the most part tends to avoid proverbial language, although scholars do not shy away completely from using such so-called clichés. Even they realize that a colorful phrase or a sapiential saying used at the right moment and without access might well add stylistic and emotive expressiveness to an erudite treatise. This is perhaps even more true, if the author intentionally varies the traditional phrase in order to make a point. This is the case, for example, in the use of the varied "spade"-expression in James Bonwick's Article on "The Australian Natives" that was published in the *Journal of the Anthropological Institute of Great Britain and Ireland*, 16 (1887), 201-210. Speaking of the belief system of Australian natives, Bonwick explains that "Wizards claim the precious gift of healing and inflicting diseases, causing rain and thunder, aiding friends and destroying foes, suddenly transporting themselves to distant places and assuming foreign forms, foretelling future events and knowing the hidden past, conversing with spirits of the dead and utilizing supernatural beings. [...] Some thrust subjects into a deep sleep, hypnotize them so that they call a spade by any other name than a spade, see visions, and reveal secrets" (p. 209). Clearly the proverbial expression "to call a spade a spade" is employed here in an innovative fashion. In fact, its meaning is reversed to express the fact that hypnotized natives are not capable of expressing the plain truth or clear reality.

Stylistically interested linguists have used the "spade"-phrase to stress that it would be better for speakers and writers to use less foreign words, euphemisms, and other types of high-polluted language. In other words, as the following three paragraphs show, people should communicate in straight-forward and plain English:

There are others [high-brow language users], and they are as numberless as the sands, who are mortally afraid to call a spade a spade because that would be the natural word, and not to be natural, in their eyes, would be common, and by this declension they would fall into the pit of vulgarity. The tendency to translate an ordinary word as it spontaneously emerges in the brain of the "genteel" speaker into a "genteel" expression gradually becomes a well-conditioned reaction, an almost automatic habit. The English language, with its abundance of synonyms, is an ideal hunting ground for such persons, with the difference that they are not hunters but poachers, who are not even aware of their offence. Once this has become an established habit the genteel expression springs from the brain without intermediate association, and the capacity for a natural conception of thought is lost, or at least seriously impaired.

> Victor Grove, "The Sociological Issue of High-Brow and Low-Brow," in V. Grove, *The Language Bar* (New York: Philosophical Library, 1950), pp. 84-96 (here p. 87).

Now read the blunders 'gainst which we've inweighed,
And when you write, these simple rules recall:
Be clear and natural, call a spade a spade,
"Learn to write well, or do not write at all."

> T.W. Kirkpatrick and M.H. Breese, *Better English for Technical Authors or Call a Spade a Spade* (London: Leonard Hill, 1961), p. ii (this is the last stanza of a tongue-in-cheek poem by the authors of this style manual).

Newsweek once came out with an unsigned article entitled "Never Call a Spade a Spade." This drew my attention at first because of the popular saying in its title. It was a reminder that different languages express similar philosophical concepts in different words and with different imageries. "To call a spade a spade" would come out in most Romance languages as "to call bread bread, and wine wine." However, I found the contents of the article equally entrancing. They dealt with the world of euphemisms, where "people expressways" is used for "sidewalks," "automotive internist" for "automobile mechanic," "activity booster" for "pep pill," "creative conflict" for "demonstration," and where a frankfurter becomes a "tube steak" while a hamburger, after going through a "Salisbury steak" phase, turns into a more modest "chopped steak." In Pentagonese, "disposal center" means "junkyard." What is at the root of euphemisms?

> Mario Pei, "The World of Euphemisms," in M. Pei, *Words in Sheep's Clothing* (New York: Hawthorn Books, 1969), pp. 208-214 (here p. 208).

But there are also two references by linguists, who argue against the message of the "spade"-phrase. After all, once in a while all of us enjoy using slang and nicknames, for example, and we don't want to call things by their proper names:

Why should people not be content to "call a spade a spade"? Their motives for using slang can seldom be analyzed convincingly, but in general they seek three things in various degrees and proportions: novelty, vivacity, and intimacy. Slang proceeds from a new way of looking at things and it exercises every form of intellectual wit and verbal ingenuity. Slang is picturesque, livens up a dull theme and administers salutary jolts or shocks to listeners. Slang increases intimacy because it allows the speaker to drop into a lower key, to meet his fellow on even terms and to have "a word in his ear".

Simeon Potter, "Slang and Dialect," in S. Potter, *Our Language* (Harmondsworth, Middlesex: Penguin Books, 1964 [1950]), pp. 130–141 (here p. 133).

Bluey
There are those amongst us who always like to call a spade "a spade", but there are others who follow a perverse and twisted path, who call black "white" and white "black", often in jest or playfulness. In this game of contraries, irony plays a major part, so that the nickname "Shorty" could be given to someone who is very short, but equally to someone who is very tall. Black may be the opposite of white, but for the other colours it is a bit difficult to decide what's what. Certainly Australians seem to feel that blue is the opposite of red, and so the nickname for a redhead is "Bluey" or "Blue". Maybe it works as a kind of verbal underlining, a way of highlighting the most obvious and noticeable thing about someone. This way of arriving at a nickname is common to English speakers around the world, but it does seem that this particular nickname for redheads is linked to Australians and has been most popular here since the late 1800s.

James Lambert (ed.), *Macquarie Book of Slang* (Sydney: The Macquarie Library, 1996 [2000]), p. 8.

There are even two proverb scholars who have effectively employed the proverbial expression for explanatory purposes. Edmund Gordon, for example, included the following footnote in one of his studies on Sumerian proverbs:

Another contrast shown by the Sumerian [proverb] collections *vis-à-vis* the Biblical proverbs is the "freedom" of language in the former, their "calling a spade a spade" in the references to sex and physiological functions. In this they show more kinship to the Arabic, Turkish and other modern Near Eastern proverbs.

Edmund I. Gordon, *Sumerian Proverbs. Glimpses of Everyday Life in Ancient Mesopotamia* (New York: Greenwood Press, 1968), p. 18 (note 27).

About twenty years later, in an introductory chapter on various aspects of the proverb, I referred to the phrase in order to explain the metaphorical nature of most proverbs and proverbial expressions:

Metaphorical proverbs also give us the opportunity to communicate in an indirect or figurative way rather than always calling a spade a spade, i.e., stating everything in a direct way. By translating a realistic situation into a metaphorical proverb, we can generalize the unique problem and express it as a common phenomenon of life.

Wolfgang Mieder, "The Proverb," in W. Mieder, *American Proverbs: A Study of Texts and Contexts* (Bern: Peter Lang, 1989), pp. 13–27 (here p. 20).

Obviously I could just as well have said "rather than calling things by their proper names," but I must admit that in 1989, when I wrote these words, I was not yet sensitized to the problematic nature of the "spade"-phrase. Its possible interpretation as a racial slur had not occurred to me at that time, and I thus made use of it as a harmless phrase to bring my point across that proverbs usually function as indirect or figurative statements. Does this make me a definite racist? Of course not. The only question that arises is whether I or other authors who have used the "spade"-expression during the past few decades should purge our writings of it? In other words, if I ever were lucky enough to bring out a second edition of my book on *American Proverbs*, would I change my "spade"-statement? As I progress writing the present book, I increasingly lean towards altering the sentence. After all, I have other ways of expressing the same idea, and why take the risk of offending one of my interested readers with a statement which they might interpret as a slur? I must, however, admit that I still find it difficult if not impossible to understand how anybody could interpret my use of the phrase in this particular context as possibly referring to black persons.

But let us return to the use of the proverbial expression in modern scholarly writings. Authors certainly like to use it as attention-getting titles, without using the phrase again in the actual text. Sometimes a sub-title clarifies the actual topic of the article, but be that as it may, the "spade"-expression signals clearly that things will be called what they are in these factual and informative publications:

Porter Shimer, "Let's Call a Spade a Spade."
Prevention, 32 (December 1980), 80.

David Tresemer, "Calling a Spade a Spade: Differences Between Spades & Shovels."
Horticulture, 60 (April 1982), 58.

William Davis, "Call a Spade a Spade."
Listener, 113 (1985), no pp. given.

Paul Surlis, "Calling a Spade a Spade; Nuclear Weapons and Sin."
Christianity and Crisis, 45 (August 26, 1985), 322–323.

Anonymous, "Calling a Spade a Spade (The Writer and Integrity)."
Index on Censorship, 15 (1986), 46–47.

Gertrud Jungblut, "'How to Call a Spade a Spade': Begründungen für monolinguale Wortbedeutungsvermittlung im Fremdsprachenunterricht."
Die Neueren Sprachen, 89 (1990), 55–68.

Wendy Woodward, "Calling a Spade a Muck Dig: Discourse and Gender in Some Novels by Christina Stead."
Geoffrey V. Davis and Hena Maes–Jelinek (eds.), *Crisis and Creativity in the New Literatures in English: Cross/Cultures* (Amsterdam: Rodopi, 1990), pp. 249–264.

M. Piskotin, "Call a Spade a Spade: The Entire Social System Must Be Overhauled."
Current Politics and Economics of Russia, 2 (1991), 101.

Brian Gartside, "Cut the Cackle, Let's Call a Spade, a Spade."
New Zealand Potter, 34 (1992), no pp. given.

Philippe Menasche, "Warm Cardioplegia or Aerobic Cardioplegia? Let's Call a Spade a Spade."
The Annals of Thoracic Surgery, 58 (1994), no pp. given.

D.C. Baines, "Not Calling a Spade a Spade: Correction to a Photograph."
History Today, 47 (1997), 36.

P.J. Tomlin, "When Is a Spade not a Spade? [Euphemisms Do Have a Place in Providing Comfort to the Distressed]."
British Medical Journal, 318 (January 23, 1999), 256.

Such "spade"-titles don't say much — they certainly don't give any precise and factual information. However, they flag the idea that the article itself will deal with the problem of calling things by their proper names, i.e., the authors wish to clarify matters for the readers on issues ranging from agriculture, politics, and society to medicine and beyond.

Here are twelve more contextualized references of the "spade"-expression found in scholarly publications of the two past decades. They once again make clear that their respective authors are totally unaware of the questionable suitability of the phrase in modern society:

We should be grateful for this honest, lucid, and elegantly written memoir. And let us specially rejoice that [George] Homans, as befits a member of the upper class, is not afraid to call a spade a spade. We need mavericks of the Right like George Homans almost as much as we need mavericks of the Left like Thorstein Veblen and C. Wright Mills. They are the salt of the earth.
Lewis Coser, "[George Homans' book] *Coming to My Senses*," *Contemporary Sociology*, 14 (1985), 429–430 (here p. 430).

If the author's [Eleanor Munro's] upbringing was modernist, the euphemistic, portentous language in which she writes about sexual matters seems maddeningly Victorian. The penises of her father and brother become "their swinging members, great and small." The inability to call a spade a spade seems detrimental to Ms. Munro's attempt to present herself as free from the paternal constraints of the past.
Joyce Johnson, "[Eleanor Munro's book] *Memoir of a Modernist's Daughter*," *The New York Times Book Review* (August 21, 1988), p. 27.

Sen. Sam Nunn, in his foreword to *The Masks of War*, says that "few of us will agree with everything in this provocative book." But this reader finds that few who know the services, and are willing to call a spade a spade, will find much with which to disagree. Carl Builder has captured the essence of the institutional personalities of the three military services.

Gerald Marsh, "[Carl Builder's book] *The Masks of War*," *The Bulletin of the Atomic Scientists*, 45 (1989), 46.

The introductory chapter of this book is entitled "Deconstructing the Monolithic Phallus." The words are set in large bold type. They make for an alarming start. Sexologists call a spade a spade, and readers who duck behind euphemism and slang when it comes to sexual awkwardness will find no refuge in this book.

Diana Souhami, "[Lesley Hall's book] *Hidden Anxieties*," *New Statesman & Society*, 4 (1991), 43.

At long last, the [communist] regime that forced writers to unnatural magicians' tricks is now gone, and a new era is dawning. Even neo-naturalists will now be able to call a spade a spade, and the others use styles and methods that would have shocked the now-defunct censor. This era, I understand, is to be the subject of this symposium [held in December, 1992, at London].

Josef Skvorecky, "Keynote Address: Eastern European Literature in Transition," *Review of Contemporary Fiction*, 17 (1997), 98-107 (here p. 107).

While, of course, formative regional influence on language cannot be excluded it would be as much of a mistake to interpret Mozart's uninhibited language (Hildesheimer 57), for instance in the Bäsle letters, merely on regional lines as is Zweig's attempt to explain Mozart's "coprolalia" as an expression of his eroticism. Vox populi, the voice of language, as Johann defined it, with its tendency to call a spade a spade and its long tradition in Germany, emphasized by the brothers Grimm, was not limited only to one region or, for that matter, to the servant class, as Einstein pointed out when he also drew attention to the fact that in the eighteenth century "all human-animalistic functions were exercised more publicly than is the case in our more civilized sanitary times." In their detailed analysis of Mozart's *Sauereyen* [filthy talk] Eibl and Senn similarly comment on the importance attributed at the time to some bodily functions, notably digestion and excretion, which were discussed in an open "matter of course" manner, *naturalia non sunt turpia* (Einstein 47).

K.A. Aterman, "Should Mozart Have Been Psychoanalysed? Some Comments on Mozart's Language in His Letters," *Dalhousie Review*, 73 (1993), 175-186 (here pp. 181-182).

His [Mohammad Chukri's] words will conclude this survey of the "unofficial" type of literary discourse, which, I hope, scholars will begin to take seriously: "[...] Noble literature about mankind may entertain, but it is useless when it comes to influencing or changing the status quo. [...] Arab regimes would like us [writers] to write demagogic texts, to go against progressive self-awareness which threatens their survival. At best they allow us to allude to but never to call a spade a spade."

    Ismail El-Outmani, "Prolegomena to the Study of the 'Other' Moroccan Literature," *Research in African Literature*, 28 (1997), 110–121 (here p. 120).

Wade also hesitates in his use of language at several key points of the conceptual article. His text and Figure 1 clearly imply to me some causal relationships between key variables, but his propositions and postulates are couched in language such as "is related to" or "are associated with." It would be less confusing for Wade to either (a) focus on exploring such simple covariation among constructs, which would yield a different article than his current speculative discussion, or (b) call a spade a spade, use language of causality, and earn points for extraordinary professional bravery.

    Ellen P. Cook, "Thoughts about Male Reference Group Identity Dependence Theory," *Counseling Psychologist*, 26 (1998), 427–437 (here p. 429).

[William] Herrick senses he is on shaky ground here. He is queasy about his act of cooperation and apologizes to those he may have inadvertently injured. But he moves quickly — too quickly I think — past the moral dilemma. Still, for a long time William Herrick has known what to call a spade when he sees one. That puts him in the best company.

    Dorothy Gallagher, "[William Herrick's book] *Jumping the Line*," *The New York Times Book Review* (May 3, 1998), p. 31.

Macaulay would no more censor the publication of Etherege than he would Plato's dialogue, but he intends to call a spade a spade and insist that Restoration drama is utterly immoral (and thereby reflects the immorality of its day). Focusing on the chief weakness in Lamb's argument, he quotes (somewhat rearranging the sentences) a passage about the characters in the comedies.

    James Fenton, "[Fintan O'Toole's book] *A Traitor's Kiss: The Life of Richard Brinsley Sheridan*," *New York Review of Books* (February 2, 1999), p. 42.

To a limited degree, reprogenetics is already practiced and accepted by a major portion of society. Each time a woman decides to abort a fetus based on the results of amniocentesis, she is choosing against the presence of certain genes in her children. And each time an abortion is chosen because the resulting child would have been mentally retarded (without other medical problems), reprogenetics is being practiced for the sole purpose of increasing the intelligence of the child that is ultimately born as a result of a later pregnancy. Why is there such a reluctance on the part of many in society to call a spade a spade in this context? One part of the answer is that the practice of reprogenetics sounds suspiciously like the discredited social theory of eugenics. Indeed, many social commentators confuse the two even though they are fundamentally different in both purveyors and goals.

Lee M. Silver, "How Reprogenetics Will Transform the American Family," *Hofstra Law Review*, 27 (1999), 649–660 (here pp. 651–652).

Nevertheless, there remains, in [Charles] Griswold's view, an unsatisfactory tension in [Adam] Smith's position. His analysis of moral qualities, together with his claim to adopt an everyday standpoint, is at odds with our disposition to "Platonize" values, to treat moral properties as features of the world. Smith's response to this difficulty, as Griswold reconstructs it in his epilogue, is to theorize without appearing to do so, to intervene in common life while at the same time warning against the damage philosophers can do when they unmask the illusions of quotidian existence. To this end, Smith conducts a "conversation" guided by the ideals of moderation, sympathy, and humanity, a style of philosophizing, which, as Griswold sees it, lacks the bluntness and directness of the Socratic method. Philosophy, Griswold seems to suggest, must be prepared to call a spade a spade and to press its inquiries beyond the limits of civility.

Susan James, "[Charles Griswold's book] *Adam Smith and the Virtues of Enlightenment*," *Ethics*, 111 (2001), 634–636 (here p. 636).

Admittedly, my harvest of references from scholarly publications is sparse in comparison to the "spade"-texts that I found in literary works and in the mass media. But this was to be expected, since scholars tend to make less use of proverbial and idiomatic language than writers of novels and plays or journalists. Nevertheless, the contextualized examples cited here show that scholars have no hesitation in using the proverbial expression "to call a spade a spade" in their publications to express the idea of writing plainly. I might add as a final note here that I have also heard it used orally during numerous committee and faculty meetings at the University of Vermont during the past three decades. Even today, at a time when our campus very consciously and responsibly addresses issues of diversity and racism, the proverbial expression is being used, albeit with only very few African American faculty members and students on this campus. When I have asked colleagues about the possible racial interpretation of the phrase, they have, for the most part, expressed surprise at this interpretation. There was, of course, one major exception, namely a colleague and friend who happens to be an African American. She truly finds the proverbial expression "to call a spade a spade" to be a racial slur. But one thing remains certain, the academic world does not appear to be particularly aware of this problematic aspect of the classical phrase in modern-day America. Scholars have reacted with concerned condemnation to such obvious racial steroetypes as "The only good Indian is a dead Indian" and "No tickee, no washee," as I have been able to show in two chapters of my book *The Politics of Proverbs: From Traditional Wisdom to Proverbial Stereotypes* (Madison, Wisconsin: University of Wisconsin Press, 1997). These proverbs against Native Americans and Chinese Americans have long been recognized as racial slurs, something that is only true to a very limited extant for the proverbial expression "to call a spade a spade" thus far.

VIII.

Use of the Phrase in the Mass Media

The internet has brought about a definite change in both diachronic and synchronic proverb scholarship. This is especially the case in finding textual references through various types of electronic databases. Obviously these modern research tools cannot completely replace traditional scholarly approaches, but they certainly make it possible to find phrasal references in many printed sources, including books, magazines, and newspapers. When I started my paremiological work some thirty years ago, I would never have been able to assemble such a wealth of references for the "spade"-phrase from the mass media as will be presented in this chapter. None of the references below have any racial implications and are thus indications that the "spade"-phrase in its original meaning of speaking plainly and calling matters by their real names is alive in the modern age. However, it is in the mass media where the proverbial expression "to call a spade a spade" has in fact appeared as a racial slur, but these occurrences will be discussed in more detail in chapters nine and ten.

The electronic search for the proverbial expression "to call a spade a spade" in the mass media has brought to light numerous valuable references, especially for the past three decades (databases usually do not go back any further than about 1970). For a scholar of the traditional school, the information found by electronic means can, at times, be somewhat frustrating, especially regarding bibliographical precision. Even though many databases include complete electronic texts of the article in question, they rather often do not provide names of authors, titles, and pages numbers. But the names of the magazines or newspapers are indicated, and the precise dates also appear. If for whatever reason someone needed to see the text in actual print, it would not be too difficult to locate it in the particular issue. Nevertheless, it would be better if more complete bibliographical information were included in the electronic media.

It should also be noted that such database searches have their limitations. It is one thing to search for the expression "to call a spade a spade," but quite another to locate intentionally varied forms with the structure "to call a(n) X a(n) X." But be that as it may, most of the contextualized references of the "spade"-phrase presented in this chapter would not have been found without an electronic search.

Before presenting this rich harvest, let me list a few older appearances of the expression that were found in the mass media without the help of a computer. They were located by lexicographers and paremiographers by chance, i.e., by having noted them down while reading a particular magazine or newspaper article. This is still an important way of finding textual references, especially in the case of varied proverbs and proverbial expressions. The earliest tongue-in-cheek reference from the mass media that I am aware of appeared in *Punch* magazine in 1884:

Law in Lavender
The peculiarly sweet scent of "the *Mignonnette* Case" at Exeter Assizes, seems to have had a strong attraction for the fair sex, "not a few of whom," says the *Daily News*, "were in the galleries of the Court," while "a few Ladies and Gentlemen of position in the neighbourhood" improved their *status* by joining the High Sheriff, who was in full yeomanry uniform, — as an officer and a sheriff, — on the Bench. "Some of the details of the case," the report goes on to say, "were hardly fit for Ladies' ears" — ahem! — then to what section of the fair sex did the ears of those in the galleries and on the Bench belong? — "but there being no controversy as to the facts, Counsel on both sides were able to pass these lightly over." And so justice put on its lavender kids, sprinkled rose-water, and accommodated the repulsive details to the susceptibilities of the audience. Excellent precedent. In future "Ladies present" will be sufficient to warn Counsel that they must find delicate synonyms, and if it is absolutely necessary to call a spade a spade, then it must be done in a whisper, the Counsel, Witness, Judge, and one Reporter coming close up to the jury-box.
Anonymous, "Law in Lavender," *Punch* (November 15, 1884), p. 229.

The indefatigable paremiographer Bartlett Jere Whiting registered the following four occurrences of the "spade"-phrase during the 1950s in major American magazines and newspapers. They make clear that the expression can in fact be used for humorous as well as serious statements:

One of the newspapers that drew the line was the San Diego *Union*, which heavily edited its wire copy [and] explained to readers that it considered the full-fleshed story too gamy for a family newspaper. Regardless of the trial's outcome or of *Confidential's* eventual fate, daily press coverage of the [obscenity] case and the increase in newsstand sales

seemed to indicate that millions of readers like to have a spade of dirt called a spade of dirt — as Dirt Spader Harrison has insisted all along.
Anonymous, "Putting the Papers to Bed," *Time* (August 26, 1957), p. 61.

He was not opposed to foreign aid in general, Ohio Democrat Wayne Hays emphasized to the House during last week's debate on the $2.9 billion foreign aid authorization bill. But he was opposed to $600,000 earmarked under the bill for Dictator Rafael Trujillo's Dominican Republic, especially as, at the very same time, Rafael Trujillo Jr. was spending a bit of his $600,000 annual allowance on a $5,500 Mercedes-Benz and a $17,000 chinchilla coat in the U.S. for Cinemagyar Zsa Zsa Gabor. Predicted Ohio's Hays, with spade-calling confidence in his congressional immunity: "If he keeps on fooling around with Zsa Zsa Gabor, who apparently is the most expensive courtesan since Madame de Pompadour, the old man is going to have to raise the ante."
Anonymous, "A Romp with Pompadour," *Time* (May 26, 1958), p. 20.

[The novelist and civil rights advocate George W.] Cable was never one to temper the "harshness of fact" for anyone, even his beloved South. He went about calling a spade what it jolly well was until it would seem that no one could ever call it anything else.
C. Vann Woodward, "Dixie Crusader," *The New York Times Book Review* (July 27, 1958), p. 6.

Why Call a Spade a Spade?
Dear Helen: My sister-in-law calls her children everything but their real names: Chum-bun, Little Poo, Squirt, Buster, Honeybunch, Funnyface, Beetlebaum, etc. Don't you think this is kind of silly? PROPER
Dear Proper: No sillier than criticizing something which is none of your business. Why call a spade a spade if a more descriptive moniker is handy? Your S-in-L evidently believes that a child by any other name is just as sweet. HELEN BOTTEL
Helen Bottel, "Helen Help Us!" *Boston Herald* (August 7, 1958), p. 30.

Unfortunately I have no references from the 1960s to report, since not even Bartlett Jere Whiting included any in his invaluable *Modern Proverbs and Proverbial Sayings* (Cambridge, Massachusetts: Harvard University Press, 1989) and the electronic databases do not go back that far. But for the following four decades there are many occurrences, and they are grouped here in chronological order by decade. Due to the wealth of materials, the length of the contextualized references has been kept to a minimum wherever possible:

1970s

In quotation of the day, economist Paul W. McCracken says of officials who shy away from using the word 'recession': I think they are ill-advised to do it. I don't think you can gain anything by playing with words. You might as well call a spade a spade.
New York Times (October 24, 1974), p. 43, col. 6.

Hurrah for James Richardson. He has had the courage to call a spade a spade [during the discussion of changes in the Canadian constitution].
R.C. McMurchy, "Richardson Praised," *The Globe and Mail* (July 5, 1978), p. P7.

Admission to hospital gives the physician time to have medical tests and x-rays performed on the child, Dr. [Ken] MacRae said. [...] He also warned physicians not to work alone but to seek the aid of social workers, public health workers, the police if necessary and other medical experts to confirm injuries which might otherwise go undetected. "Then when you talk to the parents, you can't pussyfoot around. You have to call a spade a spade." He said the physician can tell the parents he had a legal obligation to ensure that the child not be injured again.
Anonymous, "Can't Be Sued for Wrong Report of Child Abuse, Doctors Are Told," *The Globe and Mail* (September 19, 1978), p. P15.

"Why don't we call a spade a spade?" Tess suggested. Pietro pointed out that it was all very well to call a spade a spade, but it sounded ridiculous to call a relationship a relationship. Tess insisted they try it anyhow, so when Pietro bumped into Mayor Frank Rizzo one day in Philadelphia, he said, "Frank, let me introduce you to my relationship, Tess."
Russell Baker, "Mr. President, Meet My Mate," *The Globe and Mail* (January 11, 1979), p. T4.

I have always admired someone with the courage to call a spade a spade (especially in this day and age of plastic and gloss). Scott Symons'

messages ring loud and clear, and certainly have proved to be far more than a breath of fresh air after such a winter of discontent.
   Sandra L. Cattarello, "Symons Series," *The Globe and Mail* (May 8, 1979), p. P6.

Unlike many other social or economic conservatives, Mr. [Andrew] Winstanley does not shy away from qualifying himself as right-wing. Well, I see a lot of euphemisms like competitive free enterprise, or competitive economy, or capitalism. But I really like to call a spade a spade. His basic premise is simple: government interference does not work.
   Wendie Kerr, "Right-Winger Gets Foot in Door," *The Globe and Mail* (July 30, 1979), p. B2.

1980s

"Let's call a spade a spade — it's strikebreaking and we'll be taking the appropriate action," said Ken Steele, the union's regional director. Mr. Steele did not say what that action would be.
   Anonymous, "CTV to Cover Summit," *The Globe and Mail* (June 25, 1981), p. P5.

After the Argos closed out the first half of their season with their eighth consecutive loss, Wood said he feels he has to call a spade, a spade. "I find that the football team is digressing," he said. "We're a notch or two above being sandlotters. It's reached the point where it's getting to be ridiculous."
   Jeffrey Labov, "Argo Coach Losing Faith in Players," *The Globe and Mail* (August 24, 1981), p. S1.

Now, let's call a spade a spade — or, then again, let's not, since to do so might be seen as unauthentic on the part of an urban apartment dweller like myself. Better leave that to those clods out there in the backwoods with their burger joints and their off-the-rack suits.
   Richard Streiling, "Dispatching the Victim with His Own Weapon," *The Globe and Mail* (November 28, 1981), p. F7.

The CMA [Canadian Manufacturers Association] executive is to be commended for his willingness to call a spade a spade. Mr. Jean Jacques] Gagnon judges the severity of a business slump by its observed

effects, rather than by some bloodless, abstract statistical measure of gross national product.
>Ronald Anderson, "The Depressing Truth about the Recession," *The Globe and Mail* (February 23, 1982), p. B2.

Let's call a spade a spade. What the Conservatives are in fact doing is conducting a strike in the public sector. If it were Canada Post or the Toronto Transit Commission, wouldn't there be a public outcry?
>C.W. Stitt, "Re the Stalemate in Parliament." *The Globe and Mail* (March 12, 1982), p. P7.

In his [President Ronald Reagan's] willingness to call a spade a spade, he may have offended some who accept Andrei Gromyko's harsh attacks on this country but feel that any American spokesman must soft-pedal his official statements. In fact, the Soviets respect a frank statement of position and pay little attention to the weasel words of the timorous.
>Anonymous, "Reagan Lays Cards Face up," *Oklahoma City Times* (June 21, 1982), no pp. given.

Along with the one-quarter reduction in the civil service, these are all cutbacks of one kind or another. Thus the term "cutbacks" is certainly more broadly descriptive and should replace "restraint" — at the very least. But how about the media really calling a spade a spade: not "restraint," but "right-wing"?
>H.S. Ribner, "Call a Spade a Spade," *The Globe and Mail* (October 27, 1983), p. P6.

"Believe me when I say the Syrians are not as bad as you think," says Bandar. "But definitely, the Israelis are not as good as you think. We're not lobbying you to be against Israel but to call a spade a spade, make the other side feel you're even-handed, that you're willing to tell the Israelis they were wrong and you're willing to tell the Arabs that." Bandar laughs uproariously over the suggestion that he is the Saudis' version of shuttle diplomat, protesting that he isn't sure he should take the implied comparison with Henry Kissinger, with whom he socializes occasionally, as a compliment.
>M.C. Valada, "Ambassador With the Royal Touch: Saudi Arabia's Prince Bandar," *The Washington Post* (February 16, 1984), no pp. given.

Because they [lawyers] are reluctant to call a spade a spade and allow damages for mental distress as a tort (wrongdoing) independently of whether the financial settlement is reasonable or not, the courts are forced into the legal gymnastics of finding ways to get around the strictures of the "breach of contract" fiction.

    Claire Bernstein, "Business Law Judgments on Brutal Firings Making Firms Rethink Policies," *The Globe and Mail* (December 10, 1984), p. B3.

We have a secretary [William Bennett] in charge of public education who wants to essentially pay the public (in the form of tax credits) to send their children to private school. This will completely destroy the fabric of our whole public education system. Ironically, this is the same William Bennett who would limit loans to college students who otherwise cannot afford college. His advice is to tell parents that they should have used family planning. Why doesn't Bennett stop mincing words and call a spade a spade? He doesn't believe in educating the poor, the black, the Hispanic, or the handicapped. Isn't this what he is saying?

    Carolyn Birnbaum, "The Three Cs of Education," *The Los Angeles Times* (June 6, 1985), p. 4.

He [CBS lawyer Charles Walsh] said branding such efforts [blending reporting with journalistic judgments] as libelous could frighten other reporters away from investigative stories. "What reporter in his right mind will ever call a spade a spade?" Walsh asked the judge.

    Anonymous, "Suit Could Emasculate Press," *The Record, Northern New Jersey* (July 28, 1985), p. A53.

[Bill] Fabrey says he's impressed "by big things" — including ocean liners, steam engines and the George Washington Bridge — and he prefers that people call a spade a spade. "We don't like to use euphemisms like ample-figured, or plus sizes. The word is fat."

    Stephanie Mansfield, "The Really Big Story — Weight, There's More: Fashion & Society Are Making a Heavy-Duty Adjustment," *The Washington Post* (February 27, 1986), no pp. given.

Encouraged to play it safe in the past, Wilson [Sporting Goods Co.] executives say they're getting gutsier. A recent gamble: naming the company's new ceramic [tennis] racket the Ceramic. That may seem harmless enough, but Wilson has qualms that people will think of breakable pottery and shy away from the racket. So why choose

Ceramic, a name Wilson probably can't even trademark? "We want to capture this new category, and we believe the best way to do that is to call a spade a spade," says Mr. Lumley.

> Ronald Alsop, "Wilson Changes Sales Tactics to Improve Its Tennis Game," *The Wall Street Journal* (May 1, 1986), no pp. given.

It is time for the United States "to call a spade a spade" in its relations with Mexico, said Sen. Pete Wilson, R–Calif. He said the Reagan administration "needs some nudging" to develop a stronger response to the Mexican crisis, which Wilson sees as threatening the United States' economy and society.

> Benjamin Shore and Marcus Stern, "Helms' Mexico Alarm Rouses White House," *The San Diego Union–Tribune* (June 29, 1986), p. A1.

Nor is [Pieter–Dirk] Uys the only South African comic condemning his society from the stage. Believe it or not, political satire is alive and well in South Africa. "It's one of the few areas left where you can call a spade a spade," said Uys. "If television and the press were allowed to do the things we do, we wouldn't have the same impression."

> Martin Portus, "Seeing the Joke in a Black and White Issue," *Sydney Morning Herald* (January 3, 1987), p. 22.

To some, it was a natural evolution for D.C. law firms to include lobbyists and, more recently, for them to call a spade a spade — hiring non–lawyers as lobbyists. More and more, as law firms here have developed lobbying arms — either in–house or through subsidiaries — they have been shopping for access and knowledge of "the process," not for law degrees.

> Terry Carter, "An 'L'–Word Earns respect in the Capital," *The National Law Journal* (December 26, 1988), p. 24.

Peggy Noonan may want more "easy–goingness," but all this Boy–Scout stuff and the almost terminally–preppie sentimentality seems wildly out of place. No one who's seen the Bush political operation in full–throated chase believes Roger Ailes, or Lee Atwater, or, and let's call a spade a spade, Jim Baker, accepts this "easy–goingness" bull.

> David Nyhan, "Have a Nice Four Years, George," *The Boston Globe* (January 22, 1989), no pp. given.

In the program documents of the Lithuanian Communist Party congress and in the political report, the measures taken are presented as a substantial contribution in the renewal of the Communist Party of the Soviet Union and our country. But to call a spade a spade, a step was made aimed at an organizational and political split with the Communist Party of the Soviet Union.
    Anonymous, "Upheaval in the East: Gorbachev," *The New York Times* (December 27, 1989), p. A12, col. 1.

1990s

Television critic Rick Martin has done it again! He had the courage to call a spade a spade.
    Anonymous, "Bravo! Critic Doesn't Shrink from Panning TV Trash," *The Washington Times* (September 20, 1990), p. G2.

Mr. Evans: "You are a very honest man, Mr. Vice President [Dan Quayle]. You're not deceptive; you call a spade a spade. Judging from what you have just said, isn't it a fact, then, that this is laying out, head-to-head, person-to-person, [Jim] Baker to Saddam Hussein, an ultimatum? Why isn't it?"
    Anonymous, "Evans and Novak — Quayle," *Federal News Service* (December 1, 1990), no pp. given.

It [the House] referred to 1992 a measure which would allow electronic games of chance at pari-mutuel tracks after defeating 218-118 a bid by Rep. Nancy Ford, R-Nashua, to kill it. "Let's call a spade a spade, these are slot machines without a handle," she said.
    Donn Tibbetts, "House Sends Gas Tax Hike to Panel," *The Union Leader* (March 8, 1991), p. 1.

Boris Yeltsin seized control of the Kremlin yesterday and abolished much of Soviet President Mikhail Gorbachev's government in a move that all but destroyed the remnants of Soviet power. "It is best to call a spade a spade, and what is happening today on the territory of the former Soviet Union, is most certainly, a governmental coup d'état," the newspaper *Nezavisimaya Gazeta* said in a front-page article.
    Gerald Nadler, "Yeltsin Leaves Gorbachev Lame Duck," *The Washington Times* (December 20, 1991), p. A1.

Ex-IBM systems expert Julian Allen may sue the computer giant for the loss of thousands of pounds worth of enterprise allowances and unemployment benefits — a loss he blames on IBM's inability to call a spade a spade.
    Helen Arnold, "Out of Pocket Ex-IBMer Considers Legal Action," *Computer Talk* (April 6, 1992), p. 1.

Moldovan President Mircea Snegur denounced Russia for "seeking to be the policeman of the Commonwealth of Independent States" and told lawmakers at an emergency Parliament session: "We have to call a spade a spade: We are at war with Russia."
    Carey Goldberg, "Moldovan Chief Calls for War with Russia," *Los Angeles Times* (June 23, 1992), p. A8, col. 3.

"Let's call a spade a spade: Ross Perot won this debate," said ABC's Cokie Roberts shortly after it was over. Many of her counterparts at CBS, NBC and the nation's newspapers agreed.
    Thomas B. Rosenstiel, "Instant Polls Pick Winner While Debate Still Echoes," *Los Angeles Times* (October 13, 1992), p. A14, col. 5.

"Do you all personally know people who call women bitches and 'hos?" [...] "Yep," McMillian answers sheepishly. [...]. "A bitch," he says. "I mean, you call a spade a spade. It's a colloquialism. It's part of the language."
    Mary Ann French, "War of the Words," *The Washington Post* (August 15, 1993), p. G5.

Oh hell, let's call a spade a spade: Tanya Donelly meets Kim Deal for a freewheeling discussion of fronting bands, playing backup, sexual politics in the rock world and the negatives of humping trees.
    Evelyn McDonnnell, "Belly Meets the Breeders," *Musician* (September 1, 1993), p. 34.

Georgette Mosbacher won't say that she's happy to be rid of Washington, but let's call a spade a spade here. "It is the only town in the world where you can go from a B-cup to a C-cup without surgery," she tells us in an interview. [...] Mosbacher minces no words telling women to drop the mother lode on personal appearance.
    Lois Romano, "Georgette Mosbacher: The Force Is with Her," *The Washington Post* (September 10, 1993), p. G3.

Let's call a spade a spade. It is nothing but demagogy to pretend that Boris Yeltsin had the moral and political obligation to dissolve the Russian Parliament and begin one-man presidential rule.
>Mikhail Gorbachev, "Russia's Problems Can't Be Settled in Streets," *The Houston Chronicle* (October 1, 1993), p. 33.

Rush Limbaugh has the guts to call a spade a spade. He is not afraid to expose the pseudointellectual elitist snob liberals for who they are ... people who are too ashamed or naive to admit that their ideas are wrong and out of touch with mainstream America. Rush gives us a voice.
>Amonymous, "It's Easy to Understand Why They Want to Hush Rush," *The Washington Times* (August 7, 1994), p. B5.

Col. Summers is either extremely naive, or, perhaps, he is afraid to call a spade a spade.
>Anonymous, "Ample Reason to Gripe," *The Washington Post* (August 6, 1995), p. B5.

Beverly Lofton, spokeswoman for the D.C. public schools, isn't afraid to call a spade a spade, and she encourages the media to do the same.
>John McCaslin, "Inside the Beltway," *The Washington Post* (November 21, 1995), p. A5.

Peter Jennings dutifully reported that "it is very clear the president is furious." This, though, was only entertainment. McCurry had rehearsed his statement, and Jennings was pretending to clairvoyance. The important thing was that Safire had disdained the routine euphemisms, and called a spade a spade.
>John Corry, "We Are Family," *The American Spectator* (March, 1996), no pp. given.

When Can We Ever Call a Spade a Spade?
People need to stop glorifying those bums who use profanity as their only essential means of communicating [referring to the late rapper Tupac Shakur].
>Jim Cleaver, "When Can We Ever Call a Spade a Spade?" *Los Angeles Sentinel* (October 10, 1996), p. A7.

It's about time to bite the bullet, swallow the bitter medicine and call a spade a spade. Let's face it, has anyone other than its creator said it [a sculpture] was a great addition to our beautiful new airport, and worth $133,000? I doubt it.

>   Anonymous, "Airport's Sculpture," *The Providence Journal-Bulletin* (January 28, 1997), p. C4.

For an article on fabulous Jewish women who speak their minds, shoot from the hip, talk turkey, aren't threatened by their own competence, don't get nervous taking up space in a room, call a spade a spade, and, in general, take care of business — in udda woids, for an article on female role models who are OTHER than the neurasthenic American cultural distaff ideal, send in the name of a woman who has inspired you with her (fabulous, Jewish) BIG MOUTH.

>   Anonymous, "Seeking: Jewish Women with BIG Mouths," *Lilith* (March 31, 1997), p. 7.

Several Montgomery County state legislators objected last night to a proposal by Fairfax County to triple the amount of water it takes from the Potomac River by 2000. "Let's call a spade a spade," said Sen. Jean W. Roesser (R) at a public hearing on the issue in Potomac called by the Maryland Department of the Environment. "This proposal is to accommodate Virginia's massive [plans for] growth."

>   Paul W. Valentine, "Water Pipe Plan for Fairfax Stirs Concerns in Maryland," *The Washington Post* (May 22, 1997), p. D2.

Incidentally, in Biblical times Jewish descent was determined by the Jewishness of the father, not the mother. The rabbis changed that 2,000-year-old Biblical tradition. Indeed, the rabbis of the Talmud often changed the Biblical rules; they were the Reform Jews of their time. For example, in the Bible, if you violated the Sabbath by gathering sticks, the punishment was — death! (see Numbers 15:32-36). When the rabbis changed the rules, they usually did it by circuitous means, often by legal fictions (the eruv) that are no longer fashionable. We're a bit more realistic now, willing to call a spade a spade.

>   Hershel Shanks, "Tolerance vs. Halachah," *Moment* (June 30, 1997), p. 6.

[Saifuddin] Soz and other delegates agreed with the sentiment voiced by UN General Assembly President Razali Ismail of Malaysia: "Let's call a spade a spade. Over five years not enough has been done [about the environment]."

Anonymous, "India Asks West to Meet Environment Standards," *News-India Times* (July 4, 1997), p. 3.

Is there a Jew today — at least among those appointed leaders, those whose names float from crisis to crisis — who is ready to say: "Let's be Karaites and Samaritans and Christians, and let's call a spade a spade: 'We Are One' is dead, and it's better to huddle down with our own kind?"
Suzanne F. Singer, "Free Market Judaism," *Moment* (August 31, 1997), p. 8.

Japanese-American community leaders say they do not want to evoke the Holocaust at all, but simply to tell their own community's story in its own language. "We're not trying to make any comparisons to what happened in Europe," says Chris Komai, spokesman of the Japanese American museum. "We're talking about something that happened in America. We have to tell our own story in a straight forward manner. And that requires calling a spade a spade."
J.J. Goldberg, "War of Wars: A Jewish-Japanese Clash over Language and the Holocaust," *The Jewish Week* (February 27, 1998), p. 14.

Actor Anupam Kher, however, adopted an aggressive stance, saying: "It is absurd to let Pakistani artists perform here when their government has evil designs on India. We are guilty of being nice to Pakistan. It is time we called a spade a spade and stop Pakistanis from coming here."
Taani Pande, "Shiv Sena Disrupts Ghulam Ali Performance in Mumbai," *India Abroad* (May 8, 1998), p. 18.

"While a lot of us admire [Defense Minister George] Fernandes for calling a spade a spade, there has to be some discretion in keeping the equilibrium of troop deployment in the northern and eastern frontiers [of India and China]," said a military commander, speaking on condition of anonymity.
Sanjeev Miglani, "Plowing a Lonely Furrow," *News-India Times* (May 15, 1998), p. 18.

Richard Blackford is quite right to draw attention to misleading terminology, such as "ethnic cleansing", which helps to cloud perceptions of world events. Another unpleasant and misleading wartime euphemism which could happily be abandoned is "comfort women" —

women forced (by the Japanese) into prostitution during the Second World War. In a year when a complete new edition of George Orwell's work is coming out, we could remember one of Britain's foremost journalists by a more accurate use of our wonderful language and call a spade a spade again.

    Kate Baden Fuller, "Extremist Vocabulary," *The Times of London* (June 30, 1998), p. 21.

"They [some politicians] lied. You just have to call a spade a spade," said Long Hill resident Frances Desmelyk, who attended the June meeting.

    Greg Saitz, "Records Detail Case against Ex-School Chief," *The Star-Ledger* (August 6, 1998), p. 29.

Referring to the word schism, Father Aivazian says: "We must call a spade a spade — words that have been historically established become useful to understand the past."

    Ara K. Yeretsian, "The Schism of Antelias," *Armenian Reporter* (August 15, 1998), p. 3.

Let's call a spade a spade. Extreme environmental groups on the North Coast are made up of extremists. Extremists don't compromise. Just look at the stranglehold the extreme right-wing currently has on our government for another example.

    Shelly Groshan, "Extremism," *The Press Democrat* (November 29, 1998), p. G2.

The government of Israel refuses to call a spade a spade and continues to make believe that [in Lebanon] it is dealing with some minor nuisance or necessary evil.

    Moshe Arens, "A Dangerous Game," *The Jerusalem Post* (December 4, 1998), p. 8.

When two Hollywood big shots do it [i.e., plagiarize], the act is euphemistically called "a retelling" or "a replicate". But let's call a spade a spade: The new "Psycho" is a forgery, an exquisitely done one, but a forgery nevertheless.

    Joe Baltake, "New 'Psycho' Would Make Hitch Proud," *Sacramento Bee* (December 6, 1998), p. J6.

Mr. Yergin was introduced to a Tokyo audience of businessmen, bankers, reporters and scholars as "a walking think tank" and "Renaissance man." He didn't disappoint. Mr. Yergin showed his ability to call a spade a spade without insulting anyone. A recent parade of Japan-bashers has left Tokyo reeling.
Edward Neilan, "Asian Comeback," *Journal of Commerce* (December 11, 1998), p. A5.

To call a spade a spade, palaver and hypocrisy among Ohio House Republicans (and some Democrats) reached new peaks in the post-election session that ended last week.
Thomas Suddes, "Pats on Backs Overshadow Real Travesties," *The Plain Dealer* (December 16, 1998), p. B13.

On Saturday, for the second time in a week, they shot down a United Nations plane soon after take-off from the besieged Angolan city of Huambo. U.N. Secretary-General Kofi Annan was "outraged," and Issa Diallo, head of the U.N. Observer Mission in Angola, said he thought U.N. flights were being specifically targeted. [...] Yet nobody said the obvious: "Savimbi did it." Both planes were shot down over territory controlled by UNITA (National Union for the Total Independence of Angola), Jonas Savimbi's rebel army, and Savimbi has always treated the U.N. with contempt. But the U.N. never calls a spade a spade in Angola — with results that have been disastrous for the country.
Gwynne Dyer, "Angola Returns to Hell as U.N. Dithers," *The Toronto Star* (January 5, 1999), no pp. given.

TD Wants a Spade to Be a Spade in Language of Law
A call for laws to be drafted in simple, well-written English accessible to a person with average literacy was made yesterday by the chairman of the Dail Committee on Public Accounts, Mr. Jim Mitchell.
Christine Newman, "TD Wants a Spade to Be a Spade in Language of Law," *The Irish Times* (January 8, 1999), p. 8.

The diplomat in you [Deputy Prime Minister Pak Lah] may resist this, but when the need arises, your job may demand no less than a steely grip on situations. You may have to call a spade a spade. There's going to be a lot on your plate as you steer the nation out of the economic crisis into the more familiar territory of sustained and expanding prosperity.

Ahmad A. Talib, "An Open Letter to Pak Lah," *The New Straits Times* (January 10, 1999), p. 10.

He's the former altar boy who drinks and swears. Loud and amiable, Rob Hulls wants you to know he is a rough-and-tumble knockabout bloke, unafraid to "call a spade a spade." "I don't bullshit and I don't, if you like, beat around the bush," he says. As state Labor's parliamentary hit-man, his job is "to get down and get dirty."

Ewin Hannan, "Getting Down and Dirty," *The Age* (January 28, 1999), p. 13.

Unlike you, Ms. Helfgott, not everybody is prepared to "call a spade a spade." Judith S. Neaman and Carole G. Silver state, in *Kind Words: A Thesaurus of Euphemisms*, that "this fear of causing psychic pain, this desire to be well thought of leads us to use 'kind words'."

Howard Richler, "It's an Old Story: What to Call the Aged," *The Gazette* (February 6, 1999), p. 12.

"Let's call a spade a spade," [Justice Ann Walsh] Bradley said. "This is about personal ambition, politics and pettiness. Justice Bablitch and the three other justices are interested in topping the chief."

Cary Segall, "Justices Lay Bare Problems," *Wisconsin State Journal* (February 14, 1999), p. A1

John Travolta: "I'm going to call a spade a spade here: I missed the first five minutes of 'Jerry Maguire' because of the love scene. I know it's acting and Tom (Cruise) is a friend. And I know my wife (Kelly Preston) loves me, but it's hard to watch your wife. And I think it's hard for her to watch me, but I've never been that explicit in any love scene. Maybe 'Saturday Night Fever' in the backseat or something, but I didn't know (my wife) then."

Anonymous, "Some Film Stars Are Real Characters During Amour," *The Star-Ledger* (February 24, 1999), p. 3.

Mental gymnastics are not required in choosing from the menu. A half dozen antipasti ($5.95–$9,95); four pasta selections ($11.95–$12.95); and three secondi ($15.95–$16.95) are traditional favourites. Now, since a new menu is in the works, created by the newly hired chef Sam Greco, this might be an opportune time to call a spade a spade and stop fiddling with nickels. Does $5.95 lure anyone into thinking the cost is not really $6?

    Sara Waxman, "Galileo a Delicious Rediscovery," *The Toronto Sun* (March 7, 1999), p. C15.

Hats off to Likud deputy minister Michael Eitan. He is the only politician in the country who has had the guts to call a spade a spade: until proven otherwise, Aryeh Deri is a crook, a man who brought totally unacceptable norms of behavior to Israeli political life, who cost the country hundreds of millions of shekels, who took bribes, and who used public monies to purchase a jacuzzi and imported toilets for his duplex apartment. No amount of public relations can change these facts.

    Hirsh Goodman, "Moral Turpitude," *The Jerusalem Post* (March 26, 1999), p. B8.

The decision of the United States and its NATO allies to strike Yugoslavia is a very dangerous step fraught with unpredictable consequences not only for Europe but for the whole world. Let us call a spade a spade; it's an aggression.

    Mikhail Gorbachev, "U.S. Showing 'Victory Complex' in Kosovo Risky Game," *The Houston Chronicle* (March 30, 1999), p. A21.

"Because Gray Davis is so new, I think there was some reluctance among different leaders to call a spade a spade and say what they really felt," said Elena Soto-Chapa of the Mexican-American Legal Defense and Educational Fund. The good news for Davis is that he was able to push reforms through the Legislature that, if proposed by a Republican governor, would most likely have been dead on arrival.

    Ed Mendel, "Democrats Still Griping Despite Their Return to Top," *The San Diego Union-Tribune* (April 5, 1999), p. A3.

Could someone please take pity on ordinary Kiwis and form a political party dedicated to calling a spade a spade? Plain English is clearly out of favor as restless bureaucracies spawn a bewildering maze of titles and labels designed to disguise the obvious and befuddle the innocent. [...] A political party determined to call things by their plain, down-to-earth titles would win huge support from voters weary of costly rebranding for rebranding's sake.

    Anonymous, "Befuddling Nomenclature," *The Dominion* (April 15, 1999), p. 8.

Some movies are dumb. Some movies are dumber. "Lost and Found" is the dumbest. Please don't think this judgment too harsh. In this business it's important to call a spade a spade. David Spade, that is. The elfin guy who gets upstaged by a dog in every scene they share.
    Chuck Graham, "Spade Digs Himself a Deep Hole in 'Lost'," *The Tuscon Citizen* (April 22, 1999), p. L23.

"Lost & Found"? Let's Call a Spade a Flop
"Lost & Found" quickly loses its way in its attempt to copy "There's Something About Mary," and David Spade has no one to blame but himself.
    Jeff Strickler, "'Lost & Found': Let's Call a Spade a Flop," *Star Tribune* (April 23, 1999), p. E15.

"Excuse me," said a Ferret emerging from a large white house. "We in the White House prefer describing it as a 'humanitarian mission'."
"I say we should call a spade a spade," shouted a Hippopotamus, who was one of a large group of Hippopotami milling about atop a rise. "We on Capitol Hill prefer to describe it as an 'armed conflict'."
    Arthur Hoppe, "Oh, What a Lovely ...," *The San Francisco Chronicle* (May 3, 1999), p. A23 (*Alice in Wonderland* parody about war in the former Yugoslavia).

It was with great consternation that I read your [Darko Nadic's] eloquent letter to the editor. You must think Americans are stupid, as you are on the faculty of political science (or shall we call a spade a spade "on the propaganda ministry of Serbia") at Belgrade University. You, my dear Dr. Nadic, have been put into the position of the late Mr. Goebbels of Nazi Germany.
    Fred Andrews, "Holocaust Survivor Replies to Letter-Writer from Belgrade," *Florida Today* (June 16, 1999), p. A11.

"Let's call a spade a spade," said David Shambaugh, a China scholar at George Washington University here. "We have a relationship of strategic competition with China."
    Jim Mann, "Fears of Chinese Spying Only Deepen U.S. Mistrust," *Los Angeles Times* (May 20, 1999), p. A1.

"To hell with post-colonial sensitivities," said James Fergusson, a spokesman for Carlos Westendorp, the international community's High

Representative who is overseeing the implementation of the Dayton Agreement which ended the Bosnian war. "Let's call a spade a spade. You can't make any agreement stick unless you have complete power."
> Patrick Bishop, "Conflict in the Balkans," *The Daily Telegraph* (May 27, 1999), p. 20.

It's time to call a spade a spade. Without getting personal about the character of our commander in chief, it's time for Congress to stop showing fear and tell the president he does not have the authority to take this nation into an undeclared war.
> Anonymous, "Pentagon Out of Line," *The Washington Times* (June 1, 1999), p. A14.

As well as taking offense at your logic saying the president was playing word games again in "failing to 'fess up to the thefts on his watch," your cutesy language is almost as irritating as your wishy-washy statement that Clinton seems to have been "playing with words." Straight out, this editorial seems to deliberately excuse the inexcusable. Is it too hard for you to call a spade a spade and say that a serious threat to national security occurred while Clinton was supposed to be, above all else, the defender of our national security. Oh well, St. Louis has yet to be attacked.
> Kathy Gumersell, "Clinton 'Word Games' Are Outright Lies," *St. Louis Post-Dispatch* (June 7, 1999), p. D14.

I was upset after reading the June 18 article about the Canada geese roundup. It said the birds would be sent to food-processing plants to be "euthanized." Why not call a spade a spade? The geese will be slaughtered, probably like farm poultry: They'll be hoisted by their feet on an assembly line, their throats will be slit and then they'll be dumped into a vat of boiling water.
> Grace Fedor, "Geese Will be Slaughtered, not 'Euthanized'," *The Plain Dealer* (July 2, 1999), p. B8.

2000s

It's Time to Call a Spade a Spade
The first week of a new millennium is a good time for the taking of stock, but so far as television was concerned it was back to basics. The fireworks had hardly faded when the small screen brought us down to

earth with the hardiest old faithfuls in the schedulers' armoury: period drama and gardening.

Robert Winder, "It's Time to Call a Spade a Spade," *The Independent* (January 9, 2000), p. 14.

His client used the Internet to accuse Uni-Marts Inc. executives of mismanaging the convenience store chain, lawyer Bret Southard told a Centre County judge yesterday. "But so what? In this country, you have a right to call a spade a spade," Southard told Common Pleas Judge David Grine. "This is a case of [Uni-Marts] trying to address its own mismanagement by trying to blame guys posting messages on the Internet."

Tom Gibb, "Accusations Defended in Uni-Marts Libel Case," *Pittsburgh Post-Gazette* (May 25, 2000), p. C10.

"We have to take a long hard look at ourselves and decide now if we want to take a vacation or if we want to play hard for our jersey the rest of the way," United coach Thomas Rongen said. "We have to call a spade a spade. In this league you can't defend the way we are and win games. It's suicide."

Steve Spencer, "United Is Kept at Bay," *The Washington Post* (July 5, 2000), p. D1.

It's time someone has the gumption to call a spade a spade when it comes to the Brewers. The new skipper, Davey Lopes, should have stayed where he was or, better yet, sent where Phil Garner was sent: packing.

Anonymous, "Speak Out! Letters from Readers," *Milwaukee Journal Sentinel* (July 16, 2000), p. C2.

[Mayor James] Coutts said he has become increasingly upset by the council's gridlock over development of a second business park, "micromanagement" of city staff members by aldermen and a heightened political atmosphere on the council. "I'm going to start saying what needs to be said. I'm going to call a spade a spade. I've just about had it with all this political stuff," he said.

Anonymous, "Ozaukee County News Roundup," *Milwaukee Journal Sentinel* (August 20, 2000), p. Z3.

Finally! A newspaper that calls a spade a spade! The Christian Coalition has proven to be nothing but a radical, right-wing, power-hungry, partisan demagogue, losing sight of Christ's commands to "Win the lost," "Love thy neighbor" and "Judge not lest you be judged." Instead, it spends all its time and energy trying to enforce its own moral code through legislation by trying to destroy perfectly good politicians and getting its own right-wing cronies elected.

>Kathy Polleschultz, "Heavy-Handed Tactics," *Tulsa World* (November 20, 2000), no pp. given.

A series in four parts, each roughly covering a quarter of the century, "Sex in the 20th Century" identifies each of the following as incentives to sexual activity: the swinging, anything-goes Jazz Age, but also the resulting Great Depression; World War II — as well as its conclusion; marriage and divorce; popular music, dancing, beat poetry, birth-control devices, Hollywood, feminism, medical studies, Roe vs. Wade, drugs; and well, let's call a spade a spade — the availability of sex leads to sex, period.

>David Kronke, "History Channel Looks at Sex in the Last Century," *St. Petersburg Times* (April 23, 2001), p. B2.

"Medicaid was designed as a safety net," [Stephen] Moses said. "Not as an option for the majority of the country."
"We need to call a spade a spade," [Robert] Pearson added. "Medicaid is welfare and, obviously, people don't know that."

>Ed Fanselow, "Most Consumers Still Expect Medicare Will Pay for LTC Needs," *McKnight's Long-Term Care News* (August 27, 2001), p. 3.

Recruitment professionals are rarely shy of over-promotion when it comes to job descriptions. To call a spade a spade is anathema to many. A shop assistant is a "sales consultant" and a dustman is a "waste professional." Applicants for some of the dullest jobs are told they are entering a new life of thrills and endless fun.

>Jim Pickard, "Warts-and-all Hiring Policy," *Financial Times* (August 28, 2001), p. 11.

Real estate institute president Valda Walsh wants the Bracks Government to honour a promise to lower the highest stamp duty in the country. She is a successful businesswoman who drives a blue Porsche and calls a spade a spade. Valda Walsh is an energetic grandmother, who a year ago

became the second women in 70 years to be elected president of Real Estate Institute of Victoria [Australia].
  Anthony Black, "Duty Calls," *Sunday Herald Sun* (October 7, 2001), p. 77.

Even as U.S. Defence Secretary Donald Rumsfeld dispatched more than 100 military aircraft to the Persian Gulf, he still did not delineate who is the foe. "There is a real resistance on the part of western leaders to call a spade a spade," declares Joseph Farah, an American of Christian Arabic lineage.
  Robert Owen, "War Against Whom, Specifically?" *Alberta Report* (October 8, 2001), p. 10.

Reading the *Journal Sentinel's* articles on the attacks on the World Trade Center and the Pentagon, as well as on our present war against "terrorists," I wish editors would stop labeling these people just as terrorists. We have provided them with a title that makes them proud of what they have done. Let's call a spade a spade and provide them with the proper title: murderers and terrorists.
  Don Morgan, "Let's Call Terrorists What They Really Are," *Milwaukee Journal Sentinel* (October 14, 2001), p. J5.

While most restauranteurs think it's clever to stuff their menus with obscure gastronomic gobbledegook, most of us would rather call a spade a spade and order exactly what we want — even have pudding before the starter if it's what you really feel like.
  Gillian Glover, "Everyone's Eating It," *The Scotsman* (October 27, 2001), p. 25.

Would that the American media were more willing to call a spade a spade when it come to America's own sponsors of terrorism. Instead, we are regularly treated to experts with far too much practical expertise in the field. A good example is ABC News analyst Vincent Cannistraro, who also shows up frequently in other media venues (NPR's "All Things Considered" on Sept. 26) as an expert on terrorism. Cannistraro's former employer was the Central Intelligence Agency where as a high-ranking official he was in charge of the arming and training the contras in Nicaragua during the early '80s.
  Daniel Hellinger, "A Shallow Media Can Inflict Deep Damage," *St. Louis Journalism Review* (October 2001), p. 20.

[Camryn] Manheim: My family has always been very philanthropic, donating time and money to charities. But when you become a celebrity, you become inundated with requests to be on their boards, be on their letterheads. When you get honored by a charity, they're choosing you because of how much money you can bring in. Let's call a spade a spade: It's how many tables can you fill at an event. Charities are businesses; it's a racket [laughing]. Of course, they're all trying to do something very good.
    Susan Douglas, "Camryn Manheim [Interview]," *The Progressive* (October 2001), p. 33.

It has already been pointed out in the sixth chapter on "Literary Texts from the 16th to the 20th Century" that some authors have expanded the formulaic "spade"-phrase for the sake of emphasis and/or satire. Such extensions can, of course, also be found in the mass media, as the following final examples illustrate:

El Salvador has succeeded Vietnam as a Cold War pawn, and it is with dismay that those of us who remember the American entanglement in the Vietnam conflict watch the United States again put its reputation on the line. There are the same massive infusions of military equipment, with the same strange inability to keep down a desperate peasantry. There are the same mouthings of such words as "democracy" and "elections", and the same appeals to friendly countries to lend legitimacy to these frauds. The most friendly action that Canada can take on behalf of her great neighbor is to call a spade a spade, and the grave that it digs a grave. There are too many of them in Latin America.
    Andrew Gibson, "El Salvador Has Succeeded Vietnam as a Cold War Pawn," *The Globe and Mail* (March 12, 1982), p. P6.

After celebrating mass with 40 bishops and 1,000 priests, the Pope delivered his homily. He lamented that there is today a growing tendency to no longer call a spade a spade, a sin a sin.
    Stanley Oziewicz, "Nothing Can Replace God, Pontiff Tells Cheering Crowd," *The Globe and Mail* (September 11, 1984), p. P1.

But [Marlene Dietrich] on pediatricians: "I love them all. They love children. They help children. They read a baby's eyes. They call a spade a spade and a rash a rash. They concentrate on the patient. One at a time. They set their minds to not evoke fear. Their hearts must be big, sweet lollipops."

Don Freeman, "Point of View," *The San Diego Union-Tribune* (August 21, 1986), p. D15.

We are constantly warned by our intellectual leaders against the shallow assumption that America is uniquely virtuous; and, well, I have to agree. America isn't uniquely virtuous. It just happens to be worlds more virtuous than the Soviet Union and Nicaragua and Cuba and Libya and Zimbabwe and all the other despotisms, communist or non-communist, you can think of. From which it follows that America enjoys the right to call a spade a spade, an enemy an enemy, and to act accordingly, in the full light of day. Anyway, it would seem so to me; but I confess to being remorselessly old-fashioned.
    William Murchison, "U.S. Shouldn't Fear Hitting Its Enemies," *The Dallas Morning News* (October 11, 1986), p. A31.

But Rabbi Weinreb cautioned against such solutions [to the Jerusalem issue]: "I have no problems with hearing church bells ringing in Jerusalem, or with seeing mosques in Jerusalem," he said. "I have a problem with whether or not there will be synagogues in Jerusalem. I think we have to call a spade a spade, and call Judenrein Judenrein."
    Rona S. Hirsch, "Eternal Concern: Debate on Jerusalem's Fate Offered Glimpes into the Varying Views of the Holy City," *Baltimore Jewish Times* June 13, 1997), p. 30.

Remember, the guy behind the mike gets the last word. His mission, apparently, is to illuminate the olive of truth in a sub sandwich full of baloney, to call a spade a spoade, an imbecile an imbecile and keep the phone lines lighted up.
    Ken August, "Radio Name-Calling a Poor Substitute for Insight," *The Sacramento Bee* (April 11, 1999), p. N4.

The primary reason is that orthodox Christians want to get rid of a Muslim population (which happens to be ethnically different). But of course Western (Christian) owned media could not possibly call a spade a spade and a Christian terrorist a Christian terrorist.
    Rafiq Ahmad, "Postbag-Media Should Call a Spade a Spade," *Bangkok Post* (April 25, 1999), no pp. given.

Dear Inky Wretch, It would take too long — as long as some of those unreadable columns you write with all those big words you probably make up — to tell you my opinion of this year's Miss America Pageant, and, yes, it is a beauty pageant, no matter what they call it now. I will not have my words censored. Even if the pageant's wimpy sponsors censor themselves and call it something else — a Celebration of Multiculturalism or whatever. I still call a spade a spade and a beauty pageant a beauty pageant. I hope I make myself clear.

> Paul Greenberg, "Miss America Parody," *The Washington Times* (November 4, 2000), p. A12.

Call a Spade a Spade, and an Ad an Ad
I had always thought a contract was a bargained-for exchange of valuable consideration between two willing parties, and that the agreement could later be enforced if necessary. But in the non-profit sector, contracts are not always contracts. And, by the way, a charitable contribution does not always spring from the charitable impulse, nor is it always a contribution. [...] Better we should call a spade a spade when it comes to corporate sponsorships. Call it the advertising that it is. Pay the taxes on it, and leave the idea of a charitable contribution, and the English language, just a bit less sullied.

> Bruce Collins, "Call a Spade a Spade, and an Ad an Ad," *Corporate Legal Times* (December 2000), p. 7.

Olga Borodina, a Russian mezzo-soprano, is one of the finest singers in the world. She is also one of the finest singers ever. Now, most critics would rather swallow poison than make that last point, at least in public. Moderation is the name of the game. [...] But this is a bit of a cop-out: Part of the critic's duty is to call a spade a spade, or an immortal an immortal — even if "prematurely." We have no trouble saluting the past. But contemporary performers? They will have to wait their turn: from the grave.

> Jay Nordlinger, "Greatness, Here & Now," *National Review* (May 28, 2001), no pp. given.

Doubtlessly many more references of the "spade"-phrase could be found as other databases become available on the internet. But the result would basically stay the same, i.e., journalists of the regional, national, and international mass media like the proverbial expression "to call a spade a spade." They often cite it as "Let's call a spade a spade" to call for more honesty in plain English vocabulary by politicians and people in the public eye. Editors of such renowned American newspapers as *The New York Times*, *The Wall Street Journal*, *The Washington Post*, etc. seem to see nothing wrong with using the traditional phrase. Political correctness does not appear to have purged the phrase from the mass media in this country. The English-language media in Africa, Australia, Canada, Great Britain, India, and Israel also continue to use the expression without any worries that it might offend readers who possibly interpret it as a racial slur. Clearly the "spade"-phrase in its traditional meaning of calling for plain and factual language is alive and well in the mass media.

The press and its readers (as stated in letters to the editor) want the truth expressed in understandable and clear language without "beating around the bush" by employing meaningless euphemisms. Often the "spade"-expression appears in headlines to draw special attention to the fact that "It's time someone has the gumption to call a spade a spade." It does indeed at times take civil courage to express one's views directly, as Pittsburgh lawyer Bret Southard expressed it so poignantly: "In this country, you have a right to call a spade a spade." I assume that he was not aware of the possible problems with this sentence if he had stated it in front of an African-American audience. The classical phrase "to call a spade a spade" is in itself and in its traditional meaning not a slur, but it can become one in certain contexts. But that is exactly the point that the many excerpts from the mass media in this chapter are supposed to bring across. As a call for plain English in human communication the old proverbial expression continues to be an effective linguistic and metaphorical *leitmotif* in the mass media. Extremists of the political correctness campaign have not succeeded in "killing" the phrase in its use as an innocuous call for truthfulness. But we must, of course, add an important caveat at the end of this chapter: only the context in which the phrase is used can reveal whether it is in fact a harmless metaphor or whether there is an indirect racial slur intended by it. To make such an evaluation on ethical grounds, we need texts in contexts. As will be shown in chapters nine and ten, there is no doubt that the phrase has been used as a slur and that it has been understood as such. The question at the end of this chapter is, of course, once again whether the classical expression should be avoided in all contexts because of its possible racial implications? One thing is for certain, it would be impossible to read any racial interpretation into the many references of the phrase presented in this chapter dealing with national and international politics, economics, and various social issues.

IX.

Innocuous Proverbial Phrase or Racial Slur?

The previous chapter on the use of the phrase in the mass media included numerous references of the "spade"-expression that gave no hint whatsoever of an intended racial comment by the authors. So-called extreme political correctness does not appear to have had any influence on the modern use of the classical phrase. In fact, as can be seen from the following reference, even when writing about the subject of controlling what is proper language use, some journalists continue to employ it, seemingly utterly unaware of its different shades of meaning:

If you thought politics, social work and teaching were riddled with political correctness, try middle management. In general, it finds it hard to call a spade a spade and is imbued with slightly doubtful optimistic "correctness" that applauds the fact that, for example, when Richard Branson goes walkabout among his staff, he is wired up to a researcher who tells his earpiece the name and details of whoever he stops to have a quick chat with.
    Hilaire Gomer, "The Value for Employees of Management Brain-Storming," *The Daily Telegraph* (May 13, 1999), p. 69.

This unawareness or indifference to the racial interpretation of the phrase can also be found among black writers, who might simply be unaware of the problematic nature of the expression. In the following textual examples the contexts make it clear that the speakers or authors are black citizens, for the most part in fact African Americans. And yet, they use the "spade"-phrase simply in its old meaning of calling things by their proper names, i.e., making impartial and factual statements. The contexts also do not allow any racial interpretation of the phrase in these cases, and it would take political correctness to its extreme to see racial innuendos in these statements:

A black American from Canoga Park, [Rev. Kenneth] Frazier, who has never been to South Africa, told his audience [at Rancho Santiago College] of about 150 that the current unrest in that country is part of a Marxist strategy to put all of Africa under Soviet rule. [...] "I hope you're not fooled by Bishop Tutu, who, when he comes to the United States gets the red carpet rolled out," Frazier said of the Nobel laureate.

[...] "Tutu has declared by his own mouth that he's a Marxist. Why do we not have the courage to call a spade a spade?" Frazier asked.
Bob Sipchen, "Speakers Attack Apartheid, but Agreement Ends There," *Los Angeles Times* (November 28, 1985), p. 1.

"Whether classically trained or not, most of us young artists want a freedom, a glasnost, to create whatever kind of art we feel like creating. And it will be black art because we're black, not because we talk about jazz or rap or poverty or the South," says the 27-year-old [novelist Trey] Ellis, who was educated at Andover and Stanford. "We want," he goes on, "to get away from the notion of black sacred cows, that black art needs to be coddled. When we see something we don't like, we call a spade a spade. We are not wedded to the notion that the black audience needs positive images exclusively. We are wedded to the truth. And we think that the balance of the truth, when it comes out, will be positive."
David Nicholson, "Painting It Black: African American Artists in Search of a New Aesthetic," *The Washington Post* (December 10, 1989), p. G1.

"We have to call a spade a spade in Milwaukee: It's not like Selma, Ala., in the '60s, but we have institutional racism," Art Murchison said. He added, though, that minorities were impressed with Police Chief Philip Arreola and his bid for sensitivity training and introducing new recruits to the central city. "The strides he is attempting to make in our community cannot be successful if the community doesn't feel a sense of trust," Murchison said.
Katherine M. Skiba, "Victims' Families Want Officers to Stay Fired," *The Milwaukee Journal Sentinel* (October 16, 1992), p. B6.

A Georgia commission on racial and ethnic bias in the courts got off to a rocky start Friday when it drew criticism for preventing a witness from naming court personnel she felt had discriminated against her. Testifying at the first of a series of public hearings to be held around the state, Melinda Holloway, a black lawyer, attempted to name allegedly prejudiced judges in the Griffin Judicial Circuit. "I believe in calling a spade a spade," Holloway said. "A disease can kill you until you diagnose it and give it a name." She was stopped by commission co-chairman Clarence Cooper, who emphasized that the commission wanted to focus on "systematic" problems in the judicial ystem.

Mark Silk, "Panel on Bias Doesn't Let Witnesses Name Names: Lawyer Tries to Identify Prejudiced Judges," *Atlanta Constitution* (October 2, 1993), p. B5.

The traumas of the Million Man March and the O.J. Simpson verdict have forced America to focus its gaze once again on its lingering racial crisis. In sharpening our focus, they have done at least one good. By casting too bright a light on the realities of our unfinished racial agenda, they have scrambled the sordid use of coded and covert racial rhetoric by conventional politicians. We must now call a spade a spade, and, while it is good old American politics to fan racial division while pretending the opposite, it is far too risky to appear clearly to be doing so. But what exactly is the crisis which we gaze upon? For African Americans, these are genuinely the best and worst of times, at least since the ending of the formal Jim Crow laws. What is odd, however, is that, in the current rhetoric of race, the pain completely dominates the gain.

Orlando Patterson, "The Paradox of Integration: Why Whites and Blacks Seem so Divided," *The New Republic* (November 6, 1995), p. 24.

Growing up, I was somewhat timid and shy. Didn't dare challenge my parents' authority. Didn't have the nerve to call a spade a spade. Didn't possess much self-esteem. What a difference a few decades can make. Now family and friends will tell you that sometimes I have too much to say. I say this to that: The only way African-Americans of the turbulent 1960s delivered us to the so-called "good life" of the 1990s is because some folks had the gumption to rise up and speak out. Against segregation, they rose. Against unfair hiring and housing practices, they rose. Even while waging a war against attack dogs, and bricks, rocks and water pelting their bodies, they had the power to rise. Somewhere along the way, African-Americans relinquished control of that power base. Let today be the time to reclaim it.

Jeff Theodore, "Rise Up, Speak Out, Reclaim Our Power Base," *The Post-Standard* (February 26, 1996), p. A6.

By now, a resurgence of Klan activity in Alabama is being linked to the fires [at African-American churches across the South] — at least by some investigators. "The concentrated activity used to be in Georgia," said Loretta Ross, founder of the Atlanta-based Center for Human Rights Education and former research director for the Center for Democratic Renewal, which monitors hate groups. She says skinheads

— young, white supremacist Nazi-worshippers — have become the front-line warriors in racial hatred. "The older seasoned racists are hiding behind them," Ross said. [...] Ross, frustrated with the pace of investigation, said, "We need to call a spade a spade. These are hate crimes."

>Betsy M. Peoples, "No Turning Around, Say Blacks: Fires at African-American Churches Across the South Resurrect Memories of the Bad Old Days," *The Baltimore Sun* (June 16, 1996), p. F6.

Women and minorities. Blacks and women. How often have you heard the words? Whenever I hear them, I ask myself where this leaves black women, who, in effect, belong to both groups. Are they black first and women second, or what? [...] Will (white) women and their national and local organizations ever acknowledge how the civil rights struggle led by blacks created a climate in which employment equality for white women was made more acceptable? Will white women ever pay tribute to their unsung black sisters? Will they ever pay their debt? Let's hope so. Meanwhile, how about changing the words to "white women and minorities" and "blacks and white women?" Let's get real. Let's call a spade a spade.

>Richard G. Carter, "White Women Owe Huge, Unacknowledged Debt to Blacks," *The Capital Times* (August 15, 1996), p. A13.

When Eddie Murphy paid out $6.3m in cash to buy Cher's white Moroccan-inspired, Egyptian-decorated mansion with its eight bedrooms, gym, cinema, sunshine roof, swimming pool and moat, he was exactly where he thought he should be — at the top of the Hollywood Hills. Perched up there amid the Moorish towers and giant palms it could be seen for miles. This was a black artist who had hurdled racial barriers and was revelling in 1980s-style rewards. Living excessively was the best revenge. This was the outlaw on and off the screen, stage and record in the profane tradition of Lenny Bruce and Richard Pryor. He made it so fast by being quick, outrageous and savvy. He boasted with a cheeky grin that he called a spade as spade. He had his tongue around more four, seven and 12-letter words than the Spanish navy but, although he had attitude, he was not perceived as aggressive. Yet he never played Uncle Tom or the black stereotype, the number two man or the kerbsite drug addict; he was the action star (Beverly Hills Blues) or the hilarious con artist (Trading Places) and always the leading man.

>Douglas Thompson, "Who's so Nutty Now?" *The Herald* (September 21, 1996), p. 8.

Black Enterprise Magazine publisher Earl Graves thinks nothing about calling a spade a spade if he has to. He looked President Clinton straight in the eye at a recent Harlem forum on welfare reform and told him not to expect Black businesses to do the government's job. Graves was reacting to a call by Clinton for the private sector to be more aggressive and creative in providing job opportunities for those on public assistance. He didn't seem to think too much about the plea and decided to set the record straight. The publisher said studies conducted by his magazine, show that Black-owned companies are more likely than other businesses to hire and train residents of urban communities, where 43 percent of nation's poor live.

J. Zamgba Browne, "'We Won't Do Your Work for You,' Graves to Prez," *New York Amsterdam News* (March 1, 1997), p. 10.

[The Rev. Al] Sharpton [who as an African American in 1992 ran as a candidate for the United States Senate in the New York Democratic primary] may not get the acknowledgment he deserves in his lifetime. However, his name may live on for a long time. The perceived underhanded handling of the post-primary, and the ruckus Sharpton created as a result, will definitely lead to changes in rules for future elections, and will no doubt be referred to as the "Sharpton Issue." Am I lobbying, you may ask? Naw! Just calling a spade a spade! Yeah man!

Carl B. Moxie, "Lessons for the Political Future," *Everybody's: The Caribbean-American Magazine* (October 31, 1997), p. 20.

Another interesting point is the history of whites castigating Blacks who dare call a spade a spade while fighting systematic injustice. "Historically, any word of protest against a white man by a Negro was insolence or disorderly conduct," noted Richard Wright, Jr. in his 1911 Penn Wharton School doctoral dissertation entitled, "The Negro in Pennsylvania — A Study in Economic History." Wright is the father of trailblazing Black Philadelphia educator, Dr. Ruth Wright-Hayre, who died recently. In the racist milieu of American History, the First Amendment right of whites to express opinions is sacred even when factually inaccurate while opinions expressed by Blacks are suspect regardless of factual accuracy.

Linn Washington, "NAACP Hit with Criticism for Calling a Spade a Spade," *Philadelphia Tribune* (February 10, 1998), p. A2.

He [Coleman A. Young] was salty, provocative, profound. He came up from the cottonfields, up from the auto plants, up from the union ranks and became the first Black mayor of the city of Detroit. For 20 turbu-

lent, exciting, call-a-spade-a-spade years, Coleman A. Young held Motown in his hands, and when he died recently at the age of 79 after a long struggle with emphysema, New Detroit President William Beckham said, "Coleman Young is Detroit."
  Anonymous, "Coleman A. Young 1918-1997: Requiem for an Urban Giant," *Ebony* (February 1998), p. 140.

And, the recent demolition of the Ritz Theater was literally a technical knockout! They may as well have torn the whole thing down for what its [*sic*] worth. For crying-out-loud, is nothing sacred anymore? Do the perpetrators have consciences? I doubt it. Why humor us with the "Putting on the Ritz" folly, when the true intentions seem to be to crush our spirits and erase our glorious past. Sorry to sound so ungrateful, but I like to cut the bull and call a spade, a spade. I am sick and tired of Masquerades! Over the past few decades in the wake of Integration and Urban Renewal, the traditional Black Community (once a close knit community) has become utterly disintegrated and is now being trampled down in the name of progress. This dilemma is occurring all across "America the Beautiful" with the blessed assurance that Black Folk could care less, now that they have arrived in the "Promiseland." I hate to rain on our little parade Brothers and Sisters, but compared to what Dr. Martin Luther King Jr. saw on that Mountain Top thirty years ago, what we have today is "just a mirage". I don't think the man sacrificed his life, so that a few of us could wallow in the lap of luxury, while the majority of us are still struggling to be "Free at Last."
  Linda Mitchell Harper, "Designer of LaVilla Afghan Speaks Out," *Jacksonville Free Press* (April 15, 1998), p. 1.

  Most of these references deal with explicit racial matters and concerns, and yet the authors (most likely all African Americans) continue to use the "spade"-expression in its traditional meaning, i.e., without any apparent awareness that to some people, both black and white, the proverbial expression can be insulting. One would have thought that these writers would have consciously shied away from using the questionable phrase that to some readers might be offensive. But nothing is further from the truth. The proverbial expression appears as a metaphorical amplification of the claim or request that the blatant truth must be expressed at all costs. There are no signs of a racial slur in these references that deal with serious racial issues in the United States.
  Before moving on to references where the "spade"-phrase is unfortunately used as a racial slur, let me cite this following account out

of the (Malaysia) *New Straits Times* from 1996 which had been sent to me by my colleague and friend Charles Clay Doyle in this truncated form: "The trouble with calling a spade a spade is they, the spades, don't take kindly to it." He had located this text by way of a *Lexis-Nexis* database search, and when I received it, I immediately thought that I had obtained a definitely racist use of the proverbial expression, with "the spades" doubtlessly referring to Blacks. But when I located the complete text on the internet, it had absolutely nothing to do with Blacks or racial matters at all! In fact, the newspaper article entitled "Let's Make Sure Truth Prevails" deals with honest and factual newspaper reporting. Here is the text in its entirety as a superb example for the importance of contextual analysis:

The trouble with calling a spade a spade is they, the spades, don't take kindly to it. The bigger the spade, the bigger the reaction. And, as spades are wont to, some of them try to bury you, pushing criticism and truth into the ground.
It's hard being a columnist in this age of hypocrisy and bigotry. Where political correctness is an excuse for obfuscating the truth. Plain speaking is frowned upon and the fundamental right to criticise is bound, legally and otherwise, in threats, both implied and explicit.
In sports, the prerogative to freedom of expression has been compromised. Sports, where a man's worth or a team's performance is based solely on results. Defeats and bad performances meant criticism, success praise.
Time was we used to say black was black and white was white, not shades of grey. Doublespeak is the order of the day. The press of propaganda. It's all down to semantics and word play. But criticism, by its very nature, is meant to take someone or something to task. Without fear or favour, it is meant to question and expose misdeeds. Trouble is, nobody likes to be criticised even though it comes with the turf they covet. They mouth platitudes like "we can take constructive criticism, but not when it is personal." But tell me when is criticsm not personal for whoever is at the receiving end? It's an illogical inference, the irrational rage of men taking offence to being exposed for what they are. Refusing to accept it.
So too I have been faulted by individuals who think that I have gone overboard in describing how sports has lost its moral resonance. Individuals who have been the object of my criticsm. Believe me, it's so much easier to say good things and sing praises in chorus. But that would be encouraging, and living, a lie.

Many are the times that I have felt like chucking it in. Why rile and upset, make enemies, when it would be so much easier to tow the line. But then I would be cheating myself and wouldn't be able to sleep nights. After more than 20 years in the business, I am privy to information that is kept from the public. As a journalist, it is my responsibility to see that the people are informed. My conscience and love of sport insist that I continue to do so.

The point here is the people have the right to know, to be informed. We cannot nurture ignorance as a cover for incompetence or wrongs. Honesty, integrity, credibility, accountability and sportsmanship must prevail above all else. We must not forget that criticising unreasonable people and things is the intrinsic right of every citizen. It is his unavoidable responsibility — his duty.

Leaders, those in public positions, politicians in power and in opposition, sports officials, are only human. Only the critical supervision of the people will ensure that they make fewer mistakes or not give in to temptations. It's a safeguard against duplicity and deception. Against those with personal agendas who don public masks of selfless dedication when they are solely motivated, and driven, by self interest. That means free, unrestricted inquiry, seeking the truth from facts, no matter how much the opposition and the intransigence of those who would want it otherwise. Those who think that they have a caveat on reason and rhyme. On what is right for all of us. Such assumptions, that the people don't know enough or cannot comprehend, are not only presumptuous but an affront to society. Most of us are fallible and have to be told and reminded of our faults and mistakes. The people must be informed so that they will know and have that right of judgment. That is why we have newspapers to disseminate information as objectively as possible, and allow the masses to differentiate right from wrong. Truth from lies. For the public to think and reason. Otherwise, we will have more misguided souls like Frankenstein's crippled lackey, Igor, or Pavlov's canines, who are conditioned to react rather than reason. Who would use strongarm tactics, rather than the process of intelligent thought, to satisfy their masters. Mindless violence is not a tool of rational beings.

The people are no longer ignorant, cowed masses. The information revolution has seen to that. The Malaysian public, by and large, can see flagrant abuses of individual liberty and intolerence for what they are. Their silence does not mean agreement. It's often a disquiet of disapproval. Of disgust. The people, moderates and conservatives alike, may differ on social issues, but they know when the right of the individual is being trammelled.

We should get over the notion that we must not offend certain indivduals by criticising them if they so deserve. If we sincerely hope to transcend the culture of blame and shame those in position, we must first learn to accept responsibility, accountability, integrity and transparency as the creed. Criticsm — fair, just and objective — will see to it. Don't be deceived. Don't let the spades bury the truth.
    Fauzi Omar, "Let's Make Sure Truth Prevails," *New Straits Times* (November 19, 1996), p. 48.

This is a courageous indictment of political correctness in its extreme form. Clearly the truth must be told, even if it hurts at times. As the author of the essay argues quite convincingly, things must be called by their proper names at least once in a while. The journalist could use the proverbial expression "to call a spade a spade" and even the noun "spade" in Malaysia without having to worry that they would be interpreted as a racial slur in this context. Nevertheless, these references might have been somewhat problematic if they had appeared in an American newspaper, where the beginning and the end of the essay with their "spade" references might have been questioned, even though the context clearly shows that no racial slur is intended.
    And yet, as has been mentioned in various chapters in this study, the "spade"-phrase can be interpreted as a racial slur. As I indicated at the end of chapter five, two dictionaries of the 1990s make a point of alerting readers to this possible understanding of the classical phrase. It will be recalled that the first of these warnings appeared in a general phrasal dictionary, where the compiler decided to take a moral stance:

call a spade a spade, to. [...] A cliché since the nineteenth century, it acquired a slightly more sinister meaning when "spade" became an offensive slang word for a black person.
    Christine Ammer, *Have a Nice Day — No Problem! A Dictionary of Clichés* (New York: Dutton, 1992), p. 48.

But the author of a highly specialized dictionary from the era of "political correctness" actually included a reference to the stereotypical meaning of the "spade"-phrase one year earlier, this time calling for its avoidance in verbal communication:

call a spade a spade get to the point, speak plainly / straight from the shoulder / straight out, be up front / frank / on the up and up / above

board. The expression is associated with a racial slur and should be avoided.
> Rosalie Maggio, *The Bias-Free Word Finder. A Dictionary of Nondiscriminatory Language* (Boston: Beacon, 1991), p. 61.

Of course, as is so often the case with such agenda-driven dictionaries, the author failed to give any contextual examples where the "spade"-phrase is used as a racial slur! This is also the case in another invaluable scholarly observation by Philip Cohen, an expert on the multi-faceted nature of racism and its linguistic expression. He is definitely aware of the fact that the proverbial expression "to call a spade a spade" could, under certain circumstances, be understood as a racial stereotype. But he speaks in generalities, failing to give any examples of the different semantic shades of the expression. Nevertheless, his general comments, quoted here at length, will be a most fitting bridge for my presentation of contextual references of the "spade"-phrase as a racial slur. Here is what Philip Cohen has to say in general:

There are a number of reasons why such attempts [of strong-arm tactics in schools] to legislate against ideology fail. In the first place they are forced to adopt technologies of surveillance and control which are identical to those already exercised by the state and sometime to deploy them in an even more extreme form. Interestingly enough, the propaganda produced by both physical and moral forcers often explicitly mimics the discursive strategies of totalitarian power. "Racist Beware — Elwar is watching You" says one well-known campaign flyer issued by East London Workers Against Racism. Haringey Council issues an invitation for a conference on housing and ethnic minorities, entitled "Stamping Out Racism", which positions the readers as having his or her face stamped on, in sad fulfillment of George Orwell's prophecy for the world after 1984.
The battle for young hearts and minds will clearly not be won by such means. When it is no longer possible to "call a spade a spade", because the level of connotations, which is always open to multiple associations, including racist ones, has been shut down "By Order", then denotation itself becomes a mere exercise in the language game of Power. But when meanings can no longer be subject to negotiation, it becomes impossible to question or contest their ideological construction. The chronic repetition of "correct thought" is probably the quickest way to kill the development of any critical awareness; when the anti-racist message is

Innocuous Proverbial Phrase or Racial Slur? 189

only the same old slogan we can be sure that young people will not listen to it!
No one seriously engaged in anti-racist education would entertain such a purely repressive strategy. This is not unfortunately, true of some political activists, of an authoritarian persuasion. Yet they are their own worst enemies, for in their failure to understand and engage with the unconscious reasoning of racism, they run the risk of reproducing it within their own practices of representation.

    Philip Cohen, "The Perversions of Inheritance: Studies in the Making of Multi-Racist Britain," in P. Cohen and Harwant S. Bains (eds.), *Multi-Racist Britain* (Houndmills, Hampshire: Macmillan Education, 1988), pp. 9-118 (here pp. 93-94).

Cohen makes an incredibly important point here regarding the various shades of meaning of the proverbial expression "to call a spade a spade." While he does not give examples as such, he certainly states that they include racist ones. In addition, he draws attention to the fact that language in general and the "spade"-phrase in particular are governed by different levels of connotations and are therefore open to multiple associations which need to be negotiated during communicative acts, both oral and written. This is the point, of course! As has been stated a number of times already in our study, the traditional phrase "to call a spade a spade" is not a slur as such, but in particular contexts it might take on stereotypical meanings. What is needed is a more conscious and differentiating use of language rather than a mind police that outlaws the modern use of the phrase altogether. Overly zealous proponents of "political correctness" might in fact make things even worse by starting a declared crusade against this phrase which, more often than not (or even hardly ever), is anything but a racist slur. The phrase should, if at all, be used with care so that no one will feel insulted, but it need not necessarily disappear from the stock of metaphorical phrases going back to classical times. We must also keep in mind that the "spade"-phrase is part of all the Englishes spoken around the world. Anglo-American perceptions are not necessarily shared by speakers in other countries for whom the expression "to call a spade a spade" is perfectly harmless.

    But let us now turn to a number of contextualized references that make it abundantly clear that it is not always wise to make use of the "spade"-phrase. A strange introductory paragraph was used by Betty Winston Bayé in her article on "Life in the Shadows" that appeared in 1996 in the Louisville *Courier-Journal*, especially in light of the fact that the article dealt among others with the African-American writer Anatole Broyard, who "yearned to be a great writer, but not a black writer":

> He or she who laughs loudest around the old office coffee pot, on the 9th hole, or from a podium before thousands, may not be who they say they are. Maybe the stubborn impoliteness — framed merely as calling a spade a spade — ha, ha, ha — is because the speakers are spades themselves. Perpetrators, who fear ridicule if word ever leaks that — ohmygosh! — they're one of the dreaded them. No surprise. The world is overrun with people who are passing. Blacks passing as whites. Cowards passing as courageous. Knaves passing as knights. Gays passing as straights. Foes passing as friends. Fools passing as wise. Evil passing as good. Much more people than presumably frightened gays reside in closets; I was reminded of that in my recent stack of reading. Of particular note were Henry Louis Gates' essay "The True Lies of Anatole Broyard" in the *New Yorker*; reviews of David Hadju's new book, *Lush Life: A Biography of Billy Strayborn*, and Patrice Gaines' 1994 autobiography, *Laughing in the Dark*. Two wonderful writers and a brilliant composer. Each made choices with which others may quarrel, but choices that each figured were less painful than the truth.
> Betty Winston Bayé, "Life in the Shadows," *The Courier-Journal* (July 18, 1996), p. A11.

The journalist was playing with words, but she did employ the "spade"-phrase together with the slang term "spade" meaning African American. Stylistic wordplay or not, this was hardly an appropriate beginning of an article dealing with the complexities of people passing for something they are not, especially for black intellectuals and artists passing as whites or at least ignoring or hiding their ethnicity.

Perhaps U.S Senator Jake Garn also did not mean to make a racial slur in the following statement, but the context makes such an interpretation possible, especially since his attack on the political motives of Rev. Jesse Jackson appear to be racially charged:

> U.S. Senator Jake Garn said yesterday he wondered whether Rev. Jesse Jackson would have gone to Syria seeking the release of U.S. Navy Lieutenant Robert Goodman had the downed flier not been black. "I have to ask the question, 'Would Mr. Jackson have been over there if Lieut. Goodman weren't a black?' Sometimes you have to call a spade a spade," Senator Garn, a Utah Republican, said in a telephone interview from Washington, D.C., with Salt Lake City radio station KDYL.

Senator Garn said he was happy Lieut. Goodman was freed, "but the methods that were used — the absolute blatant nature of the politics involved — stink." Mr. Jackson, who is seeking the Democratic presidential nomination, headed back from the Middle East yesterday with Lieut. Goodman, whom the Syrians had called a prisoner of war. When a reporter for another radio station asked Senator Garn about his choice of words, the senator said: "That's a common phrase. It just means being candid — call things what they are." Later, Bill Hendrix, Senator Garn's press secretary, said he had been authorized to respond to reporters' questions about the senator's statement. "To construe his comment, 'Let's call a spade a spade,' as a racial slur is ludicrous at best. Those who believe it was, you have to question the mischief of their minds." "It is a term that is quite common in the West and is part of Senator Garn's vernacular," Mr. Hendrix added. "He does not apologize for it."

Anonymous, "'Call a Spade a Spade' Quip Defended by Utah Senator," *The Globe and Mail* (January 4, 1984), p. P11.

Obviously Bill Hendrix did not know anything about the much older classical tradition of the phrase, when he stressed its common currency in the West of the United States. But Senator Garn certainly made a judgmental error when he dug in his heels and refused to acknowledge the fact that his statement could be interpreted as a racial slur, especially in the context of the other questionable parts of his statement. He would have done well to apologize, no doubt about it.

Here is a second "spade"-reference directed at Rev. Jesse Jackson, this time however being blatantly racist. Little wonder that its originator signed off with the ridiculous name "innocentbystander," clearly not wanting to disclose his/her true identity. Interestingly enough the author identifies himself/herself as being African American, albeit clearly of the conservative and bigoted type:

As a Black Conservative, I cannot tell you how much we Blacks need to get rid of Jesse and Al [Gore]. [...] Jesse Jackson cannot fight you, if you fight back. Don't shrink away from liberals who call you a racist if you say something negative about Jackson, or any black person who deserves it. "Call a spade a spade", so to speak. If you think that last phrase is racist, you are exactly the kind of coward I'm trying to describe. The truth is sometimes ugly and mean. So what?

> Anonymous [innocentbystander], "Jesse Jackson Succeeds Only Because Most White People Are Cowards" (March 3, 2001), http://www.eaglesup.com/racerelations.html

This is clearly a sick use of the "spade"-phrase as a racial slur, employed as such by an African American against members of his own ethnic background who happen to have different socio-political views. Such hateful statements on the internet unfortunately do their part in spreading racial prejudices without apologies, as was discussed in the following paragraph with, however, a rather unfortunate use of the "spade"-phrase that simply does not fit in this well-intended context:

Some people argue that race does not exist in cyberspace, that misrepresentation and lack of visual data nullify the cultural signifiers that define race most strongly. The offender could be some brother who decided to liven up the POC [People of Color] bulletin board by playing white devil's advocate, for all anyone knows [this might just be the case with the internet reference cited above]. Cyberspace makes the physical properties of race more nebulous, but that doesn't have any bearing on the simple fact that people of color, no matter how distinguishable we are from the gray mass of humanity on the Net, use online services. That one can't — forgive my metaphor — call a spade a spade is both an advantage and a disadvantage. It is a disadvantage in that it miscegenates people sensitive to racial issues and those who couldn't care less in a place where race isn't apparent. [...] The advantage resembles the disadvantage: it allows POC to ambush unwitting bigots. When most noncolored people use the word race, they don't think of it in terms of themselves, because "white people" don't constitute a race in the first place. Race, to them, is a code word for what Americans used to call "the Negro problem." The most common reaction to this chauvinistic denial involves turning the other cheek about four times and then walking away. But on the Net it couldn't be easier, html willing, to create a territory for yourself instead of complaining that no one has created it for you. "White people" don't hope for acceptance from anyone; they take it for granted.

> James Hannaha, "Don't Believe the Hypertext," *The Village Voice* (November 7, 1995), p. 23.

These are unfortunately true observations about racism on the internet, but the author surely got carried away with his "play" with the "spade"-phrase. Such play with slurs is simply too painful for those who feel deeply offended by it, and it also helps to keep such racial slurs in circulation.

In the following example, a legitimate apology was quickly given after an inappropriate use of the expressions as a slur, thus bringing an immediate solution to a thoughtless remark in the heat of political debate:

The contentiousness started early, with the stadium bond issue, which passed by a 14-10 vote. "If the baseball board can afford travel to Japan and can change the terms of the original agreement with the Legislature, they can afford this as well," Supervisor Dorothy Dean said. Supervisor Michael Mayo, referring to the stadium board's plan to lease equipment, said he would like the county to use leasing for housing for the mentally ill, alcohol and other drug abuse treatment programs and other constituent services. Supervisor Anthony Czaja, however, said: "If we would vote no, we would be the biggest jerks in the state. Let's call a spade a spade." The remark raised a few eyebrows. Mayo is African-American. "I take offense, supervisor," Mayo said. Czaja said he meant no offense and apologized. Later, Czaja said Mayo told him he was joking, but Mayo couldn't be reached for comment.

Gretchen Schuldt, "County Refuses to Pay for a New Animal Shelter," *The Milwaukee Journal Sentinel* (March 21, 1997), p. 1.

Be that as it may, the racially tense situation was resolved in the most humane way possible, i.e., through open and forgiving communication.

But witness the following humorous account that Lawrence Douglas Wilder, newly elected lieutenant governor of Virginia, gave to a journalist about his effectiveness as the first African American in the Virginia Senate since Reconstruction:

"Then they had another bill holding people indefinitely for shoplifting without placing them under arrest," Wilder remembers. "My colleague from Richmond, Senator Edward Willey, said some of those held were not all that innocent. He said they wouldn't be all that lily-white [i.e., they are black]." There were snickers. "I got up and said, One thing about my colleague from Richmond. He certainly knows how to call a spade a spade." The Senate erupted in laughter and applause. And the bill was changed.

Myra MacPherson, "Douglas Wilder: Winning the Waiting Game," *The Washington Post* (February 2, 1986), p. G1.

What Senator Edward Willey had expressed with the metaphorical phrase "lily-white" was in fact a racially charged claim, as can be seen from this phraseological commentary:

lily-white Prejudiced or discriminatory against blacks; racially segregated. This term gained popularity immediately following the Civil War, especially as a description for those white people who wished no contact with blacks and attempted to thwart them from exercising their newly won rights. A group of Southern Republicans who favored excluding Negroes, not only from the Republican party, but from any political activity whatsoever, actually adopted the term as a name for their faction, calling themselves *The Lily-Whites*. The term was soon extended to describe those social organizations that had written a color ban into their constitutions.
Laurence Urdang, Walter W. Hunsinger, and Nancy LaRoche, *Picturesque Expressions: A Thematic Dictionary* (Detroit, Michigan: Gale Research Company, 1985), p. 556.

But rather than protesting vehemently against this slur, Douglas Wilder countered it with the racially meant "spade"-phrase and thereby brought about a welcome "humorous" relief of an otherwise precarious situation. As an African American, i.e., as a member of the group against whom the two slurs are intended, he found a way to diffuse matters by taking ownership of the "spade"-expression. The positive outcome saved Senator Willey from a lot of embarrassment and established Senator Wilder as an effective communicator who knew how to get beyond racial strife. This incident is, to be sure, yet another superb example to the multi-faceted connotations of the "spade"-phrase that depend very much on who uses it and under what specific circumstances. In this case, the apparent racial slur saved the situation for everybody concerned!

Talking about African-American ownership of the "spade"-phrase, here is another example by Prof. Henry Louis [Skip] Gates Jr., chairperson of the African-American Studies Department at Harvard University:

"I want to tell you about the griot," says Gates, all at once the professor signaling this-is-important-so-listen-up. In western African culture, the griot keeps the oral history of the tribe. "The role of the griot was to call ..." The self-defined "race man" stops, punctuating the pause with an irreverent laugh. "I was going to say 'to call a spade a spade'." He laughs again. This is hilarious, the idea of Harvard's prize African-American scholar using language that in another context could be seen as a racial slur. Plus, the literary scholar who testified for 2 Live Crew at the rappers' obscenity trial is not about to censor himself. "Well, I can say it. The role of the griot was to call a spade a spade, to tell the community the truth about itself. People hated the griot. The griot wasn't even allowed to be buried in the communal burial ground. That's the role of the intellectual. You have a relation of alienation from your community as well as an organic one."

>Patti Hartigan, "Harvard's Skip Gates: Guru, Griot, Gadfly. The Controversial Head of African-American Studies Has Earned a High Profile by Speaking His Mind," *The Boston Globe* (April 29, 1993), p. 53.

Of course, Prof. Gates can speak his mind and as an African American he can even ridicule the "spade"-phrase as a racial slur and use it in its non-racist meaning. He should, however, be aware of the fact that he is playing his part in promulgating the phrase in its various meanings among members of society beyond those of African-American background.

But humor and racial slurs usually don't mix, as can be seen from a report on Superior Court Judge Donald McCartin, who is positively known for his outspokenness, fairness, and integrity. He loves to make off-the-cuff remarks which, when misunderstood by those who don't know him, can very quickly be taken the wrong way:

"I don't mean them; I just say them," McCartin said. At one point during the Tirado trial, McCartin indicated he was unimpressed by a statement in which the defendant said he was so mad at the girl that he could kill her. "So what," McCartin said. "I feel like killing my wife sometimes." Defense attorney Gary Proctor says that after appearing before McCartin, you soon learn to recognize when he's joking and when he's serious. Once, McCartin recalled, he was sentencing a client of Proctor's who was black. "I was really giving her a lecture to try and convince her to straighten out," McCartin said. "I finally said, 'Young lady, it's time to call a spade a spade.' Proctor nearly passed out, and the courtroom was in a frenzy," the judge said. "It was a joke," Proctor said, "My client and I took it as a humorous remark." The judge never has minced words in sentencing defendants.

>Jeanne Wright, "A Man of Opinions: Judge's Outspokenness Has Become a Courthouse Legend," *The Orange County Register* (July 2, 1987), p. B1.

Yet not mincing words and using phrases that can be interpreted racially in the courtroom is a strange sense of humor at best. One would hope that Judge McCartin might have learned a lesson from this incident, but since he told this story as a joke to a journalist, it looks as if he did not understand the inappropriateness of the remark in this situation.

Taken seriously, intended or unintended "spade"-slurs can lead to costly litigation, as can be seen form a California law-suit:

> The suit also accuses [Mayor Armando] Rea of calling a black council member, Louis Byrd, "a little animal" and of referring to African Americans as "spades." Rea Wednesday denied ever using racial epithets against blacks and said the remarks were taken out of context. The remarks reportedly were made during a July 7 council meeting. According to an article published in the *Lynwood Journal*, which is owned by Rapid Publishing, Rea told Byrd that, unlike Byrd, he had sat quietly while African Americans dominated the council. "It's amazing how you get up and jump up and down," Rea said. "You jump up and down like a little animal here. It's true, it's true. I say it like it is. I call a spade a spade. I say it like it is."
>
> Jack Leonard, "$800-Million Civil Rights Suit Filed Against City of Lynwood Courts: Three Latino Council Members Are Named in Allegations of Discriminatory Practices Against Black Contractors and City Workers," *The Los Angeles Times* (August 13, 1998), p. B3.

It is in fact always the context that shows whether the proverbial expression "to call a spade a spade" is being used as a racial slur or not. That is exactly what extreme proponents of political correctness tend to forget in their attempt of purging the language completely from certain words and phrases, sometimes with the help of an emotionalized and linguistically uninformed mass media. But there is no need to discredit more moderate advocates of political correctness. After all, they have played a considerable role in making people become aware of hate language in the form of racial slurs that ought to be avoided. In other words, we don't need to throw out the baby with the bath water when ridiculing extremist views of political correctness:

> Some factions of the media, seizing on the most extreme examples of P.C. run amok, have portrayed the reformers as loonies. Sometimes it's too easy. Consider the case of the administrator at the University of California who sought to ban such phrases as "a chink in the armor," "a

nip in the air" and "call a spade a spade" because they contain words that might offend minorities if used in another context. But is it fair to dismiss the movement for such extreme examples?

>Jonathan Eig, "P.C. or not P.C.: Academics Debate Whether It's Right to Be 'Politically Correct'," *The Dallas Morning News* (April 4, 1991), p. J1.

With all of its faults, the political correctness movement has brought about a linguistic awareness that was not necessarily present before. It has helped to bring about a new and hopefully more responsible consciousness about human communication. People are making more humane word and phrase choices, especially in an ever more ethnically diverse environment. We can make intelligent choices about language, as was clearly expressed in this last paragraph with a reference to the "spade"-expression:

What really seems to worry people [about political correctness] is the idea that they will no longer be able to express themselves freely, that they will always have to think twice before they say anything — that they will no longer be able to call a spade a spade or a woman a girl. There will, they complain, always be something else at the back of their minds when they write or speak. The response to this, as the linguist Stanley Fish puts it, is: "There was always something at the back of your mind [for example racist thoughts] and perhaps it might be better to have this code [of political correctness] in the back of your mind than whatever was in there before." If in the back of your mind you possess nothing more than a jumble of dumb clichés and codes about the stupidity of Irish people, blacks, women — take your pick — is it really a great assault on your freedom to have to bring these things to the front of your mind? Regulating speech through the law is bound to be limited. There are those who argue that the best way to answer harmful speech such as overtly racist remarks is not through legislation but through simply creating more and different kinds of speech. [...] Progress depends on changing attitudes, and language always shapes and reflects what those attitudes are.

>Suzanne Moore, "Laughing on the Other Side of Their Faces," *The Guardian* (June 10, 1994), p. T5.

A conscious change in attitudes towards minorities, for example, will indeed bring about linguistic change. I doubt that the proverbial expression "to call a spade a spade" in its traditional meaning of calling things the way they are will die out in the near future. However, now that many speakers have become aware of the fact that in certain contexts the "spade"-phrase can take on a racist meaning, a conscious choice of not employing it in that sense would be the sensible and humane way to proceed. People will perhaps also decide to use the phrase less and less, especially since there are numerous other "clichés" available to express the same idea, as for example "To call things by their proper names," "to say it as it is," "not to beat about the bush," etc.

Obviously it is an encouraging sign that I have not been able to find many references at all that cite the "spade"-phrase as a racial slur. Many English speakers are not even aware of this meaning, and, as will be shown in the eleventh chapter, many young people don't know the classical phrase at all anymore. There is the definite chance then that the intentional use of the expression as a racial slur will decrease considerably in the future. In the meantime, it is the change of attitudes that will prevent people from employing the expression in a harmful and inhumane fashion. This has nothing to do with political correctness but with humanity, plain and simple.

X.

The Phrase in Advertisements and Cartoons

This chapter will unfortunately include only eight references from the iconographic realm of advertisements, book illustrations, and cartoons. And yet, they will once again show that the proverbial expression "to call a spade a spade" is definitely characterized by a semantic ambivalence, calling for clear facts on the one hand and making racist statements on the other.

The earliest one-page advertisement that I located appeared in the *Fortune* magazine in 1935. It is a rather "boring" black-and-white layout from a modern point of view. There is a crest on the top with a reference that the Bank of New York & Trust Company can look back on solid financial practices since the late eighteenth century. Then follows the simple headline "Call a Spade a Spade," while the ensuing text presents a factual statement on wise and secure investment practices. Implied in all of this is that the practices of this bank and its relationship with customers is based on honesty, plain and simple (Figure 1):

Call a Spade a Spade
Every security — regardless of its quality — is a speculation. If all investments were frankly called speculations, there would be less misunderstanding of their true nature. The only difference between so-called investments and an admitted speculation is the degree of risk involved. But risk, in some degree, is always present.

The individual who enters what is frankly termed a speculation, appreciates fully that he is assuming a risk. The individual who buys a "security" or an "investment" too often fails to appreciate the existence of a risk.

Such words as "security" and "investment" have an unfortunate connotation of safety and soundness. Their constant use militates against a realistic attitude toward the entire subject of investment.

No security can be regarded as permanently sound. Realization of the risk inherent in even the highest grade security is the first requirement for intelligent investment administration.

This Bank, appreciating the need for constant vigilance and continuing study of all securities, maintains an extensive Investment Research organization. Its findings serve as a guide in the investment of all

Figure 1: "Call a Spade a Spade"

trust funds and other funds in the Bank's care. We shall be glad to tell you how it can help you in your own investment or estate problems.
This is one of a series of advertisements explaining why a bank which has never marketed securities has more than 10% of its personnel engaged in investment analysis.
BANK OF NEW YORK & TRUST COMPANY
48 Wall Street · New York
Fortune (February 1935), p. 163.

One could summarize this text by stating that frankly speaking there are risks in investments, but the Bank of New York & Trust Company will give it to you straight, without beating about the bush, or, as the proverbial headline claims, by calling a spade a spade.

Another advertisement from the early 1950s is harmless enough, but it is of considerable interest due to the interplay of word and picture. It is an American political advertisement in the form of a poster from 1951. Set apart on the top is the proverbial slogan "Let's call a spade a spade!" To this is added an illustration of an "ace of spades" playing card, an indication once again that many people associate the "spade"-phrase etymologically with card games. The actual headline of the poster plays on this false assumption by stating "Congress is playing politics with YOUR INCOME!" In other words, just as in a game of cards, Congress is taking chances with taxpayers' money. The slogan, the playing card, and the headline are meant as emotionalized attention getters intended to get the readers to read the actual text and to encourage them to protest against unfair taxation (Figure 2):

Let's call a spade
a spade!
Congress is playing politics
with YOUR INCOME!

CONGRESS is about to boost *YOUR* income tax again. At the same time, purely for ulterior political reasons, still permits income tax exemption to more than 35,000 profit-making business corporations. Congress allows *ONE OUT OF TEN* corporations to pay little or no Federal income tax on their business profits. Congress lets them escape taxes of more than *ONE BILLION DOLLARS A YEAR* ... while taxing *YOU* more!
Congress adds that billion dollars onto the tax bill of *you* and every other income taxpayer. Their political chicanery is costing you money ... will soon cost *you* more unless *you demand an end to this tax discrimination.*

Figure 2: "Let's call a spade a spade!"

These profit-making businesses coddled by Congress ... in return for political favors from their leaders and promoters are ... COOPERATIVES, SAVINGS AND LOAN ASSOCIATIONS, MUTUAL SAVINGS BANKS, CREDIT UNIONS, and other cooperative banks and corporations of this kind. Even some MUTUAL FIRE AND CASUALTY INSURANCE COMPANIES are given favored tax treatment that adds to YOUR tax bill.
It is time *you* protested against Congress making a political football out of your pay check, your pocketbook, or your business income. Write your Congressman and your two United States Senators *immediately*.
The House of Representatives has ALREADY PASSED the new 1951 tax bill raising your individual and business income tax by billions, but doing absolutely nothing to tax the billions in profits of these tax-exempt corporations. This legislation is NOW before the Senate.
Make your resentment of this *tax discrimination* against *you* heard in the halls of Congress. Write your Congressman and Senators today. Demand that they tax the untaxed *first*, before increasing your or anyone else's Income Tax again.
   Write your Congressmen [*sic*] — c/o House Office Bldg.
   Write your Senators — c/o Senate Office Bldg.
       Washington, D.C.
[copy obtained from the Wisconsin Historical Society, Madison, Wisconsin]

This is quite a call to political action, and the twice used term of "tax discrimination" did its part in getting the taxpayers' temper up. The "spade"-phrase, of course, makes the claim that the taxpayers are getting straight information here. But that is it, and there clearly is no racial discrimination intended with the employment of the traditional expression.

The same is true for a British advertisement that was in use from the 1890s to the 1950s, for which I was unfortunately not able to locate an actual illustration:

Call a spade a spade
An expression with which we are nowadays brought into daily contact through the advertisement of a certain extract of coffee ("Call a spade a spade and Bransom's coffee extract the perfection of coffee"), has a very much longer pedigree than coffee itself or the name of Bransom, for the expression is found in Aristophanes. The meaning is of course obvious, viz. — Call a thing by its right name; sternly, rigorously, accurately,

204 *"Call a Spade a Spade"*

accord its fair due. [See also the fourth chapter on "The Phrase in Proverb and Idiom Collections"].
   A. Wallace, *Popular Sayings Dissected* (London: T. Fisher Unwin, 1894), p. 22.

Call A [Spade] A [Spade] And Branson's Coffee Perfection
Branson's [Bransom's?] Coffee; probably UK [United Kingdom], quoted 1952. Pictures of two spades were inserted instead of the words. "When this design was first propounded, the manufacturer was dubious. 'They'll think we sell spades,' he said. It was hailed as ... an effective poster ... The slogan is still used today [i.e., in the early 1950s]."
   Nigel Rees, *Dictionary of Slogans* (Glasgow: HarperCollins, 1997), p. 44.

It is difficult to imagine that this made an effective coffee advertisement, but perhaps the two illustrated spades helped to draw attention to the entire advertisement that mentioned the brand name in the headline and probably had a container or a cup of the coffee as an accompanying picture.
   Finally, there is the following advertisement from 1998 found on the internet by the *Apt Words Editorial Services* company. This is a service that wants to help people to write clearly and in good style, avoiding flowery euphemisms as it were. Their claim of knowing when to call a spade a spade in meaningful linguistic communication certainly is a straight-forward and absolutely non-racist use of the "spade"-phrase, and it is reminiscent of Lucian's call for factual and clear writing in historical accounts (see chapter 2):

When you want to present your ideas clearly, quickly and with style, you need
   Apt Words Editorial Services
Anyone can fill a page with words. It takes a good editor to make sure those words are right for the occasion. Now, thanks to the Internet, you have the services of a good editor right at your computer keyboard at a much lower cost than hiring an addition to your staff.
Poor writing can hurt you and your organization in many ways. It can kill a sale, irritate a customer or miscredit a staff member. You end up wasting time and money, and may not even be aware that anything is wrong. After all, you know what you meant to say. With Apt Words, you won't have to worry whether or not you are hitting the mark.

The editors at Apt Words can create written materials for you from scratch and improve what you've already written. Either way, you'll get a product that's crisp, clean and well-organized, one that follows the rules of grammar without sounding stuffy. We know when to call a spade a spade and when to call it a shovel — and we'll never call it a manually actuated earth-turning device.

Click on the topics in the left-hand column to see how Apt Words can help you.
E-mail: robert@aptwords.com
Apt Words, 3480 Ardendale Lane, Sacramento, CA 95825
(916) 485-3756
http://www.aptwords.com

This company really knows how to use the right words. After all, they are aware of the difference between a spade and a shovel, and they will always use direct words and not such high-convoluted language like referring to a spade as "a manually actuated earth-turning device." This internet-advertisement really brings the point across, and in the upper left corner it even lists the befitting 17th-century quotation "Good words are worth much, and cost little" by George Herbert. So who would not want to sign up for this clearly well-priced service? It sounds almost too good to be true, but buyer beware. The innovative use of a traditional phrase in an advertisement is only the first step to get attention for a new product, and the actual proof of the pudding is in the eating, i.e., the final perfectly written manuscript. I think I'll stick to my old fashioned and imperfect writing of my own for now.

But let us now look at a charming little French book entitled *Les Idiomatics — français-anglais* (Paris: Éditions du Seuil, 1989), edited by Geneviève Blum and illustrated by Nestor Salas. The book includes more or less literally illustrated proverbial expressions for which the French and English languages have semantic equivalents based on different metaphors. Thus the French say "Appeler un chat un chat" (see p. 92), while English speakers say "To call a spade a spade" (p. 93) which could be translated into French as "Appeler une pelle une pelle." The latter text has, of course, no common currency in the French language and would make little sense to native speakers. There are many equivalents to the "spade"-phrase in other languages, to be sure, but studying them could lead to a special comparative monograph. Suffice it here to present the two illustrations of French-English equivalents of the idea of calling things by their proper names without relying on euphemisms (Figures 3 and 4).

Figure 3: "Appeler un chat un chat"

The Phrase in Advertisements and Cartoons 207

Figure 4: "To call a spade a spade"

The "spade"-phrase does not appear to be particularly popular in cartoons, even though proverbs and proverbial expressions are frequently part and parcel of both their iconography and captions. The same is true for caricatures, and there is even a long tradition of artists, including Pieter Brueghel and Francisco de Goya for example, who have illustrated proverbial metaphors (see Wolfgang Mieder and Janet Sobieski, *Proverb Iconography: An International Bibliography* [New York: Peter Lang, 1999]). At times these pictures have been extremely helpful in the diachronic study of proverbs and their meanings, but there are also proverbial drawings where the message is not absolutely clear. This is also the case with a cartoon that appeared in the British magazine *Punch* (September 14, 1983), p. 78, as part of a one-page article by Benny Green on the new television series "Reilly, Ace of Spies." The cartoon shows the actor Leo McKern as Basil Zaharoff and Sam Neill as Reilly. The latter seems to have gotten himself into quite a pinch after having told Basil a thing or two in a frank and direct manner. Basil, having the upper hand now, has a spade in the one hand and a revolver in the other. He appears to have dug a grave and says to Reilly: "People who call a spade a spade ..." Judging by the picture, the ellipsis might well be "dig their own grave," pointing to a second proverbial expression in addition to the "spade"-phrase. But that is not all, for Reilly in his mind completes Basil's truncated statement with the probing query "... should use one?" In other words, as the super-spy he has to find a way to get out of this mess as his name "Reilly, Ace of Spies" implies (Figure 5). The word "ace" of this title must have conjured up the proverbial phrase "to have a card up one's sleeve" in the mind of the cartoonist, and why shouldn't that card be the ace of spades? The cartoon shows clearly that Reilly has something up his sleeve, and, true to the phrase's meaning and his own super-human character, Reilly is about to put a secret reserve plan into action and turn things around. Maybe Reilly or better the cartoonist was even aware of Oscar Wilde's formulation "The man who could call a spade a spade should be compelled to use one" in his novel *The Picture of Dorian Gray* (1890; quoted in chapter 6 of this study). In that case the cartoon would in fact be an impressive example of cultural literacy. But be that as it may, the cartoonist, at least in my interpretation of the cartoon, has cleverly interconnected three well-known proverbial expressions. The result is a bit enigmatic, but this interpretation of the cartoon fits the ingenious "Life of Reilly," as Benny Green entitled his essay on the intriguing character of this spy.

Clearly this cartoon represents a good amount of phraseological and iconographical fun. But there is absolutely nothing humorous about an-

Figure 5: "People who call a spade a spade ... should use one?"

other cartoon that appeared in the *Hustler* magazine (February 1979), p. 52, with the caption "I hope from now on you'll know not to call a spade a spade" (unfortunately permission to reproduce this cartoon was not granted). Obviously some bigoted white man used the "spade"-phrase as a direct racial slur against two African Americans who in turn gave the perpetrator a good beating. While the two victims of the verbal insult take pleasure in having punished the offender, the latter's wife is leading her husband away. Judging by the expression on her face, she hasn't understood the situation at all, assessing the two men in stereotypical fashion to be inferior. The unfortunate incident will have done little to overcome any racial prejudices.

The last cartoon appeared, strangely enough, in *The New Yorker* (April 3, 1989), p. 103, with the caption "'Early today the senator called a spade a spade. He later issued a retraction'." (© The New Yorker Collection 1989 Joseph Mirachi from cartoonbank.com. All Rights Reserved). The picture shows a middle-aged white man watching the news on television, and the entire cartoon is most likely meant to ridicule the extreme linguistic purification attempts by the political correctness movement (Figure 6). But then the gentleman in the cartoon seems to be perplexed by what he has just heard from the news reporter, and perhaps the cartoon is also directed at persons with such little social and humane awareness. The caption is also reminiscent of the trouble U.S. Senator Jake Garn from Utah had gotten himself into in 1984 when he had used the statement "Sometimes you have to call a spade a spade" in connection with Rev. Jesse Jackson and refused to apologize for it (see chapter 9). Even if he did not intend to make a racial slur, it would have caused no harm to acknowledge the fact that the "spade"-phrase might offend African Americans and also other citizens, for that matter. One thing is for certain, the cartoonist and the editors of *The New Yorker* obviously felt that people would understand this cartoon. This being so, we have solid proof here that there must be considerable awareness in the American population that the old proverbial expression "to call a spade a spade" can be understood as a racial slur.

Human communication on all levels is not without its problems, and there are plenty of verbal misunderstandings to go around. We should indeed be much more conscious of how we use language, and not just how we employ individual words or phrases. It behooves all of us to try to avoid hurtful or hateful language, and the "spade"-phrase definitely belongs to the set of formulaic language which needs to be carefully watched. While it is used in a non-racist way most of the time, it can be employed and understood as a racial slur in some contexts — reason

Figure 6: "Earlier today the senator called a spade a spade. He later issued a retraction." ©The New Yorker Collection 1989 Joseph Mirachi from cartoonbank.com. All Rights Reserved.

enough to use it only with care in proper contexts or to decide as an expression of free choice not to use it at all. We do not need an aggressive political correctness program for this. All that is required is respectful and humane behavior and language use among people, and a bit of understanding for those who use the phrase in its harmless original meaning. No finger pointing is necessary, but rather a bit of linguistic and humane give and take as well as forgive and forget. The repetitive and intentional use of the "spade"-phrase as a racial slur is, however, something that can and must not be tolerated.

XI.

Four Demographic Studies of the Expression

The previous ten chapters have been based on printed sources, and they have shown that the proverbial expression "to call a spade a spade" has been used for hundreds of years as a harmless metaphor for direct and plain communication instead of using indirect and convoluted euphemisms. Once the noun "spade" took on the derogatory slang meaning of a black person in the first quarter of the twentieth century, the "spade"-phrase could in certain contexts be understood as a racial slur. Even though, relatively few such references could be found in literary works and the mass media. In fact, judging by the contextualized occurrences presented in those chapters, we might almost have to conclude that the unfortunate use of the "spade"-expression as a racial slur is rather rare. One might even think that all this talk about the phrase being understood as a racist remark is simply much ado about nothing. Wish that it were so! A lack of references in the printed media is no proof that the phrase is not misused as a slur in oral communication and that it is not interpreted as such by people who are conscious of the pitfalls of careless use of language.

The best way to find out what people think of the "spade"-phrase is, of course, to employ the demographic research method used by social scientists and thus also by folklorists and linguists. I was fortunate enough to be able to solicit the help of four good colleagues and friends in distributing a questionnaire to find out what people know and think about the expression today (in the fall of 1999 to be precise). Fionnuala Williams of the Institute of Irish Studies at the Queen's University of Belfast prepared a short questionnaire that she distributed at her place of work. I also put together a questionnaire which Richard Sweterlitsch used with his Caucasian folklore students at the University of Vermont here at Burlington. Irmgard Immel handed the questionnaire out to her African-American students at Morehouse College in Atlanta, Georgia. And Alan Dundes asked the multi-ethnic students of his large lecture course on folklore at the University of California at Berkeley to complete the questionnaire as well. Obviously I owe much thanks to this support by the four professors and their students. There is no doubt that the results gained from their answers make up a very important part of this study.

When Fionnuala Williams sent me the results of the circular that she sent around at the Institute of Irish Studies in Belfast, she summarized the results in the following manner in two e-mail letters of September 1 and 2, 1999: "The spade expression is current and common here [in Belfast]. Although people are aware of the American slang meaning of 'spade', there is no move to clamp down on the use of the expression;" and "The main findings are that everybody knows it [the "spade"-phrase] in English but fewer use it; it has no equivalent (as yet) in the Irish language." We learn from these two statements that in the English language use in Ireland the "spade"-phrase is not associated with a possible racial meaning since the slang term of "spade" meaning a black person is not commonly known in this society. This would be the same case in other countries where English is spoken, and it behooves American speakers to keep this in mind when encountering innocent uses of the phrase in the Englishes around the world. It is also of interest, of course, to find out that although most people know the proverbial expression, a smaller number uses it in actual speech acts. This is something that questionnaires distributed in the United States have also shown. As is the case with other proverbs and proverbial expressions, the young generation seems to not use or be unaware of numerous traditional sayings. As cultural literacy declines, the proverbial literacy appears to be decreasing as well.

But let me now present the actual questionnaire that Fionnuala Williams had prepared for colleagues and students at the Institute of Irish Studies:

"to call a spade a spade"

Dear Colleagues & Students,

Are you familiar with the above expression?   Yes/No

Have you used it yourself?   Yes/No

— can you say on what occasion(s)?

Can you indicate any references to it in print in English, or any other language?

I ask on behalf of an American colleague and would be most grateful for any information however slight, or even negative.

Altogether 31 completed questionnaires were returned to Fionnuala Williams. Only one informant did not know the phrase, five know the expression but do not use it, and twenty-five know and use it.

Three informants cite variants with the emphatic adjective "bloody" added to it. In chapter five we had cited literary references of this variant primarily current in Great Britain. It is therefore not surprising to find these statements on the questionnaires:

When it is necessary to be blunt or plain spoken (To call a spade a spade & not a bloody shovel!)

To be brief and to the point without unnecessary detail. I have heard it used in "telling someone off" as in "I call a spade a spade — you are a bloody liar!"

People say "to call a spade a bloody spade."

Another three informants point out that a well-known variant of the "spade"-phrase is "not to beat around the bush," a text that has been shown in other chapters of this study to be used in printed references as well together with the "spade"-expression:

Used in an angry exchange to get my point across; to describe a person who is matter of fact in dealings (no beating around the bush).

Only oral [use] — in the sense of "beat about the bush," which I would use instead of "spade a spade."

The third instance is of special interest, since Fionnuala Williams recorded a conversation with the informant who was aware of the American problem with the "spade"-phrase:

Williams: "Do you use it yourself?"
Informant: "Not any more because of its political incorrectness."
Williams: "Because of the other meaning of spade? Oh, that's interesting. Well, what would you say instead? No beating about the bush?"
Informant: "When I say it I mean it."

Fionnuala Williams recorded another fascinating conversation with a professor whom she cornered in the kitchen of the Institute of Irish Studies with the questionnaire in hand:

Prof. H. [born and reared in Chicago] said he was very familiar with this expression as was his wife, whose parents were both from California but who had moved around as her father was in the military. He was surprised that his 16 yr. old daughter had never heard the expression. When I [Williams] said that this might be because of political correctness, he said he didn't think so. He had heard the word "spade" (meaning Afro-American) when he was growing up, but it was not used now & people wouldn't think of that when they heard the expression.

This visiting American colleague is, of course, solid proof for the problem with subjective speculations concerning actual language use. Much more research, especially demographic field research, would need to be undertaken before being able to claim that the slang term "spade" is not known or used any longer. Other questionnaires filled out in the United States certainly prove the opposite, as will become clear shortly and as has been shown in chapters nine and ten with racial references from the mass media.

Note in this regard this statement by an American M.A. student, who completed the questionnaire as well. Obviously this informant had quite a different idea about the "spade"-phrase than the professor cited above:

When you want to say that something is what it is; that there are no illusions or misconceptions. I have also always been curious about this expression. At first I believed that it came from card games or a reference to a shovel. However, I thought about it again in an African-American literature course I took back in the States. The phrase was included in a text (I cannot remember which though; possibly Harlem Renaissance. Claude McKoy, Langston Hughes, Zora Neal Hurston, etc.). And it made me think that it was race related. A spade in America is a derogatory term for a black person. So I thought that to say "a spade is a spade" may be saying that a black man is just a black man and could never be more and that they are all the same no matter what. This was just a thought, hope it was of some help to you. If you do find the origin, please inform me of it.

Thanks be to this eager student who took the time to write this telling paragraph. It is one of the best explanations of how the "spade"-phrase is being used or understood as a racial slur. I hope that the informant will come across my study in due time. These comments show, however, a very important aspect of doing field research in folklore and language. It is of utmost importance to know the social background of the informants. This particular informant is not expressing typical Irish views on the "spade"-phrase but rather the culturally informed thoughts of a linguistically aware and thoughtful young American student.

In fact, here is a second example along these lines, this time from a colleague in England to whom Fionnuala Williams had sent the questionnaire. This informant states his precise biographical background and indicates that at least some people in England are aware of the racial implications of the phrase:

"to call a spade a spade" — this one we're [the informant and his wife] quite familiar with. We've both heard it directly in conversations and in public places. The most frequent context we've heard it in is with regard [to] people from particular regions of England when describing them as "straight talkers", i.e., saying exactly what they mean, little sophistication in dialogue, tactlessness even. I personally have heard this used particularly to describe people from Yorkshire but [my wife] has heard it from a woman in Bromsgrove (Worcestershire) describing her husband (West Midlands accent). Both of us may have, on occasion, used it in this context in a humorous way. My father is from Yorkshire and my mother from Northern Ireland (Belfast) so there have been a few interesting reactions to each others traits which are part of regional characteristics. I have heard another context for this phrase which is, sadly, racism. Certainly in the Gloucester City area when I was young the term spade was applied to individual blacks living in the area as an insult. Someone who called a spade a spade might be someone who particularly disliked the growing presence of the black community in Gloucester — even though they've been present in Gloucester since the medieval period, albeit in smaller numbers. I'm not sure of any references to it in print but I would suggest looking at English newspapers printed at the race riots in London and the south coast (late 70's early 80's?). I would suspect that if a printed reference exists it would be there. Looking at local papers from areas with high National Front support in London would also be a possible source for this racist context. As for the born and reared aspect of your American colleague's survey, I was born in 1971 in Swindon, England, raised until two and half years in Cyprus, moved to Yorkshire briefly, then Gloucester until around eight years of age and Tewkesbury (Glos) until around fifteen years. Since then I've lived in various addresses in Worcestershire, including Worcester City until now where I live with my wife. My wife was born

in Worcester in 1966, raised in a village called Leigh Sinton (pronounced lie) not far from Malvern (Worcestershire) and has remained in Worcestershire (Malvern, Worcester and now Kempsey) all her life.
I hope this information proves useful for you and your colleague.

This most certainly is very helpful information. After all, it is an important reference to the fact that the "spade"-phrase, at least in certain contexts, is known in England as a racial slur as well.

But the following statements by seventeen informants show that the "spade"-expression is considered a perfectly legitimate phrase with which people announce that they will say what they mean in blunt fashion, no matter what proponents of political correctness were to think of it:

Referring to someone who is rather blunt. A refreshing antidote to political correctness. Better than saying "an indispensable agricultural implement!"

"He's the sort of man who calls a spade a spade." To me this is not at all uncomplimentary. I use it frequently enough. I use it to refer to people [who] are frank when others would be, in my opinion, unacceptably evasive.

To describe someone very direct; as an alternative to "to be blunt."

Referring to a person who speaks bluntly.

Being short, blunt, definite; coming to a conclusion; in business when a cut and dried decision has to be made.

When direct description is called for rather than an opaque term.

To make a point.

A cliché, but when plain-speaking is called for.

When frustrated at others using euphemisms especially to avoid talking about awkard or difficult issues.

Speaking bluntly.

Four Demographic Studies of the Expression 219

When it is necesary to be blunt or plain spoken.

To be brief and to the point without unnecessary detail.

To describe a forthright person.

Brutally honest and blunt.

To explain something or describe someone in simple terms; direct, open. frank.

When you want to say that something is what it is; that there are no illusions or misconceptions.

Referring to someone who is rather blunt.

With these positive evaluations of the phrase in its classical meaning we can make the jump across the Atlantic and take a look at how the primarily Caucasian folklore students at the University of Vermont have reacted to the "spade"-phrase. My colleague and friend Richard Sweterlitsch was kind enough to hand out the following questionnaire that I had prepared for his undergraduate students:

1. _____ (name); _____ (age); _____ (ethnicity)

1a. _____ (gender, if not clear from name)

2. Are you familiar with the expression: "To call a spade a spade"? _____ (Yes or No)

3. If your answer to #2 is No, then simply turn in this sheet with no further comments. If your answer is Yes, then please continue:

4. Approximately when and where did you first hear it? (Give country, state, city, and year, if possible, e.g., Fresno, Calif., circa 1980)

5. Have you ever used the expression yourself? If so, under what circumstances? Can you remember particular occasions when you (or someone else) used it?

6. If you know the expression, but cannot remember any specific instance of actual usage, could you make up a hypothetical situation in which the expression might appropriately be used?

7. In terms of usage, presumably the expression is used *metaphorically*. Can it also be used *literally*? If so, please explain, preferably by giving an example.

8. Do you consider the expression in any way offensive or insulting? If so, to whom? and why?

Thank you for taking the time to answer the above questions.
(If you need more space to answer any of them, please use the back)

The surprising result of this survey was that of 23 informants 15 (65.2%) indicated that they do *not* know the "spade"-phrase at all! Of the remaining eight students who are acquainted with the expression, seven claim that they do not use it, while but one informant acknowledges having employed it. Two of the young students (between 18–20 years old) state that they don't use the phrase because they really don't quite understand it:

I've heard it but never really understood it. I couldn't give an example situation.

I have never used the expression since I am not completely positive what it means.

One additional student thinks that the phrase "may be used in a card game," attesting once again to the fact that some people think of the "spades" suit of card games. And yet, there are five informants who understand the proverbial expression quite well:

I think it is something like to call a person or thing what s/he is, with no frills.

When something pretty obvious is put into question.

I can't remember how it [the phrase] was used but hypothetically it could be used in talking about someone who says he has only good intentions for others but is actually greedy or self-serving.

Anytime when you're labeling someone appropriately for a given situation, calling an alcoholic an alcoholic; if they get upset, you simply respond with I'm just calling a spade a spade.

Something obvious.

But even in Vermont, a state with only about 1% of its population being African American, at least three students (the first two from Vermont, the third from Connecticut) of the eight who know the phrase (i.e., 37.5%) are aware of its possible racist interpretation:

I personally don't find it offensive, but I suppose members of the black community may. Spade is slang for African Americans & the only time I've heard the expression it has been derogatory.

It obviously could apply to people of African decent, and have been used as a derogatory term, but I don't know about its origin.

A literal interpretation would make it offensive to blacks because a spade is a racial slur.

Clearly these three students are aware of the problematic nature of the "spade"-phrase, but they don't use it in any case. Twenty-three completed questionnaires are, of course, hardly a representative sample, but they show two significant results: the old proverbial expression does not play a major role in verbal communication of the students, and at least some of them are conscious of its interpretation as a racial slur. As rural Vermonters, they might well have become sensitized to this particular meaning through a general "Race and Ethnicity" course that students are required to attend as part of their liberal education at the University of Vermont.

From "white" Vermont we can go South to Atlanta, Georgia, where Irmgard Immel, a fellow Ph.D. student and friend from thirty years ago, is professor of German at Morehouse College, a predominantly "black" institution. She too was willing to hand my questionnaire out to her students, who returned 53 invaluable copies to her. And once again, many students indicate that they don't know the "spade"-phrase at all. To be precise, 32 of the 53 informants (60.4%) are not familiar with it (in Vermont it was 65.2%), and of the 21 students who know it 17 don't use it, leaving a mere 4 students who do cite it. More important is the fact that of the 21 informants who are acquainted with the expression, 11 think it has no racial implications, while 10 consider it a racial slur. This means that among the African-American student population knowing the phrase about 47.6% consider it a racial slur. This figure is not as high as one might have expected, and it shows that the "spade"-phrase is by no means universally considered to be a racial slur among black students.

The four students who actually use it had the following to say, indicating that they are not aware of any racial implications. It is of interest to note that one of the students is thinking of card games in relation to the "spade"-phrase:

Yes, [I have used the expression] when playing the card game of spades.

Yes, I use this expression to mean what someone or something is.

Yes, because I like hearing and knowing the plain truth. I can handle any type of situation in a mature way and intelligently. I don't want anything to be "sugar coated."

Yes, when my friends try to polish their wrong doing.

Eleven additional students clearly understand what the traditional "spade"-phrase means, even though they don't necesarily use it. They have no difficulties in describing situations in which one might use the expression in a perfectly harmless way:

When politicians accuse other politicians as liars.

The expression would refer to a judgment.

During an argument on whether or not twin A looks better from twin B: "Let's call a spade a spade and say they're both attractive."

It's like calling someone according to their action.

In a governmental arena when the act of stealing is given the name of "misappropriation of funds."

To call a spade a spade most nearly means to call it as you see it.

Someone is trying to act one way, but you know them to be another way. Then you can say what exactly they are. I call a spade a spade.

If all evidence points to an obvious outcome than one calls a spade a spade.

Somebody sees through another person's falseness and confronts the deceiver.

If a stripper were to be called a stripper, then that would be calling a spade a spade. But if someone called a stripper an exotic danser (but she's not) then that would not be calling a spade a spade.

It's used as a reminder or a warning.

These students obviously see no connection with the proverbial expression and "blackness," but this is the case in the following statements by the ten informants who consider the phrase to be a racial slur. This also means that of the 53 black students about 20% are offended by the racist implications of the "spade"-phrase, reason enough for speakers of any ethnic background to be careful in its use or, better yet, to avoid it altogether. Here is what the 10 informants give as their reasons for the negative reaction to the traditional phrase:

I have heard it used when white teachers were complaining about the academic performance of blacks and when referring to individual blacks as well. It is insulting to the group/individual being referred to.

Irreverence to black people; offensive to black people, spade is a racist word.

It can be used to discriminate. It is insulting to anyone who may disagree with its usage. It is not proper or polite.

It can be used as a slur (racial). It is offensive & insulting because the expression is a prejudgment.

It could be offensive. Spade was/is a racial slur for some races. Some people might take it the wrong way.

It means to call something what it is. If you were to look too deeply, in my opinion, one may find it insulting to blacks, although I do not see a problem.

The expression can be insulting depending upon the context in which it is used. However, this statement is based metaphorically upon stereotyping an individual or a group or ethnicity.

The phrase is offensive, if you relate it to people of color, using it as a stereotype, where you make a generalization about, say, black people, and say a spade is a spade, like all blacks are the same.

A woman was talking about a black man on television who had been arrested. Someone said "They're all the same." Then she said the saying. She was embarrassed when she saw me standing behind her (she was white). It is a sly way to say "nigger" and get away with it. On the other hand, personally I don't care.

It was used in reference to a black person. Someone said "you must call a spade, a spade," meaning you must refer to blacks as who they are. Can be insulting when used as I first heard it [this way]. I later realized that it could be used in another [non–racist] way.

    These ten comments by black students are in fact very revealing. While some of them see a definite racial slur in the phrase no matter what, others are more careful in their semantic judgments. They feel that the "spade"–phrase can be offensive and insulting, depending on the intended message and its context. And there are also those informants who recognize the possible racist implications but who acknowledge that this is but one specific meaning of the phrase. Furthermore, they are not particularly bothered by the expression, since their own tolerance level can deal with such verbal insults. The emotional maturity of these young students is truly impressive. One certainly gets the impression from their remarks that they would be quite capable of differentiating between the innocuous use of the traditional phrase and its slanderous misapplication. They most likely would not make a fuss if they were confronted by the old phrase in its basic meaning of calling things by their proper names. There is no call for extreme political correctness on their part in these comments. On the other hand, these young people and any other person offended by the use of the phrase as a racial slur have every right and obligation to call such bigots on the proverbial carpet, as it were.

This said, we can move West to the campus of the University of California at Berkeley, where Alan Dundes gave my questionnaire to the students of his large introductory folklore class. An impressive total of 198 students answered the survey, of whom 127 or 64.1% do *not* know the "spade"-phrase. That is approximately the same percentage as we found among white students of the University of Vermont (65.2%) and the black students of Morehouse College (60.4%). It can be said then from these admittedly limited three surveys that only about a third of American students today are in fact acquainted with the old proverbial expression "to call a spade a spade." I might add here that the picture is not necessarily much better in the case of other traditional sayings (see my "'Proverbs Everyone Ought to Know': Paremiological Minimum and Cultural Literacy," in W. Mieder, *Proverbs Are Never Out of Season: Popular Wisdom in the Modern Age* [New York: Oxford University Press, 1993], pp. 41–57; and Anna Tóthné Litovkina, "The Most Powerful Markers of Proverbiality: Perception of Proverbs and Familiarity with Them Among 40 Americans," *Semiotische Berichte*, nos. 1–4 [1994], 327–353).

The Berkeley campus is very ethnically diverse, and let me add here that of the 127 students who do not know the phrase, 57 indicated that they are white, 7 that they are black, and 63 that they belong to the large Asian population of the campus (including a few other minorities). But before quoting the student informants themselves, let me give these statistical figures regarding the 71 students (35.9%) who are acquainted with the "spade"-phrase:

51 white students
   33 see no racial meaning
       24 don't use it
       9 use it
   18 consider it a racial slur
       13 don't use it
       5 use it (but change it)

7 black students
   3 see no racial meaning
       3 don't use it
       0 use it
   4 consider it a racial slur
       4 don't use it
       0 use it

13 Asian students (and other minorities)
   12 see no racial meaning
       8 don't use it
       4 use it
  1 considers it a racial slur
       1 doesn't use it
       0 use it

What these figures show is that of the 71 students who are acquainted with the "spade"-phrase 53 (74.6%) don't use it at all. Also, there are only 23 of the 71 informants (32.4%) who think that the phrase is a racial slur. Interestingly enough this is quite a bit higher than the 20% of the black students of Morehouse College but not as high as the 37.5% of the white Vermont students. I hasten to add that all samples are relatively small, but perhaps we could generalize and say that about 30% of those young American students who know the "spade"-phrase are aware of its possible racist interpretation.

There are once again a few, eleven to be precise, students in California who connect the "spade"-phrase with the card game, clearly indicating that they are misinformed on its classical origin and historical transmission:

I used the expression playing cards with my mom.

I assume if you played bridge [you could use the phrase literally].

[It is used literally] in black spade in cards.

[It is used literally] in poker?

[It is used literally] if you are referring to the card symbol.

Maybe in a card game [it is used literally].

Spade referring to the playing deck of cards. Ace of spades, two of spades, etc.

[It is used literally] in a card game.

Call a spade in the deck of cards.

I suppose [it can be used literally] in a game of cards, but I'm honestly not sure of the origin — bridge?

[It is used literally] if you are referring to the card symbol.

But many Californian students understand the phrase very well, as the following thirty-six statements make perfectly clear:

Meaning that something is what it is.

Two people are discussing a situation — one is uncertain about the circumstances ... say infidelity. The other person thinks it is obvious. It is what it is. The man is unfaithful. Call him what he is — to call a spade a spade.

When calling attention to an obvious event.

To talk about being direct and honest versus using euphemistic terms.

Someone told me that a girl was ugly, and I told him to be nicer than that. He said he was going to call a spade a spade.

It is used to suggest a blunt, plain-speaking attitude.

I think the expression means to exactly name someone for what they are.

Lawyers don't lie, do they? Let's just call a spade a spade.

If a friend of mine did not want to tell me the truth about another person (afraid to offend me or hurt me), I could say — just tell me and call a spade a spade.

It means to call someone what he is. If someone is a liar, you call them a liar and name what they are.

When telling a friend to be honest about her intentions/thoughts. "You don't want to be his *friend*, you want to date him. Why don't you call a spade a spade?"

Honest and obvious fact; encouraging people to say it like it is without dancing around the point.

"Call a Spade a Spade"

It is what it is; nothing is hidden.

People use it when referring to honesty/integrity of a statement.

Calling something like it is.

If two people are talking about a delicate subject and one person tires of "beating around the bush," she might say with some exasperation or/and finality: "Let's just call a spade a spade and acknowledge (some touchy fact)."

Could be used in a situation when someone is trying to conceal something. To call a spade a spade in this instance would be pointing out what it is in reality, like skip the b.s. [i.e., bull shit].

When a person states the obvious.

If someone is an addicted smoker and denies it to me when I ask, saying he only puffs once in a while and just "likes it," I'd respond by saying: "Let's call a spade a spade. You're addicted."

When I want to emphasize a point that something appears as it is. You get what you see is an equivalent. The situation is obvious and there is no hidden meaning.

Having an argument with a friend, perhaps, who's beating around the bush and won't deal with the issue at hand directly.

I used it when I was sure a friend of mine was lying. I told her I was going "to call a spade a spade" and expose her for the liar she is.

When I said something a bit rude but true about something, I followed it up with the comment "I'm not afraid to call a spade a spade."

To state a fact that was obvious but no one else wanted to note. Saying it sucks when it rains.

If someone is being evasive about the truth.

A situation in which somebody states the obvious. To say that something is the way it is because it acts or is used in that particular way.

I would use it [the phrase] when I would want to say: "I call it like I see it." Usually used when there is a dispute about the authenticity of an object or situation. "That car is broken down, it's a lemon." "No, it's not." "Well, I think it is — I'm just calling a spade a spade."

If a girl is acting nastily or rudely and you call her a bitch, you've called a spade a spade. She's a bitch, and you called her a bitch.

My boyfriend used it:
Me: "She's a bit eccentric."
Him: "Let's call a spade a spade. She's a freak."

If someone was making excuses for something or obviously contriving a story, you could say it [the phrase] to tell him to just tell the simple truth.

To call something as you see it.

I think it's equivalent to "not beating around the bush." So, if you hear someone tell the truth simply and concisely (that might be difficult to tell), you might say the person called a spade a spade. Or if you think they're outright lying, you'd say they're not calling a spade a spade.

If someone engages in some inappropriate behavior and you say they are doing so. If that person gets upset because you said that you could say "I call a spade a spade" or "I call it as I see it."

If a friend's boyfriend is cheating on her and someone calls him a dog, I would say "to call a spade a spade."

When someone states the obvious.

It means to tell it as it is; so in any instance when someone is ambiguous about something it can be used.

After these comments regarding the traditional meaning of the expression, we come to those students who see racist tendencies in the "spade"-phrase. There are 18 white students who don't use it for that reason. Here are there explanations why they consider the expression offensive or insulting:

It refers to African-Americans. In the South it was common to call someone who is of African descent a spade.

[It is offensive] to the person who is being called a spade.

I associate the word spade with African American men — referring to a black man as a spade.

It can be [offensive] as African-Americans have derogatively been called spades.

[It is offensive] to African Americans because it is often used as slander against them.

It refers to "spade" as a black or African American.

I do know that racist remarks are sometimes made in reference to spades.

I've heard it referred to African-Americans, however because I was never familiar with the use of spade as a racist expression it does not immediately trigger offense.

I don't remember what the expression means, but possibly "spade" refers to the usage of the word that means African-American.

I think it has negative connotations towards black people in the United States.

I think I remember that it is racist in some way.

[I] guess it can be used as "spade" as an insulting remark to blacks.

[It refers to] African Americans from the term black as the ace of spades.

[I used the expression] when telling someone not to beat around the bush, or pussy-foot but to tell me what they really think or would call something. I wouldn't use it now — maybe because of political correctness. It might be [offensive] because I've heard it has been used about African Americans.

It is not offensive in & of itself, but it is often used in [an] offensive way.

I remember once hearing that it's a racial slur of some kind, but I can't remember.

I have used it in the past. I quit using it as I thought it was a racial slur.

It is a pejorative expression about black males.

These white students have identified the proverbial expression as being a racial slur, and they indicate that they don't use it in verbal communication. It is clear from their comments that they are aware of the slang term "spade" for an African American, and it is this meaning which is carried over into the interpretation of the "spade"-phrase. There are also those students who indicate on the questionnaire that they used to cite the phrase but have stopped doing so once they became aware of its secondary racist meaning, in part due to the political correctness movement.

There is only one Asian (Chinese) student who knows the phrase and considers it a slur: "[It is] slightly offensive using it in terms of color." The student comments that he/she never uses it, using instead the variant "to tell it like it is."

This leads us to the five black student informants who interpret the "spade"-phrase as a slur and who obviously refrain from using it:

Maybe in reference to African Americans [it is offensive or insulting].

[It is offensive] as a racial epithet.

I think it is offensive racially — a southern white expression referring to blacks, African Americans ... as a "nigger."

A racist way: If [there is] some black person who "looks white" [and] some observer might sneer "Oh, you're black. Let's call a spade ..."

Clearly [offensive]. It implies that black people don't want to be black or something like that.

As can be seen from many of these statements by student informants, there is plenty of uncertainty about the origin and meaning of the "spade"-phrase. To a certain degree, some folk etymologies enter into the interpretation of the expression, whether they refer to the card game or to racial matters. One thing is clear, modern American speakers don't know anything about the classical tradition of the proverbial expression. Instead, they attempt to reason out or guess at possible semantic underpinnings. By adding the slanderous and stereotypical meaning of the slang word "spade" to this, people have in the past few decades come up with the new meaning of the phrase as a racial slur. Linguists, folklorists, cultural historians, and others can argue that this is not the "real" meaning of the phrase, but the references from the mass media as well as from modern cartoons (discussed in the two previous chapters) and now the many statements by university students make it amply clear that the "spade"-phrase does not only mean to express matters in plain and direct language but that it unfortunately can also be used as an insulting racial slur. About 30% of young Americans who know the phrase think of it as being pejorative in a racial sense, and to the person they have decided not to cite it. That is a conscious and free ethical decision, and it need not be driven by some absurd political correctness legislation. As I argued earlier in this study, it is difficult if not impossible to legislate language behavior, especially when it comes to choosing individual words or phrases.

However, we can and should communicate as responsible and considerate citizens, and we must be conscious of how we use language. The proverbial expression "to call a spade a spade" is ingrained not only in the American version of the English language, but in the many Englishes of the world. No officially sanctioned campaign can purge the rich English language and its variants from this innocuous classical phrase, but people would do well in paying careful attention to the context in which they make use of it. Americans should not point the finger at English speakers from other countries who might use it in its traditional meaning. If they or any person here in the United States were to use it in such a way that someone could take offense, then it might be wise to draw that person's attention to it in a civilized fashion, thus bringing about an awareness of its possible racial implications. In the case of repetitive use as a racial slur, stronger measures by legal actions would, of course, be appropriate. But especially in the United States, where the "spade"-phrase is recognized as a racial slur by a fair number of citizens of various ethnic backgrounds, it would be wise to avoid it altogether, replacing it by other equally expressive metaphors like "to call things by their proper names," "to say (tell) it as it is," "not to beat about (around) the bush," etc. Let us have responsible and free decisions in this regard, based on the principle that all people are created equal and that they deserve to be treated with proper human respect. Rather than taking the chance of unintentionally offending someone or of being misunderstood, it is best to relinquish the old innocuous proverbial expression turned modern racial slur "to call a spade a spade" altogether.

Bibliography

The dozens of dictionaries and collections of proverbs, quotations, and slang that are referred to throughout this book are not repeated in this bibliography. They are cited with complete bibliographical information in the various chapters. This selective bibliography is meant to give an overview over the most important studies of stereotypes and racial slurs based on proverbial language. Some additional sources in various foreign languages are listed in Wolfgang Mieder, *International Proverb Scholarship: An Annotated Bibliography*, 4 vols. (New York: Garland Publishing, 1982, 1990, and 1993; New York: Peter Lang, 2001).

Allan, Keith, and Kate Burridge. *Euphemism & Dysphemism: Language Used as Shield and Weapon*. New York: Oxford University Press, 1991. 263 pp.

Allen, Irwing Lewis. *Unkind Words: Ethnic Labelling from "Redskin" to WASP*. New York: Bergin & Garvey, 1990. 143 pp.

Aman, Reinhold (ed.). *Opus Maledictorum: A Book of Bad Words*. New York: Marlowe & Company, 1996. 364 pp.

Arora, Shirley L. "A Woman and a Guitar: Variations on a Folk Metaphor." *Proverbium*, 10 (1993), 21–36.

Arora, Shirley L. "Proverbs and Prejudice: *El Indio* in Hispanic Proverbial Speech." *Proverbium*, 11 (1994), 27–46.

Bain, Read. "Verbal Stereotypes and Social Control." *Sociology and Social Research*, 23 (1939), 431–446.

Barnes-Harden, Alene Leett. *African American Verbal Arts: Their Nature and Communicative Interpretation (A Thematic Analysis)*. Diss. State University of New York at Buffalo, 1980. 186 pp.

Birnbaum, Mariana D. "On the Language of Prejudice." *Western Folklore*, 30 (1971), 247–268.

Colombo, John Robert. "Canadian Slurs, Ethnic and Other." *Maledicta*, 3 (1979), 182–184.

Cray, Ed. "Ethnic and Place Names as Derisive Adjectives." *Western Folklore*, 21 (1962), 27-34.

Daniel, Jack L. "Towards an Ethnography of Afroamerican Proverbial Usage." *Black Lines*, 2, no. 4 (1973), 3-12.

Daniel, Jack L., Geneva Smitherman-Donaldson, and Milford A. Jeremiah, "Makin' a Way outa no Way: The Proverb Tradition in the Black Experience." *Journal of Black Studies*, 17, no. 4 (1987), 482-508.

Daniels, Karlheinz. "Geschlechtsspezifische Stereotypen im Sprichwort. Ein interdisziplinärer Problemaufriß." *Sprache und Literatur in Wissenschaft und Unterricht*, 16, no. 56 (1985), 18-25.

Doyle, Charles. "Belaboring the Obvious: Sarcastic Interrogative Affirmatives and Negatives." *Maledicta*, 1 (1977), 77-82.

Dundes, Alan. "A Study of Ethnic Slurs: The Jew and the Polack in the United States." *Journal of American Folklore*, 84 (1971), 186-203.

Dundes, Alan. "Folk Ideas as Units of Worldview." *Towards New Perspectives in Folklore*. Eds. Américo Paredes and Richard Bauman. Austin, Texas: University of Texas Press, 1972. 93-103.

Dundes, Alan. "Slurs International: Folk Comparisons of Ethnicity and National Character." *Southern Folklore Quarterly*, 39 (1975), 15-38. Also in *Wise Words: Essays on the Proverb*. Ed. Wolfgang Mieder. New York: Garland Publishing, 1994. 183-209.

Dundes, Alan. *Life is Like a Chicken Coop Ladder. A Portrait of German Culture through Folklore*. New York: Columbia University Press, 1984. 174 pp.

Eble, Connie. *Slang and Sociability. In-Group Language among College Students*. Chapel Hill, North Carolina: University of North Carolina Press, 1996. 228 pp.

Eisiminger, Sterling. "A Glossary of Ethnic Slurs in American English." *Maledicta*, 3 (1979), 153-174.

Eismann, Wolfgang. "Nationales Stereotyp und sprachliches Klischee. Deutsche und Slawen im Lichte ihrer Phraseologie und Parömiologie." *Europhras 92: Tendenzen der Phraseologieforschung*. Ed. Barbara Sandig. Bochum: Norbert Brockmeyer, 1994. 81–107.

Enright, D.J. (ed.). *Fair of Speech. The Uses of Euphemism*. Oxford: Oxford University Press, 1985. 219 pp.

Esteban, José. *Refranero contra Europa*. Madrid: Ollero & Ramos, 1996. 78 pp.

Gaidoz, Henri, and Paul Sébillot. *Blason populaire de la France*. Paris: Librairie Léopold Cerf, 1884. 382 pp.

Grauberg, Walter. "Proverbs and Idioms: Mirrors of National Experience." *Lexicographers and Their Works*. Ed. Gregory James. Exeter/England: University of Exeter Press, 1989. 94–99.

Green, Jonathon. *Words Apart. The language of Prejudice*. London: Kyle Cathie, 1996. 383 pp.

Grzybek, Peter. "Kulturelle Stereotype und stereotype Texte." *Natürlichkeit der Sprache und Kultur*. Ed. Walter A. Koch. Bochum: Norbert Brockmeyer, 1990. 300–327.

Grzybek, Peter. "Blason Populaire." *Simple Forms: An Encyclopaedia of Simple Text-Types in Lore and Literature*. Ed. Walter A. Koch. Bochum: Norbert Brockmeyer, 1994. 19–25.

Hulme, F. Edward. *Proverb Lore; Being a Historical Study of the Similarities, Contrasts, Topics, Meanings, and Other Facets of Proverbs, Truisms, and Pithy Sayings, as Expressed by the Peoples of Many Lands and Times*. London: Elliot Stock, 1902; rpt. Detroit: Gale Research Co., 1968. 269 pp.

Janson, William Hugh. "A Culture's Stereotypes and Their Expression in Folk Clichés." *Southwestern Journal of Anthropoplogy*, 13 (1957), 184–200.

Kennedy, Randall. *Nigger: The Strange Career of a Troublesome Word.* New York: Pantheon Books, 2002. 226 pp.

Khayyat, Shimon L. "Relations between Muslims, Jews and Christians as Reflected in Arabic Proverbs." *Folklore* (London), 96 (1985), 190-207.

Kuusi, Matti. "The Place of Women in the Proverbs of Finland and Ovamboland." In M. Kuusi, *Mind and Form in Folklore: Selected Articles.* Ed. Henni Ilomäki. Helsinki: Suomalaisen Kirjallisuuden Seura, 1994. 148-158. Translation of "Naisen arvo Suomen ja Ambomaan sananlaskustossa." *Suomen Akatemia,* 1 (1971), 99-107.

Kerschen, Lois. *American Proverbs about Women: A Reference Guide.* Westport, Connecticut: Greenwood Press, 1998. 200 pp.

Louis, Cameron. "Proverbs and the Politics of Language." *Proverbium,* 17 (2000), 173-194.

Mieder, Wolfgang. "A Proverb a Day Keeps no Chauvinism away." *Proverbium,* 2 (1985), 273-277.

Mieder, Wolfgang. *American Proverbs: A Study of Texts and Contexts.* Bern: Peter lang, 1989. 394 pp.

Mieder, Wolfgang. *Proverbs Are Never Out of Season: Popular Wisdom in the Modern Age.* New York: Oxford University Press, 1993. 302 pp. With 38 illustrations.

Mieder, Wolfgang. "Language and Folklore [including proverbs] of the Holocaust." *The Holocaust: Introductory Essays.* Eds. David Scrase and W. Mieder. Burlington, Vermont: The Center for Holocaust Studies at the University of Vermont, 1996. 93-106.

Mieder, Wolfgang. *The Politics of Proverbs. From Traditional Wisdom to Proverbial Stereotypes.* Madison, Wisconsin: The University of Wisconsin Press, 1997. 260 pp. With 20 illustrations.

Mieder, Wolfgang. "Blasons Populaires." *Medieval Folklore: An Encyclopedia of Myths, Legends, Tales, Beliefs, and Customs.* Eds. Carl

Lindahl, John McNamara, and John Lindow. 2 vols. Santa Barbara, California: ABC-CLIO, 2000. I, 103-105.

Mieder, Wolfgang. *Strategies of Wisdom: Anglo-American and German Proverb Studies*. Baltmannsweiler: Schneider Verlag Hohengehren, 2000. 372 pp.

Mieder, Wolfgang. *"No Struggle, No Progress": Frederick Douglass and His Proverbial Rhetoric for Civil Rights*. New York: Peter Lang, 2001. 532 pp.

Monteiro, George. "Derisive Adjectives: Two Notes and a List." *Western Folklore*, 34 (1975), 244-246.

Nicolaisen, W.F.H. "The Proverbial Scot." *Proverbium*, 11 (1994), 197- 206.

Nwachukwu-Agbada, J.O.J. "'Bèkeè' [the white man] in Igbo Proverbial Lore." *Proverbium*, 5 (1988), 137-144.

Oinas, Felix. "The Foreigner as Devil, Thistle, and Gadfly." *Proverbium*, no. 15 (1970), 505-507.

Ojoade, J.O. "The White Man in African Proverbial Sayings." *Folklore Studies in the Twentieth Century*. Ed. Venetia Newall. Woodbridge/England: Brewer, 1978. 332-338.

Paredes, Américo. "Proverbs and Ethnic Stereotypes." *Proverbium*, no. 15 (1970), 511-513.

Parker, Carol. "'White is the Color'." *Western Folklore*, 34 (1975), 153-154.

Peacock, Martha Moffitt. "Proverbial Reframing — Rebuking and Revering Women in Trousers." *The Journal of the Walters Art Gallery*, 57 (1999), 13-34. With 21 illustrations.

Porter, Kenneth. "Still More Ethnic and Place Names as Derisive Adjectives." *Western Folklore*, 25 (1966), 37-40.

Prager, Carolyn. "'If I Be Devil': English Renaissance Response to the Proverbial and Ecumenical Ethiopian." *Journal of Medieval and Renaissance Studies*, 17, no. 2 (1987), 257-279.

Prahlad, Sw. Anand. *African-American Proverbs in Context*. Jackson, Mississippi: University Press of Mississippi, 1996. 292 pp.

Prahlad, Sw. Anand. *Reggae Wisdom: Proverbs in Jamaican Music*. Jackson, Mississippi: University Press of Mississippi, 2001. 302 pp.

Profantová, Zuzana. "Ethnoidentification in Conversational Genres of Folklore alias 'Locus Standi'." *Folklore in the Identification Processes of Society*. Eds. Gabriela Kiliánová and Eva Krekovicova. Bratislava: Ustav etnológie SAV, 1994. 75-81.

Profantová, Zuzana. *"Little Fish Are Sweet": Selected Writings on Proverbs*. Bratislava: Ustav etnológie SAV, 1997. 109 pp.

Quasthoff, Uta. "The Uses of Stereotype in Everyday Argument." *Journal of Pragmatics*, 2 (1978), 1-48.

Rapp, Marvin A. "'Nigger' in the Woodpile." *New York Folklore Quarterly*, 14 (1958), 16-25.

Raymond, Joseph. "Tensions in Proverbs: More Light on International Understanding." *Western Folklore*, 15 (1956), 153-158. Also in *The Wisdom of Many: Essays on the Proverb*. Eds. Wolfgang Mieder and Alan Dundes. New York: Garland Publishing, 1981; rpt. Madison, Wisconsin: University of Wisconsin Press, 1994. 300-308.

Reinsberg-Düringsfeld, Otto von. *Internationale Titulaturen*. 2 vols. Leipzig: Hermann Fries, 1863; rpt. with an introduction by Wolfgang Mieder. Hildesheim: Georg Olms, 1992. 31 pp. (introduction), 166 pp., and 150 pp.

Roback, Abraham Aaron. *A Dictionary of International Slurs (Ethnophaulisms)*. Cambridge, Massachusetts: Sci-Art Publishers, 1944; rpt. Waukesha, Wisconsin: Maledicta Press, 1979. 394 pp.

Ronesi, Lynne. "'Mightier than the Sword': A Look at Proverbial Prejudice." *Proverbium*, 17 (2000), 329-347.

Rothstein, Robert. "Jews in Slavic Eyes — The Paremiological Evidence." *Proceedings of the Ninth World Congress of Jewish Studies*. No editor given. Jerusalem: World Union of Jewish Studies, 1986. II, 181-188.

Russell, Melissa Anne. "'Kill 'em all and Let God Sort 'em Out': The Proverb as an Expression of Verbal Aggression." *Proverbium*, 16 (1999), 287-302.

Samper, David A. "Woman as Gallina — Man as *Gallo*: An Interpretation of a Metaphor in Latin American Proverbs and Proverbial Expressions." *Proverbium*, 14 (1997), 347-366.

Simon, John. "The Wit and Wisdom of Catch Phrases." In J. Simon, *Paradigms Lost: Reflections on Literacy and Its Decline*. New York: Clarkson N. Potter, 1980. 75-80.

Škara, Danica. "Linguistic Stereotypes: Crosscultural Analysis of Proverbs." *Radovi*, 22-23 (1992-1994), 127-134.

Smith, J.B. "Whim-Whams for a Goose's Bridle: A List of Put-Offs and Related Forms in English and German." *Lore and Language*, 3 (1980), 32-49.

Stanzel, Franz K. *Europäer: Ein imagologischer Essay*. Heidelberg: Carl Winter, 1997. 113 pp. With 11 illustrations.

Stanzel, Franz K. (ed.). *Europäischer Völkerspiegel: Imagologisch-ethnographische Studien zu den Völkertafeln des frühen 18. Jahrhunderts*. Heidelberg: Carl Winter, 1999. 324 pp. With 11 illustrations.

Tamony, Peter. "Chinaman's Chance." *Western Folklore*, 24 (1965), 202-205.

Tavernier-Almada, Linda. "Prejudice, Power, and Poverty in Haiti: A Study of a Nation's Culture as Seen Through Its Proverbs." *Proverbium*, 16 (1999), 325-350.

Taylor, Archer. *The Proverb*. Cambridge, Massachusetts: Harvard University Press, 1931; and *An Index to "The Proverb."* Helsinki: Suomalainen Tiedeakatemia, 1934; rpt. as *The Proverb and an Index to The Proverb*. Hatboro, Pennsylvania: Folklore Associates, 1962; rpt. again with an introduction by Wolfgang Mieder. Bern: Peter Lang, 1985. 49 pp. (introduction), 223 pp., and 105 pp.

Thompson, Billy Bussell. "Jews in Hispanic Proverbs." *Yiddish*, 6 (1987), 13–21.

Tóthné Litovkina, Anna. "The Most Powerful Markers of Proverbiality: Perception of Proverbs and Familiarity with Them Among 40 Americans," *Semiotische Berichte*, nos. 1–4 (1994), 327–353.

Widdowson, John D.A. "Language, Tradition and Regional Identity: Blason Populaire and Social Control." *Language, Culture and Tradition*. Eds. A.E. Green and J. Widdowson. Sheffield: University of Sheffield, 1981. 33–46.

Yéo, Lacina. "'Mohr', 'Neger', 'Schwarzer', 'Afrikaner', 'Schwarzafrikaner', 'Farbiger' — abfällige oder neutrale Zuschreibungen? Eine Analyse der Ethnika und Ethnophaulismen zur Bezeichnung von Afrikanern und dunkelhäutigen Menschen afrikanischer Abstammung." *Muttersprache*, 111, no. 2 (2001), 110–146.

Yusuf, Yisa Kehinde. "Proverbs and Misogyny." *Working Papers on Language, Gender and Sexism*, 4, no. 2 (1994), 25–45.

Yusuf, Yisa Kehinde. "A Semantics Classroom Connection of Connotations, Stereotypes and Misogynous Proverbs." *Proverbium*, 18 (2001), 365–374.

Zenner, Walter P. "Ethnic Stereotyping in Arabic Proverbs." *Journal of American Folklore*, 83 (1970), 417–429.

Name Index

Abate, Frank R. 76
Acton, Harold 80, 96
Ahmad, Rafiq 176
Aik, Kam Chuan 78
Allen, Irwing Lewis 235
Allen, Julian 162
Alsop, Ronald 160
Aman, Reinhold 235
Ammer, Christine 81, 84, 86, 111, 187
Anderson, Ronald 158
Anderton, Stephen 98
Andrews, Fred 170
Andrews, Robert 58
Apperson, G.L. 66
Arens, Moshe 166
Aristophanes 8, 10, 12, 15, 17, 18, 20, 21, 23, 33–37, 39, 40, 47, 49, 50, 52, 67, 69, 70, 81, 83, 86, 124, 203
Arnold, Helen 162
Aronstein, Martin J. 104
Arora, Shirley L. 235
Arrowsmith, William 34, 35
Arthur, Timothy Shay 126, 141
Asbury, Herbert 79, 133
Aterman, K.A. 149
Atkinson, J. 75
Augarde, Tony 55
August, Ken 176
Ayto, John 108

Bailey, Nathan 66, 87
Bain, Read 235
Baines, D.C. 147
Baker, Russell 156
Balchin, Nigel 73, 82, 91
Baltake, Joe 166

Barickman, Jake 5
Bark, Melvin van den 106
Barker, William 41
Barnes-Harden, Alene Leett 235
Bartlett, John 48, 49, 55, 58
Bates, William 13, 14
Baxter, Richard 7, 11, 67
Bayé, Betty Winston 189, 190
Bekker, Leander J. de 66
Bengel, Albert 24
Benham, W. Gurney 50
Bennett, Arnold 73, 140, 142
Bernstein, Claire 159
Berrey, Lester V. 106
Bertram, Anne 82, 83
Birnbaum, Carolyn 159
Birnbaum, Mariana D. 235
Bishop, Patrick 171
Black, Anthony 174
Blum, Geneviève 205
Boatner, Maxine Tull 74
Boileau, Nicolas 8, 13, 49–51, 100
Bonner, Robert J. 101
Bonwick, James 143
Borneman, Ernest 31
Bottel, Helen 155
Bouchard, Lucien 104
Brackenridge, Hugh Henry 75, 125
Bradley, David 97
Bradley, Henry 90
Brann, William Cowper 93
Breese, M.H. 144
Brookbank, George 99
Brown, Bob 107
Browne, J. Zamgba 183
Browning, Robert 3, 128, 140

Broyard, Anatole 190
Brueghel, Pieter 208
Brunvand, Jan Harold 128
Bryan, George B. 93, 127, 131, 134, 135
Buckheit, Vincenz 30
Builder, Carl 148, 149
Bulkeley, Gershom 75, 122, 141
Burridge, Kate 235
Burton, Robert 3, 10, 15, 50, 53, 54, 57, 66, 67, 70, 82, 83, 119, 140, 142
Byrd, Louis 196

Cabell, James Branch 79, 130
Cable, George W. 155
Cadogan, Mary 91
Caldeira, Judy 110
Call, Tenney 137
Camp, L. Sprague de 80, 136, 142
Carolus, Cheryl 97
Carruth, Gorton 58, 88
Carter, Richard G. 182
Carter, Terry 160
Cattarello, Sandra L. 157
Chancellor, E. Beresford 79, 132
Chapman, Robert L. 108
Chideckel, Maurice 72
Chiu, Kwong Ki 64
Chrétien, Jean 104
Churchill, Winston S. 3, 131, 140, 141
Cicero 38, 52, 70, 81
Cleaver, Jim 163
Clurman, Robert 95
Cohen, J.M. 54
Cohen, M.J. 54
Cohen, Philip 188, 189

Cole, Robert 99
Collins, Bruce 177
Colombo, John Robert 58, 235
Cook, Ellen P. 150
Cooper, James Fenimore 3, 72, 92, 126, 140
Corry, John 163
Coser, Lewis 148
Coutts, James 172
Cowie, A.P. 76
Craig, Patricia 91
Craigie, W.A. 90
Cranmer, Thomas 7, 9, 14, 15
Cray, Ed 236
Creasey, John 79, 135
Croker, John Wilson 89, 125, 141
Cumberland, R. 33, 34
Czaja, Anthony 193

Daintith, John 58
Daniel, Jack L. 236
Daniels, Karlheinz 236
Davis, Luke 100
Davis, William 147
Davison, Rebecca 58
Day, Ruby 87
Demosthenes 8, 36, 49
Dent, Robert W. 76, 114, 119
Desmelyk, Frances 166
Devas, Nicolette 80, 138
Dickens, Charles 3, 53, 66, 71, 82, 127, 140
Dietrich, Marlene 175
Donadio, Stephen 58
Douglas, Susan 175
Doyle, Charles Clay 185, 236
Dundes, Alan 5, 28–31, 213, 225, 236
Dyer, Gwynne 167

Eble, Connie 236
Edmonds, J.M. 20–22
Egerton, Hazel 58
Ehrlich, Eugene 58, 88
Eig, Jonathan 197
Eisiminger, Sterling 236
Eismann, Wolfgang 237
Eitan, Michael 169
El-Outmani, Ismail 150
Ellis, Trey 180
Engeroff, Karl 27
Enright, D.J. 237
Erasmus 2, 8, 9, 12, 13, 15–17, 21, 24, 25, 27, 28, 31, 33, 36, 37–45, 49–52, 54, 57, 62, 66–69, 71, 74, 77, 81, 82, 84, 85, 89, 102, 114, 142
Esar, Evan 103, 133, 138
Esteban, José 237
Ettlinger, John 87
Evans, Bergen 54
Evans, Ivor H. 74
Evatt. Herbert Vere 95

Fabrey, Bill 159
Fahy, Francis A. 129
Fanselow, Ed 173
Farah, Joseph 174
Fedor, Grace 171
Fenton, Alexander 96
Fenton, James 150
Fergusson, James 170
Fergusson, Rosalind 58
Flavell, Linda 82
Flavell, Roger 82
Flexner, Stuart Berg 88, 107
Forbes, C. 10
Ford, Nancy 161
Fowke, Frank Rede 18, 19
Fraser, W. 9

Frazier, Kenneth 179, 180
Freelove, William 14
Freeman, Don 176
French, Mary Ann 162
Friedman, Jeffrey 110
Fry, Christopher 54, 55, 57, 135, 142
Fuller, Kate Baden 166
Funk, Charles Earle 68

Gaidoz, Henri 237
Gailey, Alan 96
Gallagher, Dorothy 150
Galsworthy, John 3, 73, 132, 140, 141
Garn, Jake 190, 191, 210
Gartside, Brian 147
Gates, Henry Louis 194, 195
Gates, John Edward 74
Gibb, Tom 172
Gibson, Andrew 175
Gifford, Humphrey 50, 51, 53, 67, 70, 71, 77, 89, 117
Gilbert, Anthony 80, 139
Giles, H.A. 67, 69, 74
Glover, Gillian 174
Glynn, Elinor 71
Goldberg, Carey 162
Goldberg, J.J. 165
Gomer, Hilaire 179
Goodman, Hirsh 169
Goodman, Robert 190, 191
Gorbachev, Mikhail 163, 169
Gordon, Edmund I. 145, 146
Goserud, Diane 110
Gossen, Stephen 53, 65, 70
Gottschalk, Walter 27
Goya, Francisco de 208
Graham, Chuck 170
Grauberg, Walter 237
Graves, Earl 183

Gray, Martin 56
Green, Benny 208
Green, Jonathon 109, 237
Green, Roger Lancelyn 79, 94
Greenberg, Paul 177
Griswold, Charles 151
Grocott, J.C. 49
Groshan, Shelly 166
Grove, Valerie 73, 82
Grove, Victor 144
Growden, Greg 99
Grzybek, Peter 237
Gulland, Daphne M. 78
Gumersell, Kathy 171

Hannaha, James 192
Hannan, Ewin 168
Harper, Linda Mitchell 184
Hartigan, Patti 195
Harvey, Paul 68
Hawkins, Joyce M. 88
Hazlitt, W. Carew 63
Heironimus, John Paul 25, 26
Hellinger, Daniel 174
Hendrickson, Robert 84
Hendrix, Bill 191
Herbert, George 205
Herrick, William 150
Highsmith, Patricia 80, 139
Hinds-Howell, David 78
Hirsch, E.D. 55
Hirsch, Rona S. 176
Hochstein, Mort 97
Holder, R.W. 109
Holloway, Melinda 180
Holt, G. 79
Homans, George 148
Hoppe, Arthur 170
Hughes, Langston 216
Hughes, W. 89
Hulls, Rob 168

Hulme, F. Edward 7-9, 237
Hunsinger, Walter W. 77, 194
Hurston, Zora Neal 216
Huxley, Aldous 3, 73, 134, 140
Hyamson, Albert M. 65

Ichikawa, Sanki 72
Immel, Irmgard 5, 213, 221
Inui, Ryoichi 72
Irving, Washington 3, 75, 89, 125, 126, 140
Irving, William 75, 125
Ismail, Razali 164

Jacks, Beth B. 105
Jackson, Jesse 190-192, 210
James, Susan 151
Janson, William Hugh 237
Jeffares A. Norman 56
Jennings, Diane 96
Jeremiah, Milford A. 236
Joans, Ted 110, 111
Johnson, Geraldine 97
Johnson, Joyce 148
Jonson, Ben 3, 7, 50, 51, 53, 56, 57, 65, 66, 70, 71, 77, 82, 118, 121, 140
Jungblut, Gertrud 147

Kaplan, Justin 55
Kay, Joe 108
Keith, Allan 235
Kemp, William 53, 66, 70, 118
Kennedy, Randall 238
Kerr, Wendie 157
Kerschen, Lois 238
Kett, Joseph F. 55
Khayyat, Shimon L. 238
Kher, Anupam 165
Kihara, Kenzo 72
Kirkpatrick, E.M. 75

Kirkpatrick, T.W. 144
Knowles, Elizabeth 57, 58
Knox, John 7, 72, 85, 116, 140
Komai, Chris 165
Korach, Myron 85
Kronke, David 173
Küpper, Heinz 31
Kuusi, Matti 238

Labov, Jeffrey 157
Lah, Pak 167
Lambert, Barbara 5
Lambert, James 97, 145
Lamonda, Barbara 5
LaRoche, Nancy 77, 194
Lean, Vincent Stuckey 64
Leite de Vasconcellos, J. 29
Leonard, Jack 196
Leonhardt, Rudolf Walter 26
Limbaugh, Rush 163
Linfield, Jordan L. 108
Longstreet, S. 107
Louis, Cameron 238
Lovelace-Käufer, Cicely 27
Lucian 8, 12, 15, 20–24, 37–40, 49, 50, 52, 55, 56, 66, 68, 70, 81, 85, 86, 89, 204

MacInnes, Colin 109
Mackin, R. 76
MacLeod, Charlotte 80, 140
MacPherson, Myra 193
MacRae, Ken 156
Macrone, Michael 80
Maggio, Rosalie 112, 188
Mahoney, Dennis 6
Mair, James Allan 49
Major, Clarence 107
Makkai, Adam 77
Malcolm X 97, 100, 110, 111
Manheim, Camryn 175

Mann, Jim 170
Mansfield, Stephanie 159
Marprelate, Martin 7, 9, 71, 89, 117, 141
Marsh, Gerald 149
Marshall, Ed. 15, 17, 18
Martial 23, 24
Martin, Lawrence 104
Martin, Rick 161
Mathews, Mitford M. 101, 102, 106
Maugham, William Somerset 91, 94
Mayo, Michael 193
McCaig, I.R. 76
McCain, Robert Stacy 98
McCartin, Donald 195, 196
McCaslin, John 163
McCracken, Paul W. 156
McCreevy, Charlie 98
McDavid, Raven I. 106
McDonnell, Evelyn 162
McKern, Leo 208
McKinnon, Jane 104
McKoy, Claude 216
McLeish, Kenneth 35
McMurchy, R.C. 156
Melanc(h)thon 7, 14, 15
Menander 20–23, 36, 37, 39, 40, 52, 55, 70, 72, 77, 81, 83, 85
Menasche, Philippe 147
Mencken, H.L. 51, 106
Mendel, Ed 169
Menen, Aubrey 79, 135
Mesner, Susan 58
Metzger, Bruce M. 22–25
Michener, James A. 108
Mieder, Wolfgang 14, 26, 28, 48, 93, 100, 127, 131, 134,

135, 137, 146, 152, 208, 225, 235, 238, 239
Miglani, Sanjeev 165
Miller, Henry 95
Miller, Tom 104
Mine, Takuji 72
Miner, Margaret 59
Mirachi, Joseph 210
Mitchell, Gladys 95
Monteiro, George 239
Montgomery, Lucy Maud 132
Moore, Suzanne 197
Mordock, John B. 85
More, Sir Thomas 114
Morgan, Don 174
Morland, N. 79
Morris, Desmond 29
Morris, Mary 72, 88
Morris, William 72, 88
Moxie, Carl B. 183
Munro, Eleanor 148
Murchison, Art 180
Murchison, William 176
Murphy, Eddie 182
Murray, James A.H. 90
Mynors, R.A.B. 39-41

Nadler, Gerald 161
Nares, Robert 65
Neaman, Judith S. 168
Neilan, Edward 167
Neill, Sam 208
Newman, Christine 167
Nicholson, David 180
Nicolaisen, W.F.H. 239
Nordlinger, Jay 177
Nunn, Sam 148
Nwachukwu-Agbada, J.O.J. 239
Nyhan, David 160

O'Toole, Fintan 150
Oinas, Felix 239
Ojoade, J.O. 239
Omar, Fauzi 187
Onions, C.T. 90
Owen, Robert 174
Oziewicz, Stanley 175

Pande, Taani 165
Pandya, Mukul 99
Paredes, Américo 239
Parizeau, Jacques 104
Parker, Carol 239
Partridge, Eric 53, 67, 71, 103, 107, 123
Patterson, Orlando 181
Paulding, James Kirke 75, 125
Peacock, Martha Moffitt 239
Pearl, Anita 107
Pearson, Robert 173
Pei, Mario 144
Peoples, Betsy M. 182
Philip of Macedon(ia) 8, 10, 12, 15-18, 20, 23, 25, 36, 37, 43, 44, 45, 49, 52, 54, 64, 65, 68, 69, 74, 81, 85, 86, 89
Pickard, Jim 173
Pickens, T. Boone 96
Pickering, David 85
Pinckney, Darryl 108
Piskotin, M. 147
Platt, Suzy 56
Platt, William 15
Plutarch 8, 12, 16-23, 25, 37, 43, 48-50, 52, 56, 57, 68, 69, 72, 77, 81-83, 85, 88
Polleschultz, Kathy 173
Porter, Kenneth 239
Portus, Martin 160
Potter, Simeon 73, 145

Prager, Carolyn 240
Prahlad, Sw. Anand 6, 240
Priestley, John Boynton 137
Proctor, Gary 195
Profantová, Zuzana 240
Przebienda, Edward 73
Purvee, Daryl 5

Quasthoff, Uta 240

Rabelais, François 8, 13, 21, 53, 70
Rabkin, Job 98
Rapp, Marvin A. 240
Rastell, John 68, 74, 85, 113–116
Rawson, Hugh 59, 108
Ray, John 11, 63, 71
Raymond, Joseph 240
Rea, Armando 196
Reade, Compton 93
Reagan, Ronald 158
Rees, Nigel 57, 204
Reinsberg-Düringsfeld, Otto von 240
Ribner, H.S. 158
Richardson, James 156
Richler, Howard 168
Ridout, Ronald 73
Rinehart, Mary Roberts 79, 84, 94
Roback, Abraham Aaron 240
Roberts, Cokie 162
Roberts, Kate Louise 49
Roesser, Jean W. 164
Rogers, James 77
Röhrich, Lutz 27, 28
Rolet, Charles 13, 14, 21, 49, 51
Romano, Lois 162
Ronesi, Lynne 241

Rongen, Thomas 172
Rosedale, Nancy 5
Rosenstiel, Thomas B. 162
Ross, Loretta 181, 182
Rothstein, Robert 241
Russell, Melissa Anne 241

Safire, William 163
Saitz, Greg 166
Salas, Nestor 205
Samper, David A. 241
Saunders, N. 108
Scaliger, J. 10, 12
Schinke-Llano, Linda 78
Schuldt, Gretchen 193
Schultze-Galléra, Siegmar von 29
Schwarz, C.M. 75
Seabury, Samuel 75, 123
Sébillot, Paul 237
Segall, Cary 168
Seldes, George 55
Shadwell, Thomas 66, 71, 121
Shakespeare, William 8, 67, 69, 71, 77, 119, 140, 141
Shambaugh, David 170
Shanks, Hershel 164
Sharpton, Al 183
Shaw, George Bernard Shaw 93
Sherrin, Ned 56
Shimer, Porter 147
Shore, Benjamin 160
Silk, Mark 181
Sill, Edward Rowland 130
Silver, Carole G. 168
Silver, Lee M. 151
Simon, John 241
Simpson, James B. 59
Simpson, John A. 91, 92, 108
Singer, Suzanne F. 165
Sipchen, Bob 180

Škara, Danica 241
Skeat, Walter W. 19
Skiba, Katherine M. 180
Skinner, Cornelia Otis 80, 138
Skvorecky, Josef 149
Smith, Chard Powers 80, 137
Smith, Cornelia Marschall 128
Smith, J.B. 241
Smith, Joan 58
Smith, William George 67, 68, 114
Smitherman, Geneva 109
Smitherman-Donaldson, Geneva 236
Snegur, Mircea 162
Snow, Wilbert 80, 140, 142
Sobieski, Janet 6, 208
Socrates 20
Soto-Chapa, Elena 169
Souhami, Diana 149
Southard, Bret 172, 178
Spade, David 170
Spears, Richard A. 78, 82, 83, 107, 108
Spencer, Steve 172
Stanzel, Franz K. 241
Stead, Christina 147
Steele, Ken 157
Steele, W.D. 79
Stein, Jess 87
Stellwagen, Florence Marshall 139
Stern, Marcus 160
Stevenson, Burton 28, 51, 58, 59, 61, 62, 69, 114
Stibbs, Anne 58
Stitt, C.W. 158
Streiling, Richard 157
Strickler, Jeff 170
Suddes, Thomas 167
Surlis, Paul 147

Sweterlitsch, Richard 5, 213, 219
Swift, Jonathan 3, 49–51, 53, 67, 68, 70, 71, 74, 82, 89, 102, 103, 123, 140, 142

Takaha, Shiro 72
Talib, Ahmad A. 168
Tamony, Peter 241
Tarkington, Booth 131
Taverner, Richard 8, 16, 17, 25, 43–46, 50, 53, 66, 70, 71, 74, 81, 114, 115, 141
Tavernier-Almada, Linda 241
Taylor, Archer 71, 100, 242
Taylor, John 3, 53, 56, 65, 70, 83, 119, 120, 140
Taylor, Phoebe Atwood 79, 133, 142
Taylor, Ronald 27
Terhune, Albert Payson 93
Thackeray, William Makepeace 74, 93
Theodore, Jeff 181
Thompson, Billy Bussell 242
Thompson, Douglas 182
Thompson, James Maurice 128
Tibbetts, Donn 161
Tilley, Morris Palmer 40, 71, 114
Titcomb, Caldwell 95
Titelman, Gregory Y. 83
Tomlin, P.J. 148
Tóthné Litovkina, Anna 225, 242
Trapp, John 53, 67, 68, 70, 74, 89
Travolta, John 168
Trefil, James 55
Tresemer, David 147
Tripp, Rhoda Thomas 59

Trokhimenko, Olga 5
Trollope, Anthony 3, 89, 127, 128, 140
Truman, Harry S. 3, 133, 135, 140
Twain, Mark 53, 71, 82
Tzetzes, Johannes 12, 40

Udall, Nicholas 8, 16, 25–27, 44–46, 51, 64, 67, 68, 74, 77, 81, 89, 114, 115, 141
Upfield, Arthur W. 79, 95
Urdang, Laurence 76, 77, 87, 194
Usher, Mark 5
Uys, Pieter-Dirk 160

Valada, M.C. 158
Valentine, Paul W. 164
Vizetelly, Frank H. 66
Vonnegut, Kurt 3, 80, 84, 136, 140
Vulliamy, C.E. 79, 94

Wall, C. Edward 73
Wallace, A. 64, 204
Walsh, Ann 168
Walsh, Charles 159
Walsh, Valda 173
Walsh, William S. 49
Walter, Elizabeth 85
Ward, Edward 53, 70, 89, 123
Warren, C.F.S. 18
Washington, Linn 183

Waxman, Sara 169
Weiner, E.S.C. 91, 92
Wentworth, Harold 107
Whiting, Bartlett Jere 62, 71, 75, 78, 83, 114, 154, 155
Widdowson, John D.A. 242
Wilde, Oscar 3, 54, 56, 58, 84, 129, 140, 208
Wilder, Lawrence Douglas 193, 194
Wilkinson, P.R. 83
Willey, Edward 193, 194
Williams, Fionnuala 5, 213–217
Williamson, Hugh 75, 124
Wilson, F.P. 74, 114
Wilson, Pete 160
Winder, Robert 172
Witting, Clifford 73
Wodehouse, P.G. 79, 84, 132, 141
Woodin, Noel 80, 136
Woodward, C. Vann 155
Woodward, Wendy 147
Woofter, Carey 87
Wright, Edmund 58
Wright, Jeanne 195
Wright, Richard 183

Yéo, Lacina 242
Yeretsian, Ara K. 166
Young, Coleman A. 183, 184
Yusuf, Yisa Kehinde 242

Zenner, Walter P. 242

Alan Dundes
General Editor

This series will include theoretical studies of any genre or aspect of folklore—however, it will not include mere collections of data or bibliographies. The emphasis will be on analytic and methodological innovations in the consideration of myth, folktale, legend, superstition, riddle, folksong, festival, games, or any other form of folklore, as well as in any of the various interpretative approaches to folklore topics.

For additional information about this series or for the submission of manuscripts, please contact:

> Professor Alan Dundes
> Department of Anthropology
> University of California, Berkeley
> Berkeley, CA 94720

To order other books in this series, please contact our Customer Service Department:

> (800) 770-LANG (within the U.S.)
> (212) 647-7706 (outside the U.S.)
> (212) 647-7707 FAX

Or browse online by series:

> www.peterlangusa.com